W9-BGV-675

Third Reich Victorious

THIRD REICH VICTORIOUS

The Alternate History of How the Germans Won the War

Edited by Peter G. Tsouras

This book club edition is
Manufactured under licence from
Greenhill Books/Lionel Leventhal Limited, London

Third Reich Victorious
first published 2001 by Greenhill Books,
Lionel Leventhal Limited, Park House,
1 Russell Gardens, London NW11 9NN
and
Stackpole Books, 5067 Ritter Road,
Mechanicsburg, PA 17055, USA

Text and Maps © Lionel Leventhal Limited, 2002

All rights reserved. No part of this publication may be reproduced,
stored in a retrieval system or transmitted in any form
or by any means, electronic, mechanical or otherwise
without the written permission of the Publisher.

ISBN 0-7394-2643-5

Typeset and edited by Donald Sommerville

Printed in the U.S.A.

CONTENTS

ILLUSTRATIONS

illustrations appear on pages 81–96

1. September 12, 1939: Force H sorties against Lütjens' *Carrier Group III*.
2. Before the battle of Scapa Flow, 31 August 1939.
3. Kriegsmarine torpedo-boats of the *7th Flotilla*.
4. General Erich von Manstein.
5. Major General Bernard Montgomery.
6. German troops and captured British equipment at Dunkirk.
7. British troops captured by the Germans at Dover.
8. RAF aircrew on the eve of the Battle of Britain.
9. The *Luftwaffe*'s devastating attack on London on 5 July 1940.
10. Adolf Hitler.
11. Field Marshal Erwin Rommel.
12. Troops of the Egyptian Army.
13. Part of Brigadier Godfrey's 'motley force'.
14. Benito Mussolini, Halfaya Pass, Egypt.
15. Delivering supplies to the *101st Jäger Division* in the Caucasus.
16. The commander of the Soviet 53rd Army.
17. Machine-gunners of the Soviet 47th Mountain Division.
18. An Axis air attack off Gela, Sicily, July 1943.
19. Lt-Gen George S. Patton, Maj-Gen Omar Bradley, and Maj-Gen Troy Middleton.
20. German night fighters attack a British bomber over Berlin.
21. German 88mm anti-aircraft guns.
22. Me-262 in flight.
23. A B-17 being attacked by a Luftwaffe Fw 190 fighter.
24. Professor Werner Heisenberg.
25. Niels Bohr.
26. Burning buildings in London.
27. German Heinkel 177 bomber.
28. Marshal G.K. Zhukov.
29. German infantry on the defensive.
30. German 88mm gun in action in Poland.
31. Burnt out Soviet T-34 tanks.

MAPS

THE CONTRIBUTORS

DR STEPHEN BADSEY MA (Cantab.) FRHistS is a Senior Lecturer in the Department of War Studies at the Royal Military Academy Sandhurst. He is a specialist in military theory, and in media presentations of warfare. He has written or contributed to over 50 books and articles about warfare, as well as appearing frequently in television and other media.

JOHN D. BURTT is the editor of *Paper Wars* magazine, an independent review journal devoted to wargames. In his day job he is a nuclear engineering contractor for the United States Navy. However, his real love is military history. A former marine sergeant and a veteran of Vietnam, he holds a Master's degree in military history and is pursuing a PhD in the same field. He has contributed a chapter for *Rising Sun Victorious: The Alternate History of How the Japanese Won the Pacific War* and has written for *Command, Strategy & Tactics*, and *The Wargamer*, and was the original editor of *CounterAttack* magazine.

WADE G. DUDLEY holds a Master's degree in maritime history and nautical archaeology from East Carolina University (1997) and a doctorate in history from the University of Alabama (1999). He contributed chapters to Sarpedon's *Great Raids in History*, and Greenhill's *Rising Sun Victorious*. Two of his books – a short biography of Sir Francis Drake and an examination of the British blockade of the USA in the War of 1812 – will be published in 2002. He is a visiting assistant professor of history at East Carolina University in Greenville, North Carolina.

COLONEL JOHN H. GILL, US Army. Jack Gill is the author of *With Eagles to Glory: Napoleon and His German Allies in the 1809 Campaign* (Greenhill, 1992) and the editor of *A Soldier for Napoleon* (Greenhill, 1998). In addition to numerous articles and papers on Napoleonic military affairs and a chapter in *The Peninsular War* (Spellmount, 1998), he has contributed chapters to three previous Greenhill speculative history collections: *The Hitler Options, The Napoleon Options* and *Rising Sun Victorious*. He received his BA from Middlebury College in 1977 (double major: history and German) and his MA from The George Washington University in 1987 (international relations). He resides in Virginia with his wife, Lt Colonel Anne Rieman, and their two sons, Grant and Hunter.

PADDY GRIFFITH is a freelance author and publisher. His books include *The Viking Art of War, Battle Tactics of the Civil War, Battle Tactics of the Western Front*, and *The Art of War of Revolutionary Franc*e. He is currently writing a book about the desert war, 1941–42.

DAVID C. ISBY is a Washington-based attorney and national security consultant and adjunct professor at American Military University. He has a BA in history and a JD in international law. A former editor of *Strategy & Tactics* magazine, he has also served as a congressional staff member. He has designed nineteen conflict simulations and been awarded two Charles Roberts awards for excellence in this field. He has written or edited 20 books, including several dealing with World War II: *G.I. Victor*y, *The Luftwaffe Fighter Force: The View from the Cockpit*, and *Fighting the Invasion: The German Army at D-Day*.

LT COLONEL FORREST R. LINDSEY, USMC (Ret.) served nearly 30 years in the United States Marine Corps, including time in combat in Vietnam. His special assignments included nuclear weapons testing with the Defense Nuclear Agency, and service as a United Nations Truce Supervisor in Egypt and as an arms control treaty Inspection Team Leader in the former Soviet Union. His regular duties included appointments as battalion operations officer, regimental logistics officer, and commanding officer of the 5th Battalion, 11th Marines. Upon retirement from active duty in 1996, he continued working with the Marine Corps as Senior Engineer for the Marine Corps Warfighting Laboratory, responsible for weapons experimentation and precision targeting. He has written several articles on professional military issues in the *Marine Corps Gazette* and contributed a chapter to *Rising Sun Victorious*.

CHARLES MESSENGER was a regular officer in the British Royal Tank Regiment for 20 years before beginning a second career as a professional military historian and defense analyst. He is the author of numerous books, including *The Art of Blitzkrieg* (1976, 1993), *'Bomber' Harris and the Strategic Bombing Offensive against Germany, 1939–1945* (1984), *The Commandos 1940–1946* (1985), *The Century of Warfare* (1995), and biographies of SS General Sepp Dietrich (1988, 2001) and Field Marshal Gerd von Rundstedt (1991). He is also the editor of *The Reader's Guide to Military History* (2001). He has carried out numerous historical studies for the British Ministry of Defence and has written and helped to direct a number of TV documentary series.

LT COLONEL PETER G. TSOURAS, US Army Reserve (ret) is a senior analyst for the Battelle Corporation in Crystal City, Virginia. Formerly he was a senior intelligence analyst at the US Army National Ground

Intelligence Center's Washington office. He has served in the Army as a tank officer in the 1st Bn/64th Armor Regiment, 3rd Infantry Division, in Germany and subsequently in intelligence and Adjutant Generals' Corps assignments from 1970 to 1981. He retired from the Army Reserve as a lieutenant colonel in 1994 after serving as a Civil Affairs officer. His assignments have taken him to Somalia, Russia, Ukraine, and Japan. He is the author or editor of 21 books on international military themes, military history, and alternate military history, including *Rising Sun Victorious*, *Disaster at D-Day*, *Gettysburg: An Alternate History*, *The Great Patriotic War*, *The Anvil of War*, *Fighting in Hell*, *The Greenhill Dictionary of Military Quotations*, *Civil War Quotations*, *Changing Orders: Evolution of the World's Armies*, and *Warlords of the Ancient Americas*. He has also written numerous chapters in other books and many journal articles, and been interviewed frequently on television and radio.

COLONEL GILBERTO VILLAHERMOSA is a historian with the US Army's Center of Military History at Fort McNair, Washington DC. A 22-year veteran, he is a West Point graduate, Armor officer and Master Parachutist. Colonel Villahermosa was a senior graduate fellow at the Soviet Ministry of Defence Centre for Military History in Moscow under Colonel General Dmitrii Volkogonov in 1990. It was there that he first worked with the actual document upon which his chapter is based. He has served with the Armored Cavalry in Germany and the 82nd Airborne Division's light armor battalion at Fort Bragg, North Carolina. He was also a Soviet analyst at the Defense Intelligence Agency, US military representative to Georgia and Tajikistan, and advisor on Russia and Eurasia to the NATO Supreme Allied Commander Europe. Colonel Villahermosa holds Master's degrees in international affairs and philosophy of political science from Columbia University, as well as a certificate in advanced Soviet studies from the university's Harriman Institute. He has published articles on the Napoleonic Wars, the Soviet Army and the US Army in *Armor*, *Army* and *Napoleon* magazines. He has also authored a series of entries on the US military for the next edition of Scribner's *Dictionary of American History*. His first book, on the 65th Infantry Regiment 'Borinqueneers' in the Korean War, is due to be released next year.

INTRODUCTION

The Germans win World War II. It is an unsettling, even horrifying proposition for a book. It is also provoking. All too often history, and especially military history, is seen as running down an already approved and well-worn groove. We won World War II because we were meant to win it. It is a gratifying but dangerous road to travel. If we have learned anything about history it is that it we hold it in our hands like a lump of wet clay.

The actions of not only great men and women, the warlords, heroes, and geniuses, constantly shape our history, but also the actions of countless nameless people. The guard who is so bone weary but also so resolved to do his duty that he must rest his chin on his bayonet to stay awake, in his own way, is a mighty shaper of history. An army of men such as that will do great things. A soldier who carelessly falls asleep on guard, and the leadership that lets him, will also make a mark in history. Decision, reason, and character are mighty ingredients in the makeup of history. These are the rational elements of human history-making, but there are others.

These are the ephemeral qualities not subject to human construction – chance and opportunity. That they occur is powerful enough. History then is also essentially about the interplay of chance and opportunity. I have explored this concept in the companion volume to this book, *Rising Sun Victorious: The Alternate History of How the Japanese Won the Pacific War* (Greenhill, 2001). It is worth restating.

> 'The interplay between chance and opportunity is the heartbeat of war. Clausewitz touched on it when he said, "War is the realm of chance. No other human activity gives it greater scope: no other has such incessant and varied dealings with this intruder. Chance makes everything more uncertain and interferes with the whole course of events."[1] And Napoleon put his finger on the relationship, "War is composed of nothing but accidents, and... a general should never lose sight of everything to enable him to profit from these accidents; that is the mark of genius."[2] This book examines the ways not taken, the stillborn possibilities that might have grown to mighty events.'

The war against the Germans could have been lost a number of times. Each of the ten chapters in this book explores a different door leading to that dark end. Each is a self-contained examination of one particular battle, campaign, or event in the context of its own alternate reality. These are ten authors' separate approaches. Since each chapter sets in motion new events, each generates new ground from the historian's perspective. Each is to be read as if it were actual history. This approach best conveys the sense of events. If the Germans win the Battle of Britain, for example, different historical works would appear in time. These different works appear in the endnotes along with those reflecting actual events. They are woven together to present a seamless alternate history.

The use of 'alternate reality' notes, of course, poses a risk to the unwary reader who may make strenuous efforts to acquire a new and fascinating source. To avoid an epidemic of frustrating and futile searches, the 'alternate' notes are indicated with an asterisk (*) before the number. All works appearing in the bibliographies included separately in each chapter are, however, 'real'.

Also to assist the reader, the names of Allied military units are given in roman type and axis units in *italics* (with the exception of ships whose names are invariably *italicised*).

The chapters are presented in chronological order. So it is appropriate that the peril of Britain dominates the first chapters. For truly the sceptred isle was the only bar to a quick and easy victory for Hitler. In Chapter 1, 'The Little Admiral', Wade Dudley takes a unique approach reaching back deep into the century and explores the astounding consequences of a young Hitler whose military service is with the German Navy in World War I. Britain had triumphed at sea for over 300 years, defeating would-be conquerors of Europe who mercifully did not understand sea power. How would it have fared against an evil genius who fixed upon the Royal Navy as Britain's centre of gravity.

The next two chapters concentrate on other perils facing Britain in the early part of the war. In Chapter 2, 'Disaster at Dunkirk', Stephen Badsey draws a picture of the destruction of the British Expeditionary Force on the continent, a fate it missed by a hairsbreadth and the subsequent advancement of the invasion of Britain itself. Charles Messenger writes in Chapter 3 of a Battle of Britain in which a few changes in reasoning and luck would have spelled the end of Fighter Command's ability to defend the English skies.

As Hitler turned his back on a still defiant Britain and plotted against the Soviet Union, history briefly waved a great opportunity before him and then withdrew it before he knew it. Stalin contemplated attacking first in 1941. Gil Villahermosa draws a thought-provoking description in Chapter 4, 'The Storm and the Whirlwind', of massed Soviet armies commanded by Zhukov attacking into the teeth of the German forces themselves assembling for Operation Barbarossa, Hitler's invasion of the Soviet Union.

In the middle period of the war, fate then hands Britain back the key to defeat as Paddy Griffith describes how close Rommel came to snapping the hinge of three continents in 1942 at El Alamein in Chapter 5, appropriately titled 'The Hinge'. Also in 1942, in Chapter 6, 'Into the Caucasus', Jack Gill examines the fascinating possibilities inherent in Turkey's entry into the war on the side of Germany. Turkey was the largest neutral state outside of the Americas. Its entry into the war on the side of Germany in 1942 would have stretched Soviet resources at their weakest moment. John Burtt rounds out the middle period of the war in Chapter 7, 'Known Enemies and Forced Allies', with the twin battles in time – Kursk and Sicily, each a close run thing and surprisingly interrelated.

The discussion of the final period of the war, 1944–45, addresses the possibilities of air power and technology in two chapters. In Chapter 8, 'Luftwaffe Triumphant', David Isby describes the possibility for defeat of the Combined Bomber Offensive which in reality was so vital to the steady destruction of the German ability to manage and supply war. Forrest Lindsey then addresses the horrendous consequences of Germany developing the atomic bomb first. No other weapon so embodied Hitler's compulsion to destruction. It is inconceivable that, if such a weapon had been available to him, he would not have immediately and gleefully used it.

Finally, in Chapter 10, 'Rommel Versus Zhukov', I draw a scenario in which Germany could have escaped destruction as late as August 1944. The Soviet steamroller seemed invincible by then and its victory inevitable. Yet, even after the destruction of Army Group Centre, Germany theoretically had the resources to achieve at least a stalemate on the Eastern Front. It is an optimum scenario but one which shows that, absent Hitler, rational German leadership had a chance for victory – not the victory of conquest but the victory of survival.

Peter G. Tsouras
Alexandria, Virginia
2002

Notes

1, Clausewitz, Carl von, *On War*, edited and translated by Howard, Michael, and Paret, Peter, (Princeton University Press, Princeton, NJ, 1976) p. 101.
2. Napoleon, *The Military Maxims of Napoleon*, tr. Burnod (1827), in Phillips, T.R., ed., *Roots of Strategy* (Stackpole Books, Harrisburg, PA, 1985) p. 436.

1
THE LITTLE ADMIRAL
Hitler and the German Navy

Wade G. Dudley

Introduction

We are the sum of our experiences. Change any of those experiences, and you change the person. Change the person, and you may just change the world. Make that person a young Adolf Hitler, and things do get interesting...

An undying enmity, 1914–19

By early 1914, the highly militarised states of Europe needed only a spark to precipitate war. Between universal conscription and a naval arms race of staggering proportions, few German-speaking young men could have doubted that their opportunity for glory would soon be upon them. Yet, it seemed that fate would deny at least one ardent, neophyte warrior the chance to validate his manhood. Twenty-five year old Adolf Hitler attempted to join the army of his native Austria in February – the army rejected his application.

Failure was not unknown to the brilliant but erratic Hitler. He had failed to gain his certificate from secondary school, failed in numerous odd jobs in and around Vienna, and failed as an aspiring artist. This time, a desperate Hitler determined to succeed. Using the last of his money (failure had also led to poverty and hunger), he purchased a train ticket for Bavaria, intending to enlist in a Bavarian army corps. Fatefully, Hitler shared a bench with Stabsoberbootsman (senior chief boatswain) Günther Luck, returning to active duty from family leave. The garrulous Luck, impressive in his dress uniform, regaled Hitler with stories of the Imperial German Navy's rapidly expanding *Hochseeflotte* (*High Sea Fleet*). As Luck explained, ship after ship sliding down the ways meant rapid promotion for any young man intelligent enough to grasp it. The Stabsoberbootsman must have been an impressive, convincing, and somewhat generous man, for Hitler accompanied him (at Luck's expense) to the German port of Kiel. There, with the support of his new mentor, the Austrian enlisted in the German Navy.

After a brief period of basic training, Hitler found himself assigned to the light cruiser *Wiesbaden*, on which Günther Luck served as senior petty officer. In a revealing letter to his wife, Luck wrote about the young seaman's brilliance and desire to learn, and about the one thing that Hitler had to un-learn, as well:

'He is an astounding young man, and reminds me of our poor Rudie [Luck's son had been killed in a tragic accident aboard the battleship *Posen* a year earlier] in both appearance and the desire to learn. He saw a picture of our boy on my desk; now he wears that silly moustache like Rudie wore, and he reads, he reads constantly. He devoured my technical manuals in the first month on board, and asked for more. I told him to see his division officer, and was surprised to hear him mutter, "But he is a damn Jew."

My darling, where do our children learn these things? We are a nation surrounded by enemies; we are sailors who constantly battle the sea for our survival. If we hate ourselves, what is left for our enemies but an easy victory? If we let race-hatred divide our crews, will we not founder and drown? I explained this to Adolf, I reasoned with him, and I threatened to box his ears – he never had a real father to do that for him, you know – if I ever heard such words again. Then I took him to see his lieutenant and arranged for Adolf to borrow naval histories. Privately, I explained the boy's prejudice, and asked the officer occasionally to discuss the books with Adolf.

Still, I worry. He will become a man of strong convictions, strong hates, strong loves. I can only hope that the war which I feel will soon be upon us will focus that hate away from good German citizens and toward our true enemies.'[1]

Hitler thrived in his new environment. Hard work, naval discipline, and the encouragement of his mentor each played their part in a true sea-change. Hitler discovered a capability to lead others. Between charisma, rapidly developing knowledge of seamanship, and the support of Günther Luck, he quickly rose to the rank of Unteroffiziere-maat (petty officer). Perhaps more importantly, he developed a fanatical devotion to the twin institutions of the Imperial Navy and the German Empire. A voracious reader of naval history and theory when off duty, Hitler often shared those theories with his men. They, in turn, affectionately called him '*unser kleine Admiral*' ('our little admiral'), and vowed to follow him anywhere – as long as it led to a tavern in Kiel, of course.[2]

After the beginning of the Great War in August 1914, the talk of every mess in the German Navy centred upon the British fleet. The news from abroad, though not unexpected, was bleak. Within months, Great Britain had swept the seas clean of German surface units, and the few German successes did not balance the list of lost ships and forever absent comrades. Worse, the Royal Navy maintained a distant blockade of the Baltic, denying

Germany imports, particularly the nitrates needed to fuel its munitions industry and as fertiliser for its agriculture. If the war continued (and the deadlock in France showed little change as the months dragged onward) then Germany faced a harsh choice – munitions or calories, feed the guns or feed the people.

Of course, if the Imperial Navy could force Great Britain to relinquish its blockade, that choice need not be made. But, despite its aggressive building programme in the early 1900s, the Imperial Navy could not match the quantity of British ships arrayed against it.[3] Thus the admirals of the *Hochseeflotte* settled on a policy of attriting British vessels by attempting to isolate portions of the Royal Navy, defeat them in detail, and prepare the way for a final confrontation on even terms somewhere in the North Sea. That policy failed, in part because British Intelligence monitored German wireless traffic and knew exactly when the *Hochseeflotte* sailed. German planning and British Intelligence efforts set the stage for the battle of Jutland on 31 May 1916.

Hitler would have died with Luck aboard the *Wiesbaden* at Jutland, had not a curious event occurred in late March 1916. While enjoying a weekend pass, Hitler chanced to be reading a recent translation of Alfred Thayer Mahan's *The Influence of Sea Power Upon History* while sitting in a small cafe near the naval base at Kiel. He acquiesced to the request of a well dressed civilian to join him at his table, leading to a long discussion of the book in general and the importance of achieving a crushing, Trafalgar-esque victory in particular. Impressed by the young petty officer's knowledge and zeal, the 'civilian' eventually revealed himself to be none other than Erich Raeder, chief of staff to Vice-Admiral Franz von Hipper, commander of the Imperial Navy's battlecruiser squadron. When asked if Hitler would value a place on Raeder's own staff, the overwhelmed sailor could only nod an affirmative. Four days later (and suffering from a tremendous hangover, courtesy of a farewell party staged by Luck and the crew of the *Wiesbaden*) Hitler transferred to the battlecruiser *Lützow*, Hipper's flagship, as Raeder's personal yeoman. Over the following weeks, Hitler continued to impress Hipper's chief of staff with his theoretical knowledge of sea power and his fine memory for detail.[4]

Jutland not only brought the direct association of Raeder and his yeoman to an end, it almost spelled the end of Hitler, himself. In the thick of the action, ten British heavy calibre shells and a torpedo eventually crippled the *Lützow*. Even as Hipper and Raeder prepared to transfer to another battlecruiser, an internal explosion laced the deck of the doomed flagship with shrapnel. Caught in the explosion, bleeding and concussed, it would be five days before Hitler, who had volunteered to lead a damage control party, regained consciousness.

Twice during Hitler's three-month convalescence, Raeder personally visited his favourite yeoman. Though newspapers declared Jutland a tactical victory for the *Hochseeflotte* based on tonnage lost, both men realised that the

British blockade could never be broken by the weaker German fleet. This became clear during the first, and unofficial, visit. As Hitler later recorded in his autobiography, *Mein Kampf* ('My Struggle'), discussion turned to the future of the German Navy. Both men agreed that Great Britain would remain the greatest threat to Germany in this and any future war. Indeed, Hitler, upon learning of the loss of the *Wiesbaden* and its entire crew – his dear comrades! – at Jutland, took the first steps toward developing a near pathological hatred of all things British. Raeder, steeped in conservative naval tradition, still favoured the search for a single climactic battle to destroy the Royal Navy. Hitler openly agreed with the officer, but privately saw this approach as hopeless, and wondered if another means of destroying the Royal Navy was not already at hand – the *Unterseebooten* (or U-boats, Germany's submarines).[5]

At the end of Raeder's second visit, an official visit to award the petty officer the Iron Cross First Class in recognition of his valour at Jutland, the chief of staff offered to assist Hitler in any way possible. Hitler immediately requested a transfer to U-boats. Though shocked, Raeder recognised the young man's desire to strike at the hated British, something no longer possible in the *Hochseeflotte*. He not only approved the transfer, but also pulled the necessary strings to promote Hitler to probationary Leutnant-zur-See. This made Hitler somewhat of an oddity: a *Volksoffizier*, a commissioned officer raised from the ranks in an overwhelmingly aristocratic officer corps. But, as Raeder undoubtedly surmised, such would matter little in the tight confines of the submarine service.[6]

Thus, in late September 1916, Hitler reported aboard *U-39*. He thrived; in fact the only criticism recorded in his fitness reports concerned the intensity of his hatred for the British foes, a hatred that his captain feared could lead to excessive risk-taking in Hitler's zeal to sink British vessels. On the other hand, the lieutenant received the highest praise for the quickness with which he learned the complicated operation of the boat and grasped the tactics of both gun and torpedo, as well as for his leadership skills. Even the captain seemed somewhat mesmerised by the sheer intensity of the Austrian.

By January 1917, Hitler was serving as (still probationary) second watch officer of *U-39*. In that month, a new watch officer joined the boat. As with Hitler, Karl Dönitz had begun his naval career in cruisers, then transferred to submarines. The two men became fast friends; in fact, Dönitz would later credit Hitler as his role model for the boldness and inspirational leadership that characterised his career. During long watches and shared miseries, the officers often discussed the future of naval warfare. Decades later, Dönitz would recall one miserable watch in particular. With the ship running on the surface at night and both men soaked to the skin, he envisioned fleets of submarines, each boat of tremendous size, range, and destructive power, that could, perhaps, circle the globe without once rising to the surface to replenish air, charge batteries, and soak watch officers. Hitler shrugged, then pointed to the waves that often towered above the fragile vessel. What point in such fleets, he questioned, if they could not even find the enemy? What good would they serve if they could project their firepower only over short distances? First, asserted Hitler, some method of discovering the enemy at a distance was needed; then, some method of killing that enemy at a distance had to be found; then, perhaps, whining third officers could stay dry. Dönitz recalled that he laughed, and asked if adding seaplane hangars to his new submarines would satisfy his friend. Perhaps, the second officer replied, or perhaps something more would be needed.[7]

By 1917, German unlimited submarine warfare offered the only real chance of convincing Great Britain to leave the war and to end its blockade. Instead, a starving Germany watched as a new enemy, the United States, entered the alliance against it. Fortunately, the collapse of Russia allowed the transfer of forces to the West, and a renewed offensive in France held hope that the war could be ended favourably before American troops arrived in quantity. As for the navy, the *Hochseeflotte* remained useless except as a fleet-in-being, and the U-boat force shouldered an increasingly heavy load. In March 1918, Hitler received a promotion to Kapitänleutnant (Lieutenant-Commander) and a transfer to *U-71* as the executive officer of Korvettenkapitän (Commander) Kurt Slevogt. His friend, Dönitz, had been transferred to the Mediterranean, where he soon commanded a submarine of his own.

When *U-71* unmoored at Kiel in October for a new patrol, few of its crew harboured doubts that the end of the war was close. Some sailors, in fact, might well have refused to sail if not for the silver tongue of their charismatic executive officer. Hitler, having just learned that Dönitz's boat had been lost in action, called for one last strike against the English, one last blow for German honour, one last pound of British flesh to avenge dead comrades. To the last man, the crew cheered and vowed to follow their officers to Valhalla – or to Hell.[8] On 1 November their chance to see one or the other of those locations appeared near. Driven deep by British escorts after torpedoing two merchant ships in a daring daylight surface attack, depth-charges pounded *U-71*. Suddenly, a series of loud noises shook the boat, almost as if a hammer were repeatedly striking inside the vessel. Rushing from the control room to the engine room, Hitler saw that one of the quarter-ton pistons had been ripped from the engine by concussion and was banging at the thin inner wall of the boat. Knowing that if the noise did not pinpoint the submarine's location for its attackers, then the piston would soon punch through the hull and sink the vessel, he leapt to cushion the blows with his own body.

U-71 survived, and the engine was even repaired later that night. As the boat crept home, Adolf Hitler lay near death, his skull fractured in his act of heroism. Admitted to Kiel Naval Hospital on 10 November, Hitler finally regained consciousness on 15 November. The following day the doctors gave him two pieces of news that would change his life forever. First, the young officer could never again go to sea. Irreparable damage to his inner ear would impact his sense of balance for the remainder of his life, guaranteeing symptoms similar to seasickness if he even tried to stand on a rolling deck again. Second, an armistice had been signed, and though negotiations continued, Germany had lost the war.

Broken in body and stripped of his career, it would be months before Hitler could function with any normalcy again. Many people would have abandoned hope as they lay in a hospital and watched a once great nation collapse around them. Even Hitler later admitted that he felt that despair, felt the temptation to suicide. But rather than surrender, he chose to focus on the enemy who had brought him to this crisis in his life. And in those dark days of 1919, a bitter enmity for all things British began to consume Adolf Hitler. It would be the strength of this hatred that allowed a new Germany to arise.

From the ashes, 1919–39

From late 1918 through mid-1919, the Royal Navy continued its devastating blockade of Germany as the victorious allies ruminated in Paris on how best to punish their enemies and share the spoils of war. The Treaty of Versailles dismantled the German Empire, giving parts of its territory to France and the new nation of Poland. It hobbled the German military machine with limitations on manpower, weaponry, armaments industry, and even technological development. It crippled the spirit of the German people with its forced assumption of 'war guilt', demanding that they alone accept responsibility for causing the Great War.

Worse, perhaps, than all the damning clauses of that fatal treaty, during 1918 and 1919 the German people lost faith in the leadership of their statesmen, admirals and generals. The sense of betrayal from the top coupled with economic chaos led to near anarchy, controlled only by the heavy-handed police force that had once been the mighty Imperial Army. From the ashes of empire, the Weimar Republic rose to fill the political void, and in the late 1920s it actually restored a façade of economic prosperity to the nation. The economic depression which swept the globe after 1929 revealed that façade to the German people, and, discontented with the elitist Weimar Republic, they quickly called for a man of the people as their leader. His name, of course, was Adolf Hitler.

Hitler's meteoric rise owed much to his ties to the old Imperial Navy and to two officers in particular, Erich Raeder and Karl Dönitz. Raeder had rescued his protégé from the hospital at Kiel and taken him into his own home to recover from his near-fatal injuries. Two months later, Dönitz knocked on the door, having been captured rather than killed with his U-boat. His stories of ill-treatment as a British prisoner of war further strengthened Hitler's hatred of that nation. Clearly, the early months of 1919 marked the formation of the triumvirate that would build the new *Kriegsmarine* (German Navy) and found *Das Dritte Reich* (The Third Reich);

and just as clearly the least senior of the three men quickly assumed dominance of that triumvirate.

The post-Great War German Navy, limited to 15,000 officers and men and a handful of vessels (and no submarines) by the Treaty of Versailles, had little use for an officer who could no longer go to sea. Nonetheless, Raeder found a role for Hitler in the Ship Design Bureau, where he secretly developed plans for a new class of German warship, the aircraft carrier, and for the integration of new technologies into the *Kriegsmarine*.

Hitler also became the political operative of the three men, insinuating himself into a tiny political party, changing its name to National Socialist German Worker's Party ('Nazi', for short), and rapidly developing its power base through personal charisma, funds initially funnelled from the German naval budget, and the physical prowess of his 'Blueshirts'.[9] His speeches enthralled the citizenry, especially when he ripped open his tunic to display the scars earned 'for the glory of the Fatherland; for the survival of you, my German people!' The war, he harangued, had been lost by '...those who never risked their lives for the Reich, who grew fat while German children starved during the Turnip Winter and those worse winters that followed.' The future of the nation properly belonged '...with your heroes, not those cowards afraid to face the enemy's fire.'[10] With the Swastika waving above him (he designed the banner of the Nazi party himself in 1920), Hitler captivated the German people and alarmed the German government. In 1922, Hitler officially resigned from the German Navy to pursue politics full time, though the Ship Design Bureau retained his services as a civilian consultant.

In 1923, the Weimar government arrested Hitler for involvement in the Beer Hall Putsch, an attempt fronted by General Ludendorff (a senior general of the Great War) to seize control of Germany. While awaiting trial for treason, Hitler dictated his personal history and philosophic thoughts, later published as *Mein Kampf*, to fellow prisoner Rudolf Hess.[11] The judge at the trial, a secret Nazi sympathiser himself, failed to convict Hitler; offering as his reasoning that the supporters of Ludendorff had worn brown shirts instead of the blue associated with the Nazi leader. It was a popular, though wrong, decision – Hitler had, indeed, been involved in the treasonous act.

Hitler continued to build support for his Nazi Party. The economic downturn of 1930–31 provided an opportunity for the party to seize control of the government. On 13 March 1932, Hitler defeated Hindenburg (another general of the Great War) for the German presidency by claiming 53 percent of the vote to his opponent's 36.8 percent. The Enabling Act of March 1933, passed on the strength of jingoism ('Many hands have failed Germany, let two hands lead us!') and Blueshirt coercion, established the Nazis as the only German political party and Hitler as *Der Führer* (the Leader), absolute dictator of his nation.

While Hitler achieved political prominence, Karl Dönitz wore several hats within the German Navy. Officially, he served within the Ship Design Bureau, as had Hitler. Unofficially, he was the junior member of a coterie of officers that closely circled Admiral Raeder – officers committed to building a new and powerful *Kriegsmarine*. In that group, he had two roles. Dönitz is best known for the top secret development of the new submarine force. By 1932, he had secretly constructed ten small U-boats, had developed the plans for the next generation of long-range vessels, had begun training the crews for those boats, and had developed the theoretical tactics to use a U-boat fleet against Great Britain. The fruition of his efforts waited only on Hitler's seizure of the German government and the public nullification of the hated Treaty of Versailles.

Dönitz's second role has only recently been uncovered by historians. Between 1925 and 1934, he master-minded German naval intelligence. To his credit belong several major espionage efforts, including the acquisition of the plans for the Japanese 'Long Lance' torpedo. Dönitz also managed to place moles in several American and British institutions of higher education, allowing him access to (often secret) research in those countries and certainly providing Germany with schematics of the radar systems which would shortly be under development. Finally, to replace the overseas bases lost by Germany at the end of the Great War, Dönitz developed a supply system supported by sympathetic shipping magnates and industrialists in countries which could be expected to maintain their neutrality in the next round of war. In 1934 he received his richly deserved promotion to the rank of admiral from the hands of Hitler, who officially named him as Chief of Submarine Forces – an act accompanied by the public renunciation of the terms of the Treaty of Versailles.

While Hitler received the adoring accolades of the public and Dönitz submerged himself in the depths of international intrigue, Erich Raeder set the stage for the three men's vision of a new world naval order. In truth, he served as the rudder of the triumvirate, restraining the enthusiasm of Dönitz and smothering (at least visibly) the ardent Anglophobia of Hitler, while risking his own neck to siphon funds from the very public naval budget into 'black operations' and political adventurism.[12] In 1928 Raeder had become Admiral and Chief of Naval Command. At last, he had the power, if not the budget, to modernise the German Navy. In 1932 Hitler also granted him the lion's share of German military appropriations; and in 1934, the renunciation of Versailles removed the final yoke from Raeder's neck.

By 1928, Germany's Great War vintage battleships required replacements (allowed by the Treaty of Versailles as long as the replacements displaced 10,000 tons or less). Raeder proposed building three 'pocket battleships.' Mounting only six 11-inch primary guns in two turrets, they traded a third turret for speed (28 knots) and operational range (9–10,000 nautical miles at 18 knots). At the same time, he requested the building of 30 destroyers and 6 light cruisers, all trading heavier armament for extended range capability. With the Nazi Party already dominating the German parliament, his plan received rapid approval. Over the following five years, three battleships (*Deutschland*, *Admiral Scheer*, *Admiral Graf Spee*), three cruisers (*Seydlitz*, *Nürnberg*, *Wiesbaden*), and 30 modern destroyers slid down the ways. All of the vessels violated treaty stipulations in one manner or another, but the victorious allies of the Great War, distracted by global economic disaster, lacked the energy for a vigorous (i.e. military) protest.

That lack of protest, more than any other factor, allowed Hitler to disavow the Treaty of Versailles in its entirety. From 1934 to 1939, all segments of the German military rearmed with great vigour. For Raeder, Hitler and Dönitz, the time had arrived to put theory into practice. In a top secret missive to the key officers of the *Kriegsmarine*, Raeder (speaking not only for Hitler but outlining a plan that certainly bore his mark) discussed the future objectives of the navy.

'Our primary enemy, is the Royal Navy of Great Britain. We must destroy it, then land forces to subdue the English people. No nation has achieved that goal since 1066. Every nation that has tried to achieve equality with England has failed – not because of a lack of will, not because of industrial inferiority, but only because they failed to destroy the Royal Navy and its power of blockade. We shall succeed. We shall avenge our comrades who died and our children who starved at the hands of the Royal Navy from 1914 to 1919...

Phase I of our effort nears completion. A nucleus of modern surface ships is complete or near complete. Today I have ordered the conversion of the three light cruisers now under construction to aircraft carriers. Unknown to many of you, plans for light and heavy carriers have been under development since 1920, as have the plans for modern aircraft for those carriers. I have the highest assurances that the carriers will be completed by early 1936.

Phase II begins immediately. Construction has been ordered on the following ships: 2 heavy carriers, 2 pocket battleships, 2 large battleships, 3 heavy cruisers, 60 destroyers, 10 fast oilers, 10 fast replenishment vessels. Due to limitations of the economy, completion of all ships is not expected until 1942. Additionally, orders for seagoing U-boats will be placed in the next month, with an estimated delivery of five boats per month by mid-1935. Finally, the Führer has approved the formation of 30 aircraft squadrons for naval service and of a corps of marines to train for amphibious assaults...

The marine corps will consist of three divisions of light infantry plus supporting units, including a special operations battalion, an amphibious armoured brigade, and a parachutist brigade. Shipping and air assets will be allocated to provide a 100 per cent first wave lift capability to the corps. For security purposes, the corps will be designated *Schutzstaffel* ['guard detachment', abbreviated *SS*], and will officially serve as security detachments aboard ships and at bases, and as a bodyguard for the Führer. Secretly, it will begin planning and training for the potential invasion of England... [13]

We do not envision war before 1942, but we cannot ignore the fact that Great Britain or France could strike first, especially if either nation realises that the Führer intends to restore Germany to its proper place in the world. To discourage premature conflict, every effort must be made to deceive our enemy as to our future intentions. There will, on pain of death, be neither public discussion of this missive nor overt criticism of the Royal Navy... '[14]

Grandiose plans, indeed, but could Hitler accomplish them? Could he mould the entire German government to his will? The man that most Germans soon called their Little Admiral quickly discovered that a government did not perform with naval efficiency. Ruthless, he sacked bureaucrats who did not come up to scratch and simply nationalised businesses that operated inefficiently. He put the German people to work building an infrastructure of roads and railways, even airlines, second to none – and the trains did run on time. He had little time for sycophants and no time for inefficiency or internal squabbling.[15] By early 1936, Hitler had accomplished miracles both within and without Germany – and had rallied the German-speaking people of Europe to the Nazi banner.

Backed by a daily strengthening military armed from the industry of the Rhineland (re-militarised in 1934), Hitler began the *Anschluss*, the annexation of all territory that had once belonged to Imperial Germany or that now held German-speaking populations. Province by province and nation by nation, he dismantled the artificial states created by the Treaty of Versailles. And his former enemies of the Great War, Britain and France, practised appeasement – refusing to commit troops and treasure to stop the expansion of Hitler's Reich. They convinced themselves that his territorial ambitions had limits, and they were correct – to a point.

Hitler also scored three diplomatic coups during the waning years of the 1930s. He cemented alliances with both Italy (the Rome–Berlin Axis) and Japan. Both countries possessed large navies, and could challenge the Royal Navy in the Mediterranean and in the Pacific respectively. Finally, he achieved an understanding with Josef Stalin, the Russian dictator. Representatives of the two nations signed a trade treaty (with military undertones) in early August 1939. That alliance of convenience not only placed the threat of a two-front war in abeyance, it provided a much needed trading partner for Germany.

By 1939 only one portion of the old German Empire still defied Hitler's grasp: Poland. And Hitler, for the first time since 1919, wavered. His trepidation did not stem from the fact that an attack on Poland would bring Britain and France immediately to its aid, as he welcomed the conflict with the Royal Navy. Rather, as his confidant, Dönitz, later recorded, Hitler feared the failure of his army, 'Ah, Karl, at sea I am like a lion, brave and fierce, but on land I am such a coward.'[16] Only in June did he finally order the implementation of Case White, the invasion of Poland, for 1 September 1939. In mid-August, at the last joint planning session of the German High Command before the invasion, the Führer spoke with great passion. Victory, he explained to his generals and admirals, is never certain. Nothing is without risk. Hitler anticipated victory, however he ominously warned that 'we may be destroyed, but if we are, we shall drag a world with us …a world in flames.'[17]

A world in flames, 1939–45

On the eve of the invasion that would drag Europe into the conflagration which already appeared to be consuming Asia, the *Kriegsmarine* had not achieved quantitative parity with its primary enemy, the Royal Navy. Great Britain enjoyed an advantage in capital ships (battleships, battlecruisers, pocket battleships) of 15:4, in carriers of 5:4, in cruisers of 56:3, in destroyers of 159:53. Only in submarines did the advantage rest with Germany, 131:54. Both sides also featured coastal defence forces, mostly older vessels. Germany accepted it as a given that France would enter the war on the British side, but its substantial navy (6 capital ships, 1 carrier, 18 cruisers, 58 destroyers, 76 submarines) would be committed in the Mediterranean, watching Germany's reluctant ally, Italy (4 capital ships, 21 cruisers, 48 destroyers, 104 submarines).[18]

Still, Hitler, Raeder, and Dönitz realised that their navy possessed several advantages. Most of the German ships had been constructed in the past seven years, no ships were in refit, and the German admirals could dictate the tempo of initial operations. Perhaps more importantly, the Royal Navy faced obligations that stretched the length and breadth of the globe-spanning British Empire, while the numerically weaker forces of the *Kriegsmarine* could be concentrated in northern European waters. Finally, the element of tactical surprise could be exploited to the utmost.

Part of that surprise centred upon innovative carrier and U-boat tactics. By 1939 the concept of *Rudeltaktik* ('pack/group tactics'), pioneered by Dönitz and refined by Raeder, had been applied at all levels of the *Kriegsmarine*. The *Rudel* was a permanent organisation (as distinct from a task force), composed for surface forces of (ideally) a carrier, a battleship, a cruiser, and 20 destroyers supported by two fast oilers and three fast replenishment vessels. As a permanent organisation, the men and ships of each *Rudel* had served together for months (years, in many cases) and had developed a level of group expertise superior to that of any contemporary naval task force. With a top speed of 29–30 knots, a cruising range of 11–12,000 miles, a force projection radius of 250 miles, and the ability of the carrier to replace its planes while at sea (replenishment vessels carried 20 spare planes), the German carrier group would be a deadly opponent when commanded with skill and daring.

The U-boat *Rudel* consisted of ten boats, usually nine medium range Type VIIC (770 tons) and one Type IXC (1,120 tons) to operate as a command/control vessel, though two of the eleven groups functional in 1939 contained all Type IXC boats (allowing them to take station at any point in the Atlantic Basin). Dönitz (disappointed, by the way, at the failure of German industry to meet his production demands) realised that his wolf packs could not afford the heavy losses experienced by U-boats in the Great War once Britain adopted a convoy system. He also agreed with Hitler that a complete isolation of the British Isles was not feasible, and that, based upon Germany's own experience, such a blockade could not return the short-term results needed to defeat their foe. Thus he determined that the primary objective of his U-boat force was to attrite the Royal Navy – sinking merchant tonnage would be a secondary objective. Once a convoy had been spotted by a wolf pack, the radar-equipped command/control boat would race to shadow the convoy and concentrate its flock.[19] As soon as concentration had been achieved, two U-boats would target the merchantmen, drawing escorts to their location. The remaining members of the *Rudel* would sink those escorts. If the elimination of the escort could be accomplished, the defenceless convoy could be sunk at leisure (and without endangering precious U-boats). Dönitz's standing order stipulated that no attacks would take place without concentration being achieved. By the end of August 1939, six of the eleven wolf packs crowded the Western Approaches, another cruised near Gibraltar, while two crept stealthily towards Scapa Flow, primary anchorage of the Royal Navy. The time to test mettle and tactics rapidly approached.

At dawn on 1 September the German war machine smashed across the Polish border in what would be a short campaign – a proving ground for the *Blitzkrieg* ('lightning war') tactics of Hitler's generals. But Hitler's attention focused westward that morning, to London, where at 06.00 the German ambassador delivered a declaration of war to the British prime minister's office, and to Scapa Flow, where at 06.05 his German eagles would descend on the anchored British lions of the Home Fleet.

Over the past weeks, three of the four German carrier groups had scattered across the Atlantic, ostensibly to show the flag or to train. *Carrier Group* (*CG*) *I* (CV *Graf Zeppelin*, BB *Scharnhorst*, 16 destroyers, and support vessels) was on a return voyage from the South American coast, scheduled to reach Kiel on 3 September.[20] *CG II* (CVL *Günther Luck*, B *Admiral Graf Spee*, a light cruiser, 12 destroyers, and support vessels) had sailed in mid-August for the port of New York with the new German ambassador to the United States onboard. *CG III* (CVL *Gorch Fock*, B *Admiral Scheer*, a light cruiser, 14 destroyers, and support vessels) neared the Straits of Gibraltar, en route to Italy. Only *CG IV* (CVL *Fritz Heinzen*, B *Deutschland*, a light cruiser, 11 destroyers, and support vessels) remained in port through the waning days of August, only to slip its moorings quietly late on 30 August for a run to the North Sea.

By the evening of 31 August, *CG II* had detached DD *Hans Lody* to convey the ambassador to New York, then reversed its course and steamed to within 150 miles west of Scapa Flow. *CG I* had slowed its journey home, and cruised some 200 miles northeast of the British naval base. Since nearing British territorial waters, it had been shadowed by HMS *Sheffield*; but, low on fuel, that ship had broken contact (with an exchange of friendly signals) earlier in the day. *CG IV*, after a rapid passage through the Skagerrak, held position 150 miles southeast of Scapa Flow. At 01.00 on 1 September commanders of the three naval forces announced the existence of a state of war between the Third Reich and its arch-nemesis, Great Britain. Personal messages from Hitler and Admiral Raeder called for vengeance upon the fleet that had starved German children in 1919, and exhorted men and officers to make the opening blow of the new conflict a victory 'für Führer, für Reich, für Volk!'

At 06.03, the first wave of planes – four Me Bf 109T fighters, eight Fi 167 torpedo bombers, and eight Ju 87C dive bombers from *CG II* – screamed over the unprepared British Home Fleet at Scapa Flow.[21] Within minutes, 14 fighters, 21 torpedo bombers, and 24 dive bombers from *CG I* and *III* joined the assault. By 06.30, the last of the raiders had departed, unable fully to evaluate damage to the Royal Navy because of the heavy pall of smoke blanketing the harbour. And that damage was severe. Two fleet carriers, *Glorious* and *Ark Royal*, burned fiercely before sinking. Two Great War vintage battleships, *Queen Elizabeth* and *Warspite*, had slipped beneath the cold waters minutes after taking two torpedo hits each. BC *Renown*, its magazine penetrated by a bomb, exploded, then sank in seconds – over 1,000 men died with it alone. BB *Royal Sovereign*, serving as flag for the Home Fleet, lost its A-turret to a bomb and its propellers to a torpedo. The final tally of the German surprise attack was three capital ships, two carriers, a heavy cruiser, and three destroyers sunk for the cost of four planes. Additionally, of the remaining seven veterans of the British battleline at anchor that morning, all except the battlecruiser *Hood* carried some mark of German bombs and torpedoes, while Bf 109s had savaged every plane at Scapa Flow's airfields. Even then, the trial by fire of 1 September for the Home Fleet was far from complete.

Expecting additional attacks from the German carriers, survivors of the Home Fleet sortied for southern bases and their own air cover. But the German carriers had no intention of risking a second attack. After recovering planes, *CG I* steamed for Kiel and the first of many 'heroes' welcomes' for the *Kriegsmarine*. *CG II* made maximum speed for the South Atlantic and *CG IV* moved at flank speed toward Halifax, Nova Scotia. Torment by air for the Home Fleet had ended for the day, but their disorganised flight stumbled into the waiting U-boats of *Submarine Groups I* and *V (SG I, SG V)*. Vice-Admiral Kurt Slevogt, commanding *SG I*, was a model of Teutonic efficiency that day. He applied the convoy attack paradigm to the Home Fleet, using one submarine as a decoy while others

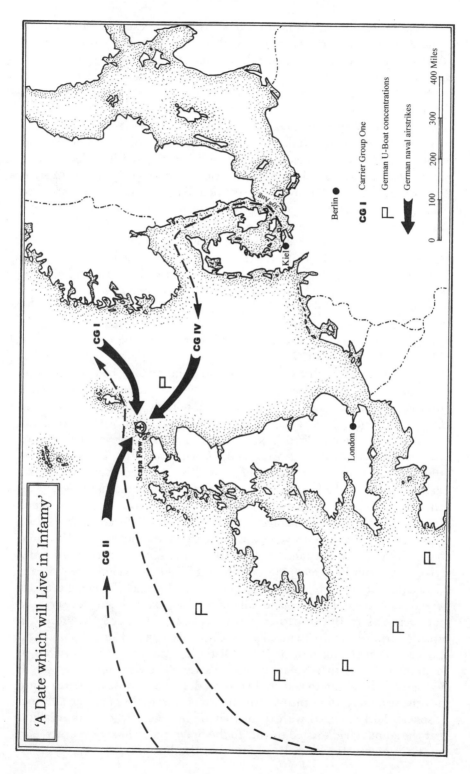

'A Date which will Live in Infamy'

CG I — Carrier Group One

▯ — German U-Boat concentrations

➤ — German naval airstrikes

Berlin ●

Kiel

Scapa Flow

London ●

0   100   200   300   400 Miles

lined up shots on its would-be attackers. By 23.00 Slevogt's tally included eight destroyers and three cruisers without the loss of a single U-boat. *SG V*'s commander failed to control the engagement. Committing his own boat to the attack early in the day, he paid the ultimate price. Two more of his boats fell to British depth charges, though it is probable that one of them managed to attack the *Royal Sovereign*, damaged and under tow, which capsized at 16.51 that afternoon when a single torpedo struck it amidships.

Throughout the remainder of September, as German armoured and infantry forces ground Poland beneath metal tracks and hobnailed boots, the *Kriegsmarine* ran amok in the Atlantic. U-boats savaged the Western Approaches, sinking 30 convoy escorts (including 18 fleet destroyers), three cruisers, and thousands of tons of merchantmen for a loss of only four submarines. *CG II* added three cruisers (*Exeter*, *Ajax*, and *Achilles*), four destroyers, and numerous merchantmen to the bag while operating near the mouth of Uruguay's River Plate. It then refuelled at neutral Montevideo before sailing for the North Sea and home. *CG IV* closed Halifax in mid-September, launching an air raid on its weakly defended harbour and shipyards before being warned clear of North American waters by the United States.[22] *CG III*, however, established a new milestone in naval history on 12 September: the first carrier versus carrier battle.

Since 1 September, *CG III* had been operating near the Straits of Gibraltar, interdicting British and French shipping (France had declared war on Germany on 3 September). By remaining in the same area, Vice-Admiral Günther Lütjens engaged in several risks, notably the concentration of enemy submarines and perhaps night attacks against his group by light forces from Gibraltar or French North African ports. However, he hoped to lure two British carriers, *Furious* and *Hermes*, from the British base at Gibraltar to the open sea where they could be engaged. By dawn on the 12th, his task force had evaded or destroyed five submarine contacts, and he ordered an unhappy withdrawal to the northwest. But at 10.23, scout planes reported that British Force H (three battleships, the two carriers, two cruisers, and a dozen destroyers) was not only at sea, but was on the same course as *CG III* at a distance of only 100 miles! Lütjens quickly ordered a strike force launched, retaining only four Bf 109s for Combat Air Patrol (CAP). His attack wave had no sooner cleared the deck than his radar detected a covey of British planes inbound. The next half hour revealed the true weakness of British carriers – their planes. The Fairey Swordfish, a biplane torpedo bomber with a top speed of less than 150mph, stood no chance against the modern Bf 109s. Of the 23 attackers, 15 fell victim to the fighters before they began their attack run. The remainder persevered, two actually surviving to launch their torpedoes (both missed) before falling into the sea. Only 14 of the 69 British airmen survived to become German prisoners. Lütjens dined with them that night, one of the flyers recalling that the admiral had toasted them: 'To the bravest men I have ever met, and damn the criminals who make you fly that deathtrap.'[23]

While the Germans rescued the downed flyers, their attack wave made contact with Force H. Brushing aside the pitiful British CAP, German torpedoes and bombs sank *Hermes* and severely damaged *Furious*, but not without a price. Of the 15 bombers involved in the attack, seven failed to return to *CG III*, and three of those that did return were so riddled with anti-aircraft fire as to be useable only for spare parts. Clearly, attacking a prepared British fleet with such a small number of planes would cost the German light carriers dear. Lütjens carefully considered that fact as Force H limped for home and *CG III* sped away to replenish its planes from its supply vessels in safety.

The Polish campaign ended on 27 September, a visible testament to the power of the German *Wehrmacht* and *Luftwaffe*. When coupled with the successes of the *Kriegsmarine*, German victories offered Hitler the opportunity for considerable diplomatic suasion. In mid-October, he hosted a meeting of several non-aligned European nations in Warsaw (amid the physical evidence of his nation's military prowess), including Belgium, Luxembourg, Holland, Denmark, Norway, Sweden, Finland, Hungary, and Romania. Hitler proposed the creation of a multi-lateral treaty between these nations and Germany. Each nation would enjoy favoured trade status with the Reich and would benefit from its protection against external threats. In return, Hitler requested rights of military passage through signatory nations and long-term leases of land for naval and air bases. Finally, he warned that in these dangerous times no nation could afford to straddle the political fence, and that Germany would deal with its enemies as easily as its friends.

On 19 October 1939, Germany, Finland, Hungary, and Romania signed Hitler's Danzig Pact. After a 24-hour conquest of Denmark on 11 November (according to a statement by Raeder, 'to defend the Baltic sea lanes from probable Anglo-French blockade'), Norway and Sweden reconsidered their stance and belatedly signed the treaty. Of course, the interdiction of the North Sea trade lanes by *CG I* and various U-boat groups during October and November probably helped Norway reach its decision.

On land, the winter of 1939–40 developed into the *Sitzkrieg*, or phony war, as the French slowly mobilised behind their 'impregnable' Maginot Line. Meanwhile, British shipping, guarded by the Royal Navy and Royal Air Force, convoyed the British Expeditionary Force (BEF) to France and Belgium. Twice the German Navy tried to interfere with the convoys, only to discover the vulnerability of both carrier groups and U-boats to concentrated enemy air power. *CG I* lost two destroyers and 28 planes, as well as suffering light damage to the *Graf Zeppelin* on 6 December, while *SG I* lost four boats, including the expert Admiral Slevogt, in the shallow Channel waters in early November. This established the pattern for the surface war at sea over the dark months of winter. Where British land-based air operated, the German carrier groups did not. Outside that range, those groups operated with a fairly free hand. In particular, the German Navy dominated the North Sea (especially after establishing its own land-based air in Denmark and Norway) and the Atlantic–Mediterranean shipping lanes.

Desperate to open the shipping lanes to the Mediterranean, allied surface forces sortied against the *Kriegsmarine* four times, losing two battleships, the only French carrier, four cruisers, and 16 destroyers in exchange for a German cruiser and two destroyers (all three lost to French carrier planes). British and French submarines fared just as badly, 20 being lost in the area over the winter months. Unknown to the allies, the excellent German radar almost always identified the submarines before they submerged to attack, operators immediately vectoring destroyers against the would-be assailants.

The North Sea presented a different set of problems for both sides. In mid-October, Hitler had declared the North Sea–Baltic sealane an open trade route, as long as merchant ships kept their bows pointed away from England. In addition, he removed all port duties and tariffs on goods entering Germany. American industrialists could not resist the strong profits in a lane not threatened by the U-boats operating near the British Isles. German trade with the United States boomed, that with Britain declined. Unless the Royal Navy could regain control of the North Sea, it could not stop the trade. Worse, the accidental torpedoing of an American luxury liner by HMS *Sealion* on 18 December threatened to turn American public opinion against Great Britain. Events in Europe stymied American President Franklin Delano Roosevelt, who strongly supported Great Britain, but faced an election in 1940 and an obviously growing wave of support for Germany among voters.

In early January, the Royal Navy attempted to take advantage of the short northern nights and the absence of *Graf Zeppelin* from *CG I* (in Germany for repairs following the engagement of 6 December) by sending a Task Force composed of BC *Hood*, two heavy cruisers, and 12 destroyers into Norwegian waters. In near absolute darkness, an alert *Scharnhorst* used its radar to place accurate fire on the British force, then directed its ten destroyers in launching their Long Lance torpedoes into the inky night. Only one cruiser and five destroyers escaped this novel use of the new radar technology. For the gallant *Hood*, unscathed at Scapa Flow in September, luck had expired. A magazine explosion doomed the ship and its entire crew, as well as any chance for Britain to close Germany's Baltic trade lanes.

By May 1940 the British situation had deteriorated at all levels. The Royal Navy had lost seven capital ships, four carriers, 28 cruisers, and 96 destroyers (most of these to U-boats while escorting convoys). With supply lines to the East Indies interrupted, shortages in several strategic materials and petroleum products threatened to slow or stop British industry. British land forces in the Mediterranean operated on shoestring logistics, British naval forces in Gibraltar and Malta hoarded precious munitions and consumables. From India to Singapore, from Canada to Australia, raw materials stockpiled and economic collapse threatened in numerous market sectors. And the United States, trapped between isolationism and German gold, remained unwilling to come to the aid of its old ally.

On 10 May 1940 Britain's struggle took a turn for the worse as Germany unleashed its military might on the Low Countries and France. By 26 May the BEF and isolated portions of the French Army stood with their backs to the Channel near the port of Dunkirk, praying for a miracle that never came. Pushed by Hitler to drive the hated British from the Continent forever, the *Wehrmacht*, ably supported by the *Luftwaffe*, slammed ever forward, closing the last Channel port on 29 May. General Erwin Rommel of *7th Panzer Division* accepted the official surrender of the BEF the following day. The Royal Navy, aided by many gallant civilian vessels, had managed to evacuate fewer than 30,000 British soldiers, most without even rifles, while suffering heavy losses from German land-based air.

France surrendered on 22 June, Hitler dancing a jig as French representatives signed the terms of surrender in the same rail car in which Germany had been shamed in 1918. The terms were harsh: occupation by German troops for an indeterminate period, loss of the provinces of Alsace and Lorraine, disbandment of France's army and air force, surrender of its navy to Italian forces (Italy had at last joined the war – after Germany had beaten France), reparations (the amount to be determined 'at a later date'), and forced participation in the Danzig Pact.

By mid-July, the *Luftwaffe* had relocated its forward air bases to France. On 28 July Hitler unleashed Operation Eagle, designed to drive the Royal Navy from the Channel coast and the Royal Air Force from the Channel skies. Supported by three carrier groups from the North Sea, the German Air Force smashed shipping and repair facilities as well as major airfields throughout eastern England. On 23 August Prime Minister Winston Churchill quietly ordered the remnants of the Home Fleet to Canada, then broke the news to Parliament with those famous words, 'Sometimes blood, sweat, and tears are of little avail… '

In the early morning hours of 18 September 1940, English residents near the coasts of Sussex woke to the sound of numerous planes flying inland. Many rushed to their cellars, waiting for the inevitable bombs. But this time, the German payloads fell softly from the sky. Parachutists of the *Wehrmacht*'s veteran *7th Flieger Division* seized critical road junctions and towns, isolating a long stretch of England's coastline, while their comrades of the *SS Parachute Brigade* dropped directly (and with heavy casualties) onto four British airfields, allowing the rapid deployment of reinforcements from the *Wehrmacht*'s *22nd Air Landing Division*. At dawn, units of the British Home Guard, supported by the pitifully few remnants of the regular army gutted at Dunkirk, watched with horror as German tanks swam from the sea alongside the flat-bottomed landing craft of the *SS 'Liebstandarte'* and *'Das Reich' Divisions*.[24] The British troops fought bravely, but short of experience and equipment, and isolated by the German parachutists to their rear, the issue was never in doubt. By the end of the day, *SS* troopers from the beaches had linked with their fellows from the skies, securing a perimeter that included the port facilities at Brighton and Worthing.

Over the next two weeks, the SS slowly expanded the perimeter against determined resistance and piecemeal counter-attacks. From captured air bases, the *Luftwaffe* dominated the skies. During that time, German armoured units and heavy artillery rapidly off-loaded at the captured ports while infantry battalions poured across the beaches. On 2 October *XXX Panzer Corps* (two armoured and a motorised infantry division) burst from the bridgehead to capture Portsmouth, then drive to Bristol, isolating British forces in Devon, Cornwall, Somerset, and Dorset. The two divisions of the SS, strengthened by an armoured and a motorised division, struck north to surround and isolate metropolitan London. Three days later, the SS *'Wiking' Division* staged a successful amphibious assault on the mouth of the Thames estuary, isolating London from the sea. Taking advantage of the confusion attending *Wiking*'s landings, German forces of the SS corps completed the encirclement of the city on 8 October.

By the third week of October, the British government was still refusing to surrender despite the occupation of most of England by German forces. Hitler therefore ordered his army to reduce London. For a week, the city witnessed heavy fighting. Only when Churchill, the stub of a cigar clutched in his lips, died defending a barricade near Buckingham Palace did British resistance finally cease.

A puppet government, formed by Hitler, signed the formal surrender on 11 November 1940, on the deck of the cruiser *Wiesbaden* in Scapa Flow. Reduced to a third-rate power under permanent German garrison, Britain was not even allowed to join the Danzig Pact. Though scattered fighting continued in former British protectorates around the Mediterranean basin for several months (and a resistance movement would plague Germany for many years), the opening episodes of World War II in Europe had ended.

The *Kriegsmarine* continued to grow through 1945, earning additional glory while supporting the seizure of the Azores and the occupation of South Africa in 1941. Germany remained neutral after the Japanese surprise attack on the United States in December of that year, its relations with the United States souring only after Germany seized British Honduras in early 1942. In June 1943, amid growing concern at the threat of militant communism, Hitler invaded a prepared Russia. Though the navy's carriers and U-boats contributed little to the campaign (other than escorting the troopships of the SS, which fought bravely wherever committed but notably at Murmansk, Leningrad, and Sevastopol), its Research and Development Section effectively ended World War II.

In December 1939, a German scientist, Albert Einstein, had penned a note to Grand Admiral Raeder (Einstein's niece was engaged to Raeder's grandson) asking if the navy would be interested in a new explosive device based on 'heavy water' research. Fascinated by the potential, Raeder spoke with Hitler who immediately saw the possibility of combining the new explosive device with rockets then under development.[25] In August 1945, as Americans struggled ashore on the Japanese home islands, Hitler obliterated Moscow (along with Josef Stalin and most of the members of his government) with two nuclear weapons mounted on V-3 guided missiles. Russian resistance collapsed as quickly as what little remained of its national government. World communism died overnight, an unsuccessful experiment never to be resurrected. The small states formed from the carcass of the USSR joined the Danzig Pact nations now firmly under Germany's hegemony.

Today, the *Kriegsmarine* lives on, though Hitler died in 1947, victim of die-hard British assassin Ian Fleming. Karl Dönitz, as Hitler had specified, took his place as dictator of the Reich. Though Americans will remember his time as Führer in connection with the Cold War, the Honduras Missile Crisis, and the guerrilla war in Afghanistan, no German will ever forget that Dönitz's first official act was to lead his nation in a month of mourning for the Little Admiral who had lifted the German people from the misery of Versailles to the glory of the Atomic Age.

The reality

Hitler lost World War II in part because he never understood naval power. Thus, he allowed the Royal Navy to survive and the *Kriegsmarine* to wither. The lessons of history are as clear today as they were in 1939: as long as Great Britain and its naval power survive, no mainland nation will ever be able to establish hegemony over western Europe. Sea power must never be under-estimated – and the same goes double for British spirit.

To change Hitler, I introduced the one thing that he clearly lacked – a strong male role model, Stabsoberbootsman Günther Luck (and I am sure that readers with naval service will agree that no one can change a young man as quickly or as effectively as a senior petty officer). Luck, as with any effective leader, showed Hitler how to maximise his natural talents and taught him to love something greater than himself – the Imperial Navy. He instilled discipline in the young man (a quality that Hitler lacked in reality). Perhaps most importantly, Luck's death at the hands of the Royal Navy gave new direction to Hitler's anger – a direction which spared Germany the self-destructive anti-Semitic impulse forever tied to the real Hitler, and forever a leading cause of Germany's failure to win World War II.

Bibliography

Great Naval Battles: North Atlantic, 1939–43 (Strategic Simulations, Sunnyvale, CA, 1992).

Hill, J.R., ed., *The Oxford Illustrated History of the Royal Navy* (Oxford University Press, Oxford, 1995).

Mulligan, Timothy P., *Neither Sharks nor Wolves: The Men of Nazi Germany's U-boat Arm, 1939–1945* (Naval Institute Press, Annapolis, 1999).

Vause, Jordan, *Wolf: U-boat Commanders in World War II* (Naval Institute Press, Annapolis, 1997).

Von der Porten, Edward P., *The German Navy in World War II* (Ballantine Books, New York, 1969).

Wegener, Vice-Admiral Wolfgang, *The Naval Strategy of the World War*, translated by Holger H. Herwig (Naval Institute Press, Annapolis, 1989).

Notes

*1. Quoted in Siegfried Junge, *Young Man Hitler* (Green Ville Press, New York, 1993), pp. 14–15.

*2. *Ibid.*, p. 18.

3. In August 1914, the German navy featured 17 modern battleships (dreadnoughts) and five modern battlecruisers; the Royal Navy floated 22 dreadnoughts and nine battlecruisers. The British also maintained superiority in pre-dreadnoughts (which could not stand against modern battlecruisers, much less battleships) and lighter fleet units.

*4. Raeder, Erich, *We Were Sailors Once and Young* (Institut der Kriegsmarine, Berlin, 1958), pp. 142–5.

*5. This is the earliest known mention of Hitler's future fascination with innovative military technology or 'wonder weapons.'

*6. In fact, Hitler served his first tour with the duties of a Fähnrich-zur-See (midshipman), regardless of his rank. Those duties were simple: watch, learn, and do as little harm as possible!

*7. Dönitz, Karl, *In the Little Admiral's Footsteps*, 5 Volumes (Institut der Kriegsmarine, Berlin, 1973), Vol. 1, p. 98.

*8. Junge, *Hitler*, p. 28.

*9. Hitler formed the Blueshirts as an activist political cadre from former naval enlisted men and officers. Sometimes characterised as 'thugs' and 'monsters,' they provided visible intimidation when Hitler's charisma failed. Purged of 'undesirables' (notably, those officers who threatened Hitler's own power) on the 'Night of the Long Knives' in 1934, the remaining Blueshirts later became the founding members of the Reich's elite SS corps (roughly comparable to the American or British Marines, though they often spearheaded land campaigns as well as conducting amphibious operations).

*10. Letter to 'Mein Bobo,' 18 November 1921; Family Papers, Stuttgart.

*11. The original edition of *Mein Kampf* rang with Hitler's hatred of Great Britain. Later impressions and translations approved for sale abroad, were 50 pages shorter than the original. Raeder had strongly suggested that the inflammatory rhetoric be eliminated so as to reduce potential British alarm at Hitler's government and thus avoid a naval armaments race.

*12. The inscription on the Raeder Memorial in Berlin translates thus, 'Those who serve in silence often deserve the loudest acclaim.'

*13. The SS constantly expanded through 1945. By that year, it included four light amphibious divisions, two armoured divisions, two airborne divisions, three corps and an army headquarters, and its own air groups, as well as standard supporting elements.

*14. *Kriegsmarine* Files (Top Secret), Raeder, Directive 318, 1 May 1934.

*15. His relief of Hermann Göring, commander of the *Luftwaffe* in 1937, for interfering in naval air operations is typical of Hitler's reactions to such squabbling. Subsequently, the Nazis tried and convicted Göring for 'crimes against nature and the state' and sentenced him to service in a penal battalion (waste not, want not). Göring 'redeemed' himself during mine-clearing operations in Poland, and was buried in Stuttgart Military Cemetery with full honours.

*16. Dönitz, *Footsteps*, Vol. 2, p. 280.

*17. Guderian, Field Marshal (ret.) Heinz, *Hitler and His Panzer Leaders* (German Military Press, New York, 1958), pp. 75–78.

18. Till, Geoffrey, 'Retrenchment, Rethinking, Revival, 1919–1939' in Hill, *The Oxford Illustrated History of the Royal Navy*, 340, provided the data for British, French, and Italian naval strength in 1939.

*19. Thanks to Dönitz's espionage, Germany began the war with effective radar. Unfortunately, the bulky equipment and short supply of sets dictated that only capital ships, carriers, and command/control U-boats could be equipped with them in 1939.

20. Ship abbreviations are: CV for carrier, CVL for small carrier, BB for battleship, B for pocket battleship, BC for battlecruiser, CA for heavy cruiser, CL for light cruiser, and DD for fleet destroyer.

*21. In 1939, the armoured flight deck of a German light carrier was crowded with 22 planes: six fighters, eight torpedo bombers, and eight dive bombers. In late 1940, two Flettner 282 helicopters (for air/sea rescue), two fighters, and six dive bombers replaced the torpedo bombers. A *Graf Zeppelin* Class carrier sported an equal mix of fighters, torpedo bombers, and dive bombers among its 48-plane air group. Though Fl 282s also joined this class in 1940, it retained its torpedo bombers until 1942.

*22. Hitler formally apologised to the understandably concerned president of the United States, promising to observe a strict neutral zone extending 200 miles from the North American coast. It is the only diplomatic apology ever rendered by Adolf Hitler. Of course, he did present the commander of *CG IV* with the Knight's Cross upon his return to Germany.

*23. From an interview with Johnny 'Boy' Griffen, survivor of the carrier engagement of 12 September 1939, by the author (English Ghetto, Marseille, France, 1971).

*24. Two battalions, some 96 tanks, of the SS Panzer brigade had been equipped with snorkels and special waterproofing, allowing them to be dropped offshore and to advance across the seabed to emerge from the sea alongside the landing craft of the infantry. [In reality, the German army designed such tanks for the never implemented Operation Sea Lion, and actually used them during the invasion of Russia.]

*25. Einstein-Raeder, Elise, *Heavy Water, Deadly Fire* (Finkle Press, Madgeburg, 1983), pp. 153–68. Professor Einstein-Raeder also defends the use of the first atomic bombs against Moscow, speculating that had the United States possessed similar weapons of mass destruction in 1945 it would have used them against Japan rather than incur the nearly 1,000,000 casualties necessitated by the invasion of that country.

2
DISASTER AT DUNKIRK
The Defeat Of Britain, 1940

Stephen Badsey

The new government

At 11 o'clock in the morning of Friday 10 May 1940, three men met in the Cabinet Room of Number 10 Downing Street to decide the future fate of their country. The result of their decision was to be the catastrophic surrender of Britain to Nazi Germany, just 70 days later. Historians have tended to be kind to these men, especially as two of them died without knowing the consequences of their actions. Particularly in Germany, it has been argued that Britain's defeat was virtually inevitable in the face of the formidable Third Reich. But given the narrow margin of victory, concealed at the time by Nazi propaganda, a case can be made that things might have happened otherwise.

Of the three men present at that fatal meeting, Neville Chamberlain, Prime Minister and head of the Conservative government since 1937, had taken Britain and its Empire to war in September 1939 against all his own hopes and expectations. Chamberlain had championed the policy of 'appeasement', believing that another world war would give Britain only the choice between military defeat by Germany and economic domination by the United States. Already in February 1940 the Treasury had warned that its gold reserves would be exhausted within two years. When forced into war, Chamberlain still hoped to avoid a repetition of the monstrous casualties of the First World War. As in 1914, Britain sent a small British Expeditionary Force (BEF) to France; but British strategy relied on the French Army, together with the Royal Air Force (RAF) and Royal Navy, to defend against the Germans, while hoping for some kind of negotiated solution. One American journalist complained that 'there is something phony about this war',[1] and the expression stuck. Now the Phony War was over, and with it Chamberlain's tenure of office.

Earlier that morning, the long awaited German offensive in the west had begun. Aircraft of the *Luftwaffe* were attacking targets in France, and also in Belgium and the Netherlands, both of which had abandoned their neutrality and asked for French and British help. The first Allied troops were driving across the Belgian frontier to meet the Germans, the BEF among them, while the RAF's Advanced Air Striking Force (AASF), based near Rheims, joined in the contest for the skies. But Chamberlain's fall from power had begun two days earlier, as Parliament debated the disastrous Anglo-French campaign in Norway against the Germans, launched in early April. Ill equipped and ill organised, the Allies had been heavily defeated. In the House of Commons, Chamberlain faced an open revolt from many of his own Conservative Party, who made it clear that he must resign.

Under the British system of ministerial responsibility, arguably the man most to blame for the Norway debacle was also present in the chamber. Winston Churchill, First Lord of the Admiralty, had been dismissed from the same post in 1915 after a similar failed amphibious exploit, the Gallipoli landings. A suspect figure in his own party for many years, the foremost critic of appeasement and opponent of the Nazis, Churchill was also an undeclared leader of the revolt against Chamberlain, and a popular candidate for Prime Minister. From the war's start, he had viewed Nazi Germany as the enemy of western civilisation, an evil thing to be destroyed. The Labour and Liberal opposition leaders were also prepared to enter a coalition government under Churchill.

But Churchill was not Chamberlain's first choice. Also present was the Foreign Secretary, Edward 3rd Viscount Halifax, who was also the choice of King George VI and of most of the Conservative Party. Lord Halifax was a deeply religious, highly intelligent, fox-hunting member of the British political and social establishment, who had championed appeasement but had finally been convinced of the need for war. Churchill called him the 'Holy Fox', and it was an apposite name. Like both Churchill and Chamberlain, Halifax's policy was to preserve Britain and its Empire. His view of the war was that men of good will should negotiate terms, and he had already made repeated secret approaches to Hitler. A colony or province here, a trade agreement there, and an honourable peace could be arranged.

This view of Germany as just another participant in the game of international politics could hardly have been further from the way that most British people saw the Nazi threat. But Britain in 1940 was not a particularly democratic country. Only in 1928 had all adults been given the vote, while many richer people held more than one vote each. Also, little in recent European history suggested that democracy had much future. The aristocratic, church and establishment figure of Halifax counted for much among the power brokers of London. Government from the House of Lords was unusual – the last occasion had been Lord Salisbury in 1902 – but it was not unconstitutional. A wartime coalition government also had little appeal for Chamberlain; the coalition of 1915 had broken the Liberal Party, which had never held independent power since, and had now declined into obscurity. Churchill himself was the grandson of a duke and had moved twice between political parties, and was hardly, therefore, a democratic figure. He could not easily be dismissed for his role in the failure over

Norway, nor could he be ignored, but he was not in a position to demand power.

All three men left contradictory and self-serving accounts of that critical Downing Street meeting. What is a matter of record is that Halifax emerged as the new Prime Minister of a continuing Conservative administration. There would be no coalition government. Churchill's price was a high one: while remaining at the Admiralty he became government spokesman in the House of Commons. Anthony Eden, an old political ally of Churchill, took over the War Office. Halifax remained Foreign Secretary as well as becoming Prime Minister. Chamberlain was appointed Lord President of the Council, retaining membership of the War Cabinet as well as leadership of the Conservative Party. The opposition was left feeling sour and frustrated.

Manstein's plan

As these decisions were taken, the BEF was rolling forward from its base at Arras into Belgium as part of French 1st Army Group. But its commander General Lord Gort and his senior officers made little secret of their pessimism regarding the French 'Plan D', which intended for 1st Army Group to meet the German onslaught head-on. In a telegram to the War Cabinet shortly before his death in battle on 2 June, Gort described how the collapse of the Belgians and the speed of the German advance 'coincided almost exactly with the estimate of the GHQ Intelligence staff.'[2] This British pessimism, together with their military weakness, in turn produced even greater pessimism and lack of trust from the French and Belgians.

Even after the Battle of France began, BEF Headquarters and the political and military leadership in London never lost their belief that the real target of any major German attack would not be France at all. The British argued that the Germans had found the experience of the Western Front too terrible to consider repeating, and understood that Britain, with its control of ocean trade routes, was a much greater threat to Germany than France. The British therefore expected any German attack to be aimed chiefly at the Netherlands and Belgium, to capture naval and air bases on the North Sea coast. From there, submarine and air attacks could be mounted against Britain, perhaps followed by an amphibious invasion of East Anglia.

This fear prompted invasion scares in October 1939 and again in April 1940 that disrupted British training and defensive planning. As German agents arrived to provide information for a possible landing, British counter-intelligence picked them all off without difficulty. But try as they could, the British intelligence services could find out no details of the German invasion plans, for the simple reason that none existed. Instead, they were picking up whispers of three developments. One of these was Führer Directive 6, of 9 October 1939, Hitler's order for the invasion of the Netherlands and Belgium, given the rather dull codename of 'Case Yellow' by *Armed Forces*

High Command or *OKW* (in the German staff system all plans were either 'cases' or 'solutions' to problems). The second development was that Hermann Göring, a keen reader of British and American thrillers, had obtained a translation of Erskine Childers' novel *Riddle of the Sands*. Written in 1903, this described a German plan for a surprise invasion of East Anglia by barges across the North Sea, under cover of fog. The story caught Göring's imagination, and it was soon the talk of official Berlin. The third development was the early planning by *Naval Headquarters* (*OKM*) under Grand Admiral Erich Raeder for the invasion of Norway. As an afterthought to this, the *Kriegsmarine* drew up an outline for an invasion of Britain, which was passed to *Army Headquarters* (*OKH*) for comment.

German plans for an invasion of Britain might have ended there, had it not been for two events in January 1940. The first was that the original Case Yellow plan was compromised by the 'Mechelen Incident'. A flight by two *Luftwaffe* staff officers carrying the plans for Case Yellow developed engine trouble and landed near Mechelen in neutral Belgium on 10 January. The officers destroyed some of the plans, but the Belgians did pass a summary on to the French. Next, a feeling among senior German officers that Case Yellow was inadequate found its voice in the form of General of Infantry Erich von Manstein, chief of staff of *Army Group A* who, on meeting Hitler to receive a decoration for the Polish campaign, explained his own misgivings. Hitler ordered a revision of Case Yellow that produced a much more ambitious plan. Led by seven of Germany's ten Panzer (armoured) divisions, the main thrust would be made through the Ardennes forest in Luxembourg and southern Belgium by *Army Group A*, with the objective of defeating the French outright. The attack into the Netherlands and Belgium expected by the Allies would be a secondary move by *Army Group B*, while the remaining *Army Group C* watched the Maginot Line.

OKW's response to Manstein's intervention was a balance of acknowledgement that he had done the right thing with a reluctance to tolerate bypassing the chain of command. Although many of his ideas went into the revision of Case Yellow, Manstein himself was removed from *Army Group A* on a technicality, and slated to command *XXXVIII Army Corps*. Since this was refitting in central Germany, someone in *OKW* decided on a humorous twist, by placing Manstein in charge of an Army conference on the possible invasion of Britain, together with a joint Army-Navy working party on amphibious craft. Without a talented senior officer such as Manstein to lead it, this working party might well have come to nothing.

Manstein started from the premise that the new Case Yellow would succeed, that Germany would control the Dutch and Belgian coast, and that much of the French Army would be neutralised. There were three approaching date-windows during which tides and other factors were optimal for a landing in southern England: early June, mid-July, and mid-September. It seemed impossible that France could be defeated by June, while the September date was too late to be sure of the weather. Only the

July option was credible, and this would surely mean invading Britain while simultaneously fighting the French.

After two weeks Manstein's working party reached – without knowing it – the same conclusion as every official British study since the 1860s: the invasion of Britain was not a realistic military operation. The reasoning was simple. For an invasion to take place on a large enough scale to overcome British land forces, the invader needed undisputed control of the seas, nullifying the Royal Navy. But in this case Britain could be starved into submission in a matter of months, making an actual invasion unnecessary. There were, of course, two new factors to be considered. One was that a protracted submarine campaign would increase the chances of the United States entering the war on the British side, as had happened in 1917. The other factor was air power. Manstein consulted experts in the *Luftwaffe* and *Kriegsmarine*. Discounting fantasies and partisan statements from both services, the answer came out as the same. The *Kriegsmarine* was not remotely strong enough to defeat or even deter the Royal Navy in its own home waters. The *Luftwaffe* could do enough damage to keep the British away from an invasion force, but only on a very narrow front and for the shortest and most direct crossing.

Manstein soon discovered that German amphibious capability was virtually non-existent. The *Kriegsmarine* had plans to use an incredible mixture of vessels from cross-Channel ferries to fishing boats, with pontoons and Rhine barges towed by minesweepers and other small craft, (much as in Childers' novel), including a motorised barge known as the 'Type A' or 'Prahm'. Most of these barges could barely survive the bow-wave of a passing British destroyer without capsizing. The Army's engineers offered an experimental troop-carrying hydrofoil capable of 50mph, the prototype for which already existed. With Manstein's prompting, ten more were built before the Navy halted the project in April, claiming that the craft were unseaworthy.

Manstein also remembered early experiments with amphibious tanks, and called for assistance from General der Panzertruppe Heinz Guderian, the unofficial but acknowledged leader of the Panzers. Guderian arranged help in the form of the deputy commander of *3rd Panzer Division*, Colonel Walter Model, and under the pretext of preparing for crossing the River Meuse, the conversion of some Panzer III tanks began. Rather than go direct to *Luftwaffe Headquarters* (OKL), Manstein also sought out Major General Kurt Student, the acknowledged specialist in paratrooper and glider warfare. Student had no doubt that he could get his forces, perhaps as much as a division, across to East Anglia or southern England by air.

Manstein's study concluded that if Case Yellow succeeded, then a combined air and sea campaign against Britain could be mounted in late June, culminating in the landing in mid-July of no more than one army corps of four divisions or 50,000 men across the Straits of Dover. Capturing a major port on the first day was critical. Even then, within three or four days the Royal Navy would cut the English Channel, and the landing forces would run out of fuel, ammunition and reserves. Either the landing itself must break the British will to fight, or the *Luftwaffe* must keep the Royal Navy and RAF at bay. Model, a keen bridge player, referred to this plan facetiously as Manstein's 'Small Slam'. Manstein himself gave it the most English name he knew as 'Case Smith', submitted it to *OKW* in the expectation that it would be filed and forgotten, and in February went off to command *XXXVIII Army Corps*. The plan's existence leaked to the British intelligence services, who took it seriously. As the British argued, 'how could it be supposed that *OKW* had not in its pigeonholes some masterpiece of staffwork providing in minutest detail for the successive stages of an invasion of England?'[3]

The Battle of France

The world now knows the consequences of Manstein's ideas for the changes to Case Yellow. In an astonishing campaign, everything by way of luck fell for the Germans and against the French. Guderian as commander of *XIX Panzer Corps* led the advance of *Army Group A* through the Ardennes with almost miraculous speed. On 13 May from Sedan to Dinant three separate Panzer corps, supported by almost 2,000 *Luftwaffe* aircraft, forced the line of the River Meuse against the weak French Second Army. Within three days, seven Panzer divisions were driving westwards across France to the English Channel, scattering the Ninth Army as they did so. On 20 May Guderian's leading forces of *2nd Panzer Division* reached the sea at Abbeville, simultaneously slicing through the BEF's over-long supply lines and isolating most of 1st Army Group in Belgium.

All this was in the future when, on the afternoon of 10 May the BEF started its move into Belgium, with II Corps under Lieutenant General Sir Alan Brooke leading. As the motorised 3rd Infantry Division under Major General Bernard Montgomery reached its pre-arranged positions near Louvain it found these already occupied by the Belgian 10th Division, which opened fire in the belief that the arriving British were German paratroopers. While Montgomery was sorting this out, I Corps under Lieutenant General M.G.H. Barker came up on the right of II Corps at Wavre, and, by the morning of 12 May the BEF was in position. Its front line consisted of four motorised divisions of tough long-service volunteers, the equal of anything the Germans could put against them. Shortage of tanks was a problem, but the British A12 Infantry Tank Mark II Matilda was almost invulnerable to German tank and anti-tank guns. In reserve with III Corps under Lieutenant General Ronald Adam were two further motorised divisions, which included Territorial Army (TA) troops less well equipped and trained than the regulars, plus three TA infantry divisions. Three further second-line TA divisions sent to France as pioneers were kept well in the rear. At the same time, French Seventh and First Armies came up into line to the north and south of the BEF in accordance with Plan D.

It was a text-book move – which unfortunately put the best Allied forces exactly where the Germans wanted them.

The next days were spent in irate political discussions. In particular, the defensive positions dug by the Belgians did not correspond – in places by several miles – with their locations on French and British maps. At a first meeting with King Leopold III and his staff in Brussels, Lieutenant General Brooke's fluent French (he had been born and raised in France) only served to confirm British suspicions. Meanwhile, both the Belgian frontier defences and the small and inexperienced Dutch Army were being smashed by the German thunderbolt. On 10 May the Belgian fortress at Eben Emael fell to a surprise attack by German glider troops, so opening the way through to Liège. Major General Student's paratroopers of *7th Air Division*, dropped miles behind the lines, created chaos throughout the Netherlands, capturing critical locations. By 12 May *Sixth Army* was across the River Meuse (called the Maas at this point) and driving for Brussels. The BEF held its positions, confident that, with First Army on its right, it could stop the German charge. But its Air Component, which had begun with six squadrons of Hawker Hurricane fighters, had already lost almost a third of its aircraft, and three further squadrons were demanded from Britain.

Far away from the BEF, an incident occurred that had lasting consequences for the British. In October 1939 the War Cabinet had envisaged the RAF carrying out strategic bombing of the Ruhr in the event of a German attack. But despite Bomber Command's own enthusiasm, Halifax proved even more unwilling than Chamberlain to risk retaliatory German bombing of British cities. Then, on the afternoon of 10 May, three Heinkel 111 bombers attacked what they believed was the French military airfield at Dijon. They never realised that they had actually bombed Freiburg-im-Breisgau, a little German town just inside their own border, killing 13 women and 22 children. The Germans were genuinely shocked by what seemed an Allied act of terror bombing, made all the worse by repeated Britain and French denials. Hitler declared that such attacks 'would be answered by fivefold retaliation against French and British towns.'[4]

On Tuesday 14 May BEF Headquarters got its first news of two Allied disasters. To the southeast there had been the French failure at Sedan, where the German armour was across the Meuse in force. Responding to urgent French requests for support, the Advanced Air Striking Force sent successive waves against the German bridgeheads. By the end of the day, of 63 Fairey Battle light bombers in action, 35 had been lost. If this were not bad enough, in the north Seventh Army had begun to pull back from Dutch soil. The government of the Netherlands, its country and armed forces helpless against the German attack, announced that afternoon that its surrender would come into effect next morning. Just as the announcement was made, a *Luftwaffe* raid tore the heart out of Rotterdam.

Early on Wednesday 15 May the Prime Minister, who had taken to

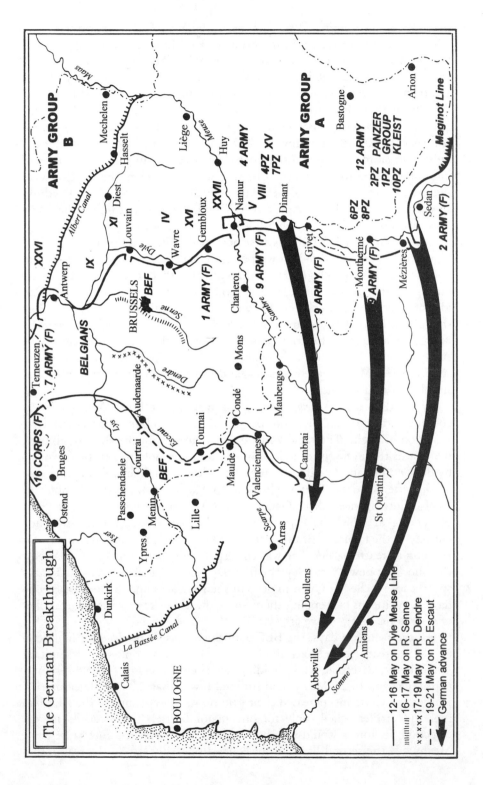

The German Breakthrough

ARMY GROUP B

ARMY GROUP A

PANZER GROUP KLEIST

12 ARMY

4 ARMY

4PZ XV
7PZ

2PZ
1PZ
10PZ

6PZ
8PZ

2 ARMY (F)

Maginot Line

Arion

Bastogne

Maas

Mechelen

Hasselt

Diest

Liège

Huy

Meuse

Namur

Dinant

Givet

Sedan

Mézières

Monthermé

2 ARMY (F)

9 ARMY (F)

9 ARMY (F)

9 ARMY (F)

XXVI

XI

IX

IV

XVI

XXVII

V

VIII

Louvain

Wavre

Gembloux

Dyle

Antwerp

BEF

BRUSSELS

Senne

Charleroi

Sambre

1 ARMY (F)

Mons

Maubeuge

Condé

Cambrai

St Quentin

BELGIANS

7 ARMY (F)

Terneuzen

16 CORPS (F)

Bruges

Ostend

Dunkirk

Calais

BOULOGNE

La Bassée Canal

Ypres

Menin

Lille

Passchendaele

Courtrai

Audenaarde

Dendre

Escaut

Lys

Yser

BEF

Tournai

Maulde

Valenciennes

Scarpe

Arras

Doullens

Abbeville

Amiens

Somme

12-16 May on Dyle Meuse Line
16-17 May on R. Senne
17-19 May on R. Dendre
19-21 May on R. Escaut
German advance

sleeping in his command bunker beneath Whitehall, was woken by a telephone call from French Prime Minister Paul Reynaud, who explained in English that the Germans had broken through at Sedan and that the battle was lost. To Halifax, Reynaud's outburst made no sense, as well as being completely at variance with the confident official press statements issuing daily from Paris. Nevertheless, he took his alliance duties seriously. At the morning's Cabinet he instructed Kingsley Wood, the Secretary of State for Air, that the RAF should provide most of the British support. A further ten fighter squadrons were transferred to the AASF, and Fighter Command intensified its patrols across the Channel. That afternoon, the AOC-in-C of Fighter Command, Air Chief Marshal Sir Hugh 'Stuffy' Dowding, submitted a formal letter of protest to Wood, pointing out that he had only 34 squadrons left, and not the 52 deemed necessary to defend Britain.

One of General Lord Gort's first acts after BEF Headquarters reached Lille had been to establish his own personal headquarters with a tiny staff in one of several small villages. He had no direct contact either with 1st Army Group or First Army; indeed, for several days French staff officers had no idea of where he was to be found. An establishment figure like Halifax, Gort thought of himself as a simple soldier and as an old-fashioned commander-in-chief, whose main function was to maintain the tone and style of the Army, defend it against politicians, and leave the details of battles to subordinates. Many contemporaries, and most historians, have seen him as simply out of his depth.

By 15 May as *Sixth Army* reached the BEF on the River Dyle, Gort was convinced that not only was the Belgian Army crumbling, but so was First Army on his right. The rapidly made new plan was for the BEF to fall back westwards from one river or canal line to another, holding off the Germans by day and moving by night, to regain the line of the Canal de l'Escaut east of Lille after six days. That Wednesday 15 May evening, Gort's flamboyant chief of intelligence, Major General Noel Mason-Macfarlane, gave a press conference at which he explained that the battle was already lost, due entirely to the failure of Britain's allies and the Chamberlain government for refusing to rearm earlier. The war correspondents barely had time to digest this shocking news. Next day, the first day of the British retreat, the Panzer spearheads reached St Quentin deep in their rear. 'I hope to God the French have some means of stopping them and closing the gap,' wrote Gort's chief of staff in his diary, 'or we are *bust*.'[5]

For the next five days, the BEF performed − as its predecessor had done in the retreat from Mons in 1914 − that most difficult of military manoeuvres, a retreat while holding off a close pursuit. Never seriously threatened, up to 21 May it had suffered fewer than 500 battle casualties. But, as the Germans increased their grip on its lines of supply, the BEF had fuel and artillery shells only for one major battle. If it attacked in any direction, its forces would simply run dry and empty in a matter of days. Meanwhile the second-line TA divisions, supposedly safe in the rear, found themselves in the path of the onrushing Panzers of *Army Group A*, which scattered them with hardly a pause. Gort's response was to form battlegroups under senior officers from any troops available. Mason-Macfarlane commanded 'Macforce', while the BEF's base at Arras was defended first by 'Petreforce' under Major General R.L. Petre of the second-line 12th Eastern Division, and then by 'Frankforce' under Major General H.E. Franklyn of 5th Infantry Division. It was rough and ready, but it would hold for a few days.

The peril in which the BEF found itself was not understood by the War Cabinet. Largely cut off from information, its members continued to think of *Sixth Army*'s attack into Belgium as the main German thrust, and were reassured by French official pronouncements (increasingly detached from reality) that any German breakthrough was a minor one. On 20 May the Chief of the Imperial General Staff, General Sir Edmund Ironside ('Tiny' Ironside from his impressive bulk and height) arrived at Gort's headquarters with orders for the BEF to attack southwestwards, an idea of which he was soon disabused. Warning was also given to the Royal Navy on 20 May that evacuation of the BEF through the Channel ports might be needed. A suggestion from Churchill of also using civilian craft or 'little ships' was turned down by Halifax as likely to alarm the population. Indeed, the main concern of the War Cabinet was that the British people should not learn too much of what was happening.

Both Hitler and his generals later pretended that the spectacular Panzer drive across France had always been their intention. Historians have known for decades that this was not true, although the advance from Sedan to Abbeville was the preferred option of the more ambitious Panzer leaders. In fact several attempts were made by *OKW* to halt the Panzers as they far outdistanced the footslogging bulk of the German Army. Finally out of supplies and badly over-extended, Guderian called an unofficial rest day on 21 May and then next day swung northwards towards the Channel ports. By nightfall the leading elements of *1st* and *2nd Panzer Divisions* had reached the outskirts of Boulogne and Calais. Dunkirk, the last major port still secure for the British, was only 25 miles away along the coast.

Hitler and his service chiefs met on 20 May to congratulate themselves on the success of Case Yellow and to plan the next phase of the defeat of France, an exploitation southward in 'Case Red'. Since the Navy had contributed little to the Battle of France, Grand Admiral Raeder raised the invasion of Britain with Hitler after the meeting and again next day, but Hitler was not interested and Raeder himself knew that the idea was impractical. All this changed a day later, with the news of a major German disaster.

Case Sea Lion

Late on 20 May, after considerable shouting and telephoning, Gort agreed to a British attack next day southeastwards from Arras to be made by two divisions, in conjunction with a French attack coming northwards from Amiens to meet it, so cutting the German Panzer corridor in two. Entrusted with the British attack was Major General Gifford 'Q' Martel, a veteran armoured warfare specialist commanding 50th Northumbrian Division. Such was the state of the BEF's reserves that Martel had to scrape together troops from five different divisions, plus 1st Army Tank Brigade of two battalions (including a handful of the precious Matildas). His attack was made by two battlegroups mixing armour, infantry and artillery, swinging parallel to each other a few miles apart, counter-clockwise round to the west of Arras before setting off southeastwards, altogether about a division's worth of troops.

On the morning of 21 May neither Martel nor Franklyn knew that four Panzer divisions had already driven past the open southern flank of the Arras defences, and that another was approaching fast. This was *7th Panzer Division*, commanded by one of the political appointees that Hitler found useful to curb the power of the German military aristocracy. Major General Erwin Rommel was not a Nazi Party member, but owed his position to his support for Hitler and his military advice to the *SA* in the 1930s. His reward for this, and for commanding Hitler's escort in the Polish campaign, had been one of the precious Panzer divisions. Lacking any experience with armour, Rommel was also vain and ambitious (he took his own publicity photographs in action), and Goebbels' propaganda machine was preparing to lionise him. Rommel had been lucky on the Meuse, getting his division across despite a near failure. Now he had allowed *7th Panzer Division* to become strung out into four widely separate columns: his armoured regiment leading – mainly Czech-built Panzer 38(*t*) tanks – followed separately by his two infantry regiments in trucks, and then the artillery and the bulk of the divisional transport, all moving on a collision course with Martel's attack.

The first clash came during mid-afternoon. Rommel's armour missed Martel's columns entirely and ended up northwest of Arras, completely out of touch. Then the two British battlegroups slammed into the remaining columns, tanks against unsupported infantry. Realising too late what was happening, Rommel positioned himself on the high ground west of Arras – marked as 'Rommel's Hill' by the massive monument erected since the war – and tried to scrape together a defence. Urgent radio appeals brought his tanks racing southwards, only to run into an anti-tank screen positioned by Martel for that very purpose. A few minutes later, and the British tanks were over Rommel's Hill and into the division's supply train, creating havoc. Rommel's aide Lieutenant Most described how 'he died before he could be carried to cover beside the gun position. The death of this brave man, a magnificent soldier, touched me deeply.'[6] Only later did Martel learn that it had all been for nothing. Just before his attack commenced, the French had informed Gort that they could not move until the next day, and the Panzer corridor was still open. Two nights later, Gort pulled Martel and Franklyn's divisions back from Arras, covering the southern flank of the pocket into which the BEF was being squeezed.

The loss of most of *7th Panzer Division* meant considerable German redeployment. On 22 May the Germans also learned of a new British plan, 'Operation Dynamo'. The information came from several sources, including a high-ranking British officer who was also a German agent. The attack at Arras had been only the preliminary to Dynamo, which was an elaborate Anglo-French trap involving six fresh divisions (one of them Canadian) together with massed Matilda tanks, ready to attack as the Panzers advanced further. On top of the existing anxieties at *OKW* this was simply too much. Next day, Göring asked Hitler that the *Luftwaffe*, not the Army, should have the triumph of wiping out the BEF. On 24 May Colonel General Gerd von Rundstedt, commanding *Army Group A*, told Hitler of Dynamo. Hitler's reaction was that the *Luftwaffe* should have its head, permitting Rundstedt an 'administrative halt', and a rather more cautious advance next day. It was only years later that Dynamo was revealed as a British deception plan, and that the cherished German spy had been a double agent. It bought the British perhaps a day; but this would turn out not to be enough.

Also on 23 May Hitler summoned his service chiefs once more to demand a plan for the invasion of Britain. What exactly had changed his mind is unknown, but revenge for Rommel was certainly uppermost in his ranting, bitter speech that day. Under pressure from *OKH* and *OKW*, Grand Admiral Raeder reluctantly put forward 'Case Lion' for landing two complete armies – over 260,000 men, 30,000 vehicles and 60,000 horses – on a broad front from Ramsgate to Weymouth. This was violently rejected by Hitler when Raeder (who was hoping to scotch the idea altogether) explained that it could not be mounted until September, and only then if the *Luftwaffe* could achieve complete air supremacy. Faced by Hitler's demands for an alternative, *OKW* admitted with some embarrassment to the existence of Manstein's 'Case Smith'. On 25 May Manstein was summoned by Hitler and ordered to implement his plan, pulling his *XXXVIII Army Corps* out of the line to do so, while Göring was told that his new priority was to defeat Britain by bombing from the air. In London on the same day, the Chiefs of Staff Committee, chaired by the First Sea Lord, Admiral Sir Dudley Pound, advised the Prime Minister that 'should the enemy succeed in establishing a force, with its vehicles, firmly ashore, the Army in the United Kingdom, which is very short of equipment, has not got the offensive power to drive it out.'[7]

Führer Directive 16, authorisation for what was now 'Case Sea Lion,' was signed by Hitler on 1 June. With battles continuing in France, Belgium and even Norway, Manstein had just over six weeks to make Sea Lion a reality and, as he soon found out, the 'full powers' that Hitler had granted him only provoked hostility and resistance from others. *OKW* promised two fully equipped infantry divisions, *6th Mountain Division* and *17th Division*. Student, his arm in a sling from a wound sustained in Rotterdam, was more than happy for his *7th Air Division* and the gliders of the *Airlanding Assault Regiment* to take part. Indeed, Student wanted an immediate airborne landing in southern England, but with his troops still spread all over the Low Countries this was not a practical proposition. Göring promised 750 Junkers 52 transport aircraft for July, enough to lift at least one division and keep it resupplied by air. The final element of the *XXXVIII Army Corps* was – at Hitler's insistence – a reformed and renamed *7th 'Rommel' Panzer Division*, for which Manstein obtained the command for Colonel Model. Air support would come at first from *Second Air Fleet* under Colonel General 'Smiling Albert' Kesselring, joined later by *Third Air Fleet*.

Disaster at Dunkirk

Also on that fateful Saturday 25 May Lord Gort took the decision that doomed the BEF. On 21 May a series of angry inter-Allied meetings had taken place at Ypres, at which the French proposed a plan not unlike the fictitious 'Dynamo,' for an offensive by eight French, British and Belgian divisions from north and south to close the Panzer corridor, starting on 26 May. As if to underline the way that nothing was working for the Allies, General Georges Billotte commanding 1st Army Group drove off from that meeting and was almost immediately killed in a car crash. Over the next three days, the French plan simply fell apart under the pressure of the German advance and mutual Allied recriminations. By Saturday all that was left of it was Gort's promise to take part the following day, launching 5th Infantry Division and 50th Northumbrian Division south once more.

Meanwhile to the north, II Corps' safety depended on the Belgians holding their line between Courtrai and the sea against the onslaughts of the German *Eighteenth Army*; if they broke, Lieutenant General Brooke had nothing to plug the gap. Montgomery's troops had captured a German map showing that, with the Netherlands out of the war, a major offensive by *Eighteenth Army* was threatening to cut the BEF off from the sea. Evacuation seemed the only option, but as Allied communications broke down, neither Gort nor Halifax thought to warn King Leopold of the British plans.

All day, Gort sat silent at the plank trestle table in the small farmhouse that was his headquarters. He had received no advice or even contact from London, other than vague exhortations from the War Cabinet. He had been out of touch with all French commanders since the Ypres conference. Word came that Boulogne had fallen; Calais was about to fall; if the French attacked at all it would be with just one division; Martel had only two Matilda tanks left. At about 18.00 he looked up and gave his order, 'Send them over to Brookie!'[8] Gort still gave the French every chance: rather than pulling out of the line at once to move northwards to II Corps, both 5th

Infantry Division and 50th Northumbrian Division would move next afternoon, just in case the promised French attack from the south materialised. Of course it did not, but still the French never forgave Gort for his decision, and, as things turned out, neither did the British. Even so, from what he knew at the time, it is hard to argue that Gort's decision was either wrong or disloyal to his allies.

Gort followed this military decision with a political one: to make public the view that the BEF had been stabbed in the back. Mason-Macfarlane returned to London to confer with General Sir John Dill, about to succeed Ironside as CIGS. On 28 May Mason-Macfarlane briefed correspondents in London on War Office orders, announcing that the BEF was about to go down fighting, betrayed by its allies and by politicians. The shock of next morning's newspapers went round the country, and destroyed what little trust remained between the Halifax government and the Army. With nothing left to hide, on 29 May the British government made public a telegram from King George VI to Gort supporting the stab in the back story. 'Faced by circumstances outside their control in a position of extreme difficulty,' the King's message read, 'they are displaying a gallantry that has never been surpassed in the annals of the British Army. The hearts of every one of us at home are with you and your magnificent troops in this hour of peril.'[9] That evening General Dill secured for Mason-Macfarlane a slot on BBC radio following the 9 o'clock News. Speaking anonymously as 'a senior BEF commander', Mason-Macfarlane repeated the same message, that the BEF had fought hard but been lost through no fault of its own. There were now those in the Halifax Cabinet, perhaps the Prime Minister among them, who genuinely expected some kind of military coup.

By 26 May while its reserves fought to hold the line together with the French, the main body of the BEF had retreated to a battlefield that its senior officers knew intimately from the First World War, the Ypres-Messines ridges. Reconnoitering personally that morning, Lieutenant General Brooke discovered a gap of some 4,000 yards between his forces and the French 60th Infantry Division to the north. Racing to BEF Headquarters, Brooke obtained immediate command of the 50th Northumbrian Division and 5th Infantry Division, ordering their brigades into the line. On the evening of 27 May the Belgian government requested a cease-fire from the Germans. Given a few hours' warning, Brooke ordered Montgomery to seal the gap. Working largely in darkness and under fire, Montgomery pulled 3rd Infantry Division out of line and steered it northwards directly behind II Corps' front from one end to the other, while only a few hundred yards away the Germans probed and hammered at the British positions. It was a virtuoso display of manoeuvre that, in other circumstances, might well have saved the BEF. But it was all happening about half a day too late. As its brigades followed 50th Northumbrian Division to block the German attack, 5th Infantry Division was being spread too thin; it could hold off two divisions, but not three. Next morning, German infantry of *18th Division* worked their way onto Kemmel Hill, while to the north five German divisions were driving unopposed along the coast towards Dunkirk.

Even when trapped, the regular divisions of the BEF were a formidable fighting organisation. Short of everything from fuel to ammunition, commanders gathered their men together with TA and French units that had attached themselves during the retreat, and prepared to die game. The evacuation of rear area personnel from Dunkirk had begun on 26 May (the real 'Operation Dynamo'), on the same day that troops of *2nd Panzer Division* reached the port area from the southwest. Late on 28 May Montgomery's extraordinary 3rd Infantry Division was tasked to clear a path through to the Dunkirk beaches together with the few remaining tanks of the French 2nd Light Mechanised Division, with the rest of II Corps closing in behind it like a protective fantail.

Despite Göring's predictions, with the shorter range to southern England favouring the RAF, and Fighter Command's new Supermarine Spitfires coming fully into play, the *Luftwaffe* took its heaviest daily losses of the campaign. Ordered to stay in France, the Air Component and AASF were shot out of the sky or had their airfields over-run. By next day the BEF had secured five miles of coastline together with about half of Dunkirk port. But it was too late to form a coherent British defensive front, there were just too many holes in the line. That afternoon the German *216th Division* from the east met *20th Motorised Division* at Bevern, and the BEF was cut in two. Lord Gort died a soldier's death when his personal headquarters was over-run by infantry of *6th Panzer Division*. There were no survivors, and there seems little doubt that his sacrifice was deliberate.

With only partial use of Dunkirk, which was contested between 48th South Midland Division under Major General Andrew Thorne (aided by French 68th Infantry Division) and *2nd Panzer Division*, the British escape was always going to be costly, especially as the ships had to come so close inshore. The cruiser HMS *Ceres* was sunk, together with ten destroyers, among them HMS *Kelly* commanded by Captain Lord Louis Mountbatten, which blew up with all hands lost.

No division of the BEF escaped intact, and fewer than 68,000 disorganised and demoralised men were transported back to Dover. Others continued to escape almost until the capitulation of France on 22 June. In particular, the 51st Highland Division, serving on attachment with the French on the Saar, had a heroic fight clear across the country, its last stand taking place at the little port of St Valery-en-Caux on 10 June from where the Royal Navy rescued 2,000 men.

Over 150,000 British soldiers became prisoners, including Lieutenant General Brooke, together with Martel and five other divisional commanders. Montgomery himself left through Dunkirk on 1 June. After a night's sleep, he went to the War Office, demanded to see General Dill, and started lecturing him on what had gone wrong. As famous for his tactlessness as his military skill, Montgomery might have got away with this in different circumstances. Instead, Dill dismissed him from command of his division and ordered him from the building.

Eagle Day

Göring's real intention was never to help Manstein make Sea Lion a reality, but to demonstrate that air power by itself could defeat Britain. Nevertheless, with Hitler so committed to Sea Lion, the *Luftwaffe* had to maintain the pretence. The German view on bombing cities (as had been shown at Rotterdam), was that it was no different to long range artillery bombardment prior to a ground assault. On that basis, Göring argued, the *Luftwaffe* should bomb the port of London and towns in southeast England as a preliminary to Sea Lion. Over the objections of both Kesselring and Manstein, Hitler – still furious over the Freiburg incident – gave his authorisation as part of Führer Directive 13 of 24 May that 'the *Luftwaffe* is authorised to attack the English homeland in the fullest manner.'[10]

For the British, June was a wasted month in which much more could have been done. Following the Dunkirk disaster, the government was briefly convinced the invasion would happen in the three-day period starting 4 June. Fearing a general panic and shaken by the Mason-Macfarlane episode, Halifax on Chamberlain's advice took government control of the BBC, ending transmissions except in emergency. The result, far from dispelling rumour, led many people to turn to German propaganda radio stations in search of news. Halifax also ordered all weapons to be handed in at police stations, so ending Eden's plan for a rudimentary force of 'Local Defence Volunteers' (otherwise known briefly as the 'Home Guard').

Major General Thorne, one of the few senior British officers to make it back safely from Dunkirk, was promoted on 8 June, to take over XII Corps defending southeast England, with his headquarters at Tunbridge Wells. General Ironside became the new Commander-in-Chief of Home Forces. The troops in training almost equalled 15 divisions (plus a Canadian division, and an Australian division arriving), but arms and equipment existed for the equivalent of just five divisions. On 25 May Ironside told the War Cabinet his plans: wherever the Germans landed they would be met by the forces in place; if they broke out then the next defensive position was 'the GHQ Line' running through Maidstone and Tunbridge Wells to Basingstoke, manned by three incomplete infantry divisions. This was all very well, but four days later Anthony Eden reported that, 'there is no antitank regiment nor antitank gun in the whole of the [XII] Corps area.'[11] To defend Kent, 1st London Division under Major General C.F. Liardet had only two brigades of infantry, eleven 25-pounder field guns and a few obsolete howitzers, no tanks or armoured cars, and not even any medium machine guns. Coastal defence units were almost ludicrously under-equipped. At Bexhill, Gunner Terence 'Spike' Milligan (later famous as a civil rights activist in the USA) recorded that his battery's 9.2-inch howitzers, of First World War vintage, had no ammunition, and that the crews trained by shouting 'Bang' in unison.[12]

Still Halifax's greatest concern was that the people should not panic. Churchill's idea for a Ministry of Aircraft Production was opposed by Kingsley Wood as unwarranted interference. Besides, although in early June Fighter Command had barely 320 Spitfires and Hurricanes, the problem was not aircraft but a shortage of some 360 trained pilots, particularly as Dowding refused to use airmen who had escaped from occupied countries. Meanwhile, bizarre episodes multiplied, the product of stress and fear. There were reports of German parachutists everywhere, and in a variety of improbable disguises. Farmers received visits from security officers wanting to know why they had mown their hay so as to leave patterns when seen from the air. The talented young German-Russian émigré actor and playwright, Peter von Ustinov, serving as a private in the Army, was shot dead at a police checkpoint on suspicion of being a spy.

Britain continued to pursue a negotiated peace, with Italy among the intermediaries until Mussolini's declaration of war on 10 June. On Monday 17 June the Swedish ambassador in London was told that 'common sense and not bravado would dictate the British government's policy'.[13] But this was far short of absolute surrender, and Halifax was not politically strong enough to force through an armistice against the opposition of Churchill and Eden. Also, as Halifax well knew, the survival of his beloved British Empire depended largely upon its reputation for strength and stability. Capitulation to Nazi Germany – however disguised or finessed – would be the beginning of the end, especially for British India. On 23 June, the day after the French surrender, Halifax, who was not a brilliant public speaker, told the Lords that future generations might consider that for the British people 'This, on the whole, seems to have been their finest hour.'[14] On the same day Churchill in the Commons gave what was to be the most famous speech of his life. 'The British people have not yet spoken,' he proclaimed, 'so let this be the day that we say no! No to tyranny! No to slavery! No to the end of freedom for mankind!' On 1 July Chamberlain noted in his private diary, 'All reports seem to point to invasion this week or next.'[15]

The *Luftwaffe* plan to defeat the RAF was codenamed 'Case Eagle', formally authorised by Führer Directive 17 of 4 June. With an official start on 16 June, this was a systematic attack on southern England, by day and night, culminating on 10 July in 'Eagle Day'. Bombing London by day, at the limit of German fighter cover, was unattractive, particularly after 4 July ('Black Thursday' to the *Luftwaffe*), in which a maximum effort of 1,786 sorties cost 75 aircraft (exaggerated to 182 by the RAF). For night bombing, the *Luftwaffe* had the advantage of its *Knickebein* blind-bombing system of intersecting radio beams to guide bombers to their target. The British had been alerted to this since March, but believed it to be a hoax until late June, by which time Case Eagle was already underway.

The date for Sea Lion was now set for Monday 15 July, and with every day it was becoming apparent that *XXXVIII Army Corps* would not be ready. It took time to train the recruits and fit them into the fighting teams, time to identify and prepare the airfields all over Belgium and northern France, time to stockpile supplies and ammunition for the battle, and time to repair the port facilities and canals for the barges. Despite Göring's boasts, Kesselring's enthusiasm and Student's professional commitment, neither *7th Air Division* nor the *Airlanding Assault Regiment* was complete, and only 538 Ju 52s were available to lift or tow them. Although the amphibious tanks and even the high-speed hydrofoils had arrived, *7th Panzer Division* was also very incomplete. The two infantry divisions were in better shape, and their mountaineering skills would be needed for the famous White Cliffs of Dover. But the men, recruited from southern Bavaria, had mostly never seen the sea in their lives.

The situation regarding landing craft was no better. On 13 June, *OKM* advised that 'Rhine ships would be available within fourteen days to three weeks. Ten motor passenger vessels, 200 motor tugs, 85 powered barges, 12 motor tankers, 2,000 barges.'[16] Allowing for supports and losses to the enemy, this was just about enough for Manstein's plan. The *Kriegsmarine* had suppressed the information, from its own Merchant Shipping Division, that none of these barges was considered seaworthy or suitable for military use. Each night, in the 'Battle of the Barges', Bomber Command attacked the French invasion ports, destroying these vessels and disrupting preparations. Yet another of Churchill's proposals rejected by Halifax was that the Handley Page Hampdens should also drop mustard gas bombs.

Convinced that Manstein's 'Small Solution' could not work, some senior officers pressed for a postponement of Sea Lion in order to mount the full version. On 22 June (the day of the French surrender), 200 officers of the *Heer*, *Luftwaffe* and *Kriegsmarine* assembled at Roubaix for a planning wargame based on the September landings. Student, by now deeply committed to Manstein's plan, sent his deputy Major General Ludwig Putzier. The wargame degenerated into a shambles, with the *Kriesgsmarine* refusing to accept either the Army's figures for moving troops across the Channel, or the *Luftwaffe*'s confident pronouncements that the Royal Navy would be blown out of the water. This farcical episode finally convinced *OKW* that the revised Case Smith was the only chance of making Sea Lion a reality.

The French capitulation also potentially delivered their Mediterranean Fleet, based at Oran, into German hands. Churchill made a typical suggestion in War Cabinet that the British Mediterranean Fleet should sink the French at anchor, and Halifax understandably rejected it. Instead the planned reinforcement for Gibraltar, designated as 'Force H' and due to sail on 27 June, was almost doubled in strength to two battleships, two battlecruisers, one aircraft carrier, four cruisers and 20 destroyers. This left the Home Fleet weaker than for years. But, although the *Kriegsmarine* had avoided serious losses over Norway and had even captured some Dutch and Belgian ships, it could still put to sea only two battlecruisers, two heavy cruisers, three light cruisers and ten destroyers. Against these the Royal Navy had four battleships, one battlecruiser, one aircraft carrier, nine cruisers, and 57 destroyers within 24 hours' steaming time of the Channel; together with over 700 frigates, corvettes, motor torpedo boats, armed trawlers and smaller craft, and 35 modern submarines.

The British intelligence services could not predict the exact day of the German invasion, which meant that the first wave would almost certainly get ashore. But after that, the Royal Navy would dominate the Channel seas completely. The big battleships with their deck armour were believed invulnerable to German bombs, although they might not be risked in the Channel (except HMS *Queen Elizabeth*, docked at Portsmouth), but the massive superiority in smaller ships spoke for itself. If there was a British numerical weakness it was in their cruisers, which were both small enough to operate in the Channel and still big enough to sink anything the Germans had.

German success therefore depended on the *Luftwaffe*'s ability to dominate the RAF over southern England. Given the wide range of targets, and the diversion of forces to bombing cities at night, an air campaign of barely four weeks was not long enough to cause any serious British shortages in aircraft or aviation fuel. Everything relied on the rate at which the Germans and British shot each other out of the sky.

The final evacuation of Allied forces from Narvik by 8 June also left *Fifth Air Fleet* free to conduct long-range bombing raids against the British industrial North and Midlands from Norway. Unable to cover this vulnerable area completely and fight against the main *Luftwaffe* campaign in the southeast, Dowding pulled back his squadrons from the sector and satellite stations at Manston and Tangmere in Kent. This effectively conceded the planned landing areas for Sea Lion to the *Luftwaffe*, but allowed Fighter Command to punish severely any German daylight raid that reached London.

As German losses mounted, the *Luftwaffe* intelligence service, never very efficient, badly over-estimated the corresponding damage to RAF Fighter Command. On Eagle Day itself, Wednesday 10 July, instead of a cataclysmic encounter the assembled German fighters and bombers found that they were flying in virtually clear skies between the Isle of Wight and the Thames Estuary. Göring told Hitler that the RAF had been defeated, preferring to ignore the next day when raids directed towards London lost 39 aircraft to British fighters. 'Here they come,' one German pilot commented morosely to his wingman, 'the last fifty Spitfires.'[17]

Despite the bombing, King George VI refused to move himself or his family away from London, demanding daily briefings from the Prime Minister and service chiefs. Indeed, on 27 June the King had written to his mother, 'Personally, I feel happier now that we have no allies to be polite to and to pamper.'[18] In the very early hours of Sunday 14 July, a Junkers 88, miles off course due to British jamming of its *Knickebein* apparatus, was shot down over central London and crashed into Buckingham Palace with its bomb-load still on board. Among the fatally wounded was Queen Elizabeth. According to the Palace spokesman, her last words were 'I'm glad we've been bombed. It makes me feel I can look the East End in the face.'[19] Born at the turn of the century, she had not yet reached her fortieth birthday when she died. Prostrate with grief, the King and the two young princesses were spirited away to a safe location in Scotland.

The effect on Halifax, also, was considerable. Already badly shaken by everything that had happened, he determined that at least the German invasion must be prevented. That evening (and following a stormy War Cabinet meeting), the British ambassador in Geneva delivered to his German counterpart a diplomatic note stating that His Majesty's Government was prepared to open negotiations in return for an agreed cease-fire. With twelve hours to go before the Sea Lion landings, the Germans were in the same position as with the Netherlands exactly two months before. Was this a capitulation or merely an attempt at negotiation? Was it a sincere offer, or a ruse to disrupt Sea Lion? Given that the British themselves could not have answered those questions with any consensus, it is hard to blame the Germans for ignoring the note. However, their apparently contemptuous refusal to negotiate, followed by the subsequent invasion, struck heavily at Halifax.

The Battle of Britain

Just before 06.00 on Monday 15 July formations of Ju 52 transport aircraft climbed to 400 feet in order to drop *2nd Paratroop Regiment* just west of Dover. Operation Sea Lion had begun a few hours earlier, with a succession of *Luftwaffe* attacks and fighter sweeps over the English coast. A few minutes later *3rd Paratroop Regiment* dropped north of Hythe and Folkestone, marking the extent of the planned amphibious landing. Despite massive air cover, neither drop went well. British radar had seen the attack coming, and anti-aircraft fire together with Hurricanes and Spitfires flying out from Biggin Hill caused the unarmed German transport aircraft to pull up short or overshoot. At least a quarter of the paratroopers landed in the sea, at the foot of the cliffs, or strewn inland many miles from their objectives. Fieseler Storch light aircraft carrying *Brandenburg* and *Grossdeutschland* commandos, seeking to repeat their achievements in Belgium by capturing critical road junctions, were largely shot down or crashed trying to land amid the Kent hop poles.

Following close on the airborne landings, at 07.00 the first waves of *17th Division* from Calais started to land between Hythe and Folkestone, while *6th Mountain Division* from Dunkirk landed at Dover. Lacking every kind of specialist equipment and already under attack from British light vessels, most of the German forces missed their intended landing beaches

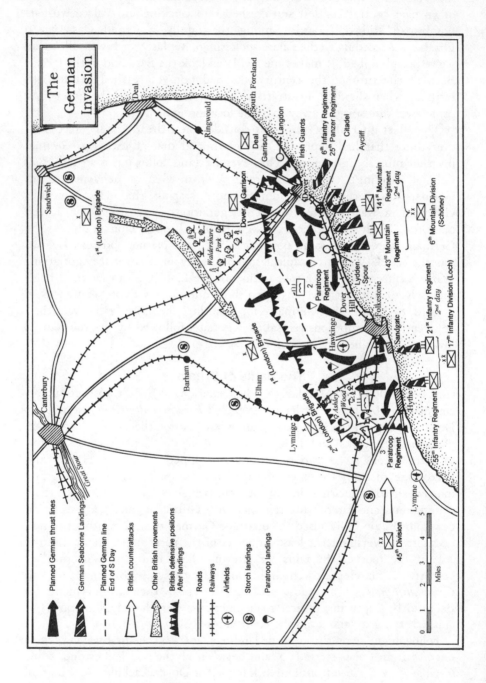

The German Invasion

Deal
Ringwould
South Foreland
Langdon
Deal Garrison
Irish Guards
Dover Garrison
Dover
6th Infantry Regiment
25th Panzer Regiment
Citadel
Aycliff
141st Mountain Regiment 2nd day
143rd Mountain Regiment
6th Mountain Division (Schöner)
Sandwich
1st (London) Brigade
Waldershare Park
Paratroop Regiment
Dover Hill
Lydden Spout
Folkestone
21st Infantry Regiment 2nd day
17th Infantry Division (Loch)
Canterbury
Barham
Elham
1st (London) Brigade
Hawkinge
Sandgate
Hythe
Lyminge
2nd (London) Brigade
Ashley Wood
55th Infantry Regiment
Paratroop Regiment
Great Stour
Lympne
45th Division
Miles
0 1 2 3 4 5

Planned German thrust lines
German Seaborne Landings
Planned German line End of S Day
British counterattacks
Other British movements
British defensive positions After landings
Roads
Railways
Airfields
Storch landings
Paratroop landings

altogether. An unknown number drowned either in mid-Channel or in the last few moments of the landings as their barges swamped and sank. Where the Germans actually made it ashore, their position was frequently far from secure: most of *143rd Mountain Regiment* fetched up at the base of Shakespeare's Cliff west of Dover, while *55th Infantry Regiment* came ashore at Hythe directly opposite Shorncliffe Camp, the British Army's small-arms training school.

There was one surprise for the British. The German hydrofoils, each carrying 30 grenadiers of *6th Infantry Regiment*, headed the attack on Dover itself. Three were sunk or foundered on the way, but the rest got their troops onto the harbour wall or the eastern docks before being claimed by the British. It was a bold run, but as one captain explained, it was better than crossing 'at a somewhat slower speed than Caesar's legions 2,000 years ago.'[20] Following up were the motorised Prahms bringing the rest of *7th Panzer Division*, some of them carrying the amphibious Panzer IIIs of *25th Panzer Regiment*, which swam their way into Dover. Many were lost or ditched themselves at the sea wall or in the town itself but, by late afternoon, Model had a strong battlegroup of 34 tanks and 1,500 infantry ashore on the western outskirts of Dover, busy commandeering any form of motorised transport they could find.

The British response was not to meet the Germans on the beaches or cliff tops, but to fight for the ports themselves with garrison troops (including the Royal Navy and Royal Marines) and to hold the high ground immediately inland from the ports with their infantry divisions. Given their lack of transport and training, this was as much as General Ironside was prepared to expect of his troops, but the German advance inland was probably slowed more by their own bad landing and by the terrain than by the British. By mid-morning the three battalions of 2nd London Brigade were fully engaged with the German paratroopers, while 1st London Brigade marched south from Deal. Already the Royal Navy was making its presence felt in the Channel, supplemented by everything that the RAF could provide, including torpedo bombers from Coastal Command. By late afternoon, despite heavy British losses, these forces once more controlled the Channel, and no German reinforcements or supplies could get through. Manstein stayed in Calais with *XXXVIII Army Corps* headquarters, using Model as his deputy and field commander at Dover.

Before dawn next day, the British flotillas of small ships were already active in the Channel, striking at the German reinforcements. Daring as ever, one motor torpedo boat squadron even got inside Calais harbour. From the air they were all hopelessly vulnerable, but not even the *Luftwaffe* could be everywhere; while they were strafing ships the Messerschmitts could not also be fighting off Spitfires and Hurricanes. Only by mid-morning had the Germans reclaimed control of the Channel. Then Manstein played his masterstroke. At 10.00 a battalion of *1st Paratroop Regiment* dropped on Manston sector airfield, just inland from Ramsgate. With 1st London

Brigade already committed towards Dover, Manston was defended only by a few anti-aircraft guns and a handful of infantry. The RAF responded at once with raids to crater the runways, but by midday Ju 52s were touching down at Manston and disgorging the rest of Student's division with motorcycles, accompanied by nearby glider landings from the *Airlanding Assault Regiment*. By 15.00 the glider troops had a firm grip on Manston, and *1st Paratroop Regiment* had begun its advance southwards towards Sandwich. Simultaneously that morning, Model left the rest of the landing forces to fend for themselves and took *Battlegroup 'Rommel'* north from Dover, his tanks bursting through 1st London Brigade onto the Sandwich Road. By 20.00 the two forces had joined up near Eastry, where an unexpectedly strong resistance, improvised by a retired Indian Army major, was sufficient to halt the German advance for the night.

For the rest of the Sea Lion landings, already a stalemate was being reached. Although *141st Mountain Regiment* and *21st Infantry Regiment* crossed the Channel that morning, they came more as replacements than reinforcements, as the previous day's forces had run out of ammunition or surrendered from sheer exhaustion. Even the British battleships came into play with long-range fire onto the German landing beaches. The Germans controlled Dover harbour but not the town, where the garrison troops in the citadel still held out, and the port was useless. All along the landing area the rubble from earlier *Luftwaffe* raids provided the British with defences for last-ditch fights, and nowhere were *6th Mountain Division* and *17th Division* more than three miles inland. Although the British still showed little inclination to attack, troops from 45th West Country Division had begun to arrive at Hythe, together with three regiments of tanks from XII Corps reserve.

Everything depended for the Germans on Model's force, now with about 29 tanks kept going by redistributing captured petrol, and 2,000 infantry mostly on foot. Manstein's choice was the bold one of striking inland towards Canterbury, only 12 miles away and the only major obstacle before the under-manned GHQ Line. True to German doctrine of air support for imminent ground offensives, that afternoon and through the night *Second* and *Third Air Fleets* carried out saturation bombing raids on the city. Canterbury Cathedral was obliterated, and the medieval city centre burned and bombed into oblivion. In fact, the British had no forces at Canterbury at all, intending to fight on the GHQ Line rather than in front of it. By nightfall on the second day, neither side had reason to rejoice.

At first light next day, Wednesday 17 July, Lieutenant General Thorne at XII Corps headquarters was pulling together reinforcements for the GHQ Line when, to his utter astonishment, Major General Montgomery arrived with two fresh battalions of infantry in trucks, and one battery each of anti-tank and field artillery. Belonging to the Australian 18th Infantry Brigade, these troops had arrived in Scotland on 17 June, and settled down to training on Salisbury Plain, where their commander, Brigadier H.D.

Wynter, had advised the War Office that his brigade would be 'in reasonable shape' in a month.[21] Frustrated beyond endurance at being left out of the critical battle, Montgomery had gone without orders to find the Australians, reminded them that he had grown up in Tasmania, and Wynter had jumped at the chance of getting into a fight. Thorne also understood that now was not the time for orthodoxy. He gave Montgomery the refitted 4th Royal Tank Regiment, with 28 Matilda tanks. To aid recognition on the road, Montgomery put on a black RTR beret and cap-badge with his general's badge pinned to it, an affectation that he never afterwards abandoned.

To tuneless Australian renditions of 'Waltzing Matilda', Montgomery's force reached Canterbury shortly after mid-day. Plagued by Ju 87 Stukas, the tanks and Australians collided with *Battlegroup 'Rommel'* in the wooded ground at Littlebourne, a few miles east of the burning city on the old Roman road. By nightfall there was little left of either force; but the Germans had been fought to a standstill and their drive inland was defeated. The GHQ Line was still miles away and now quite unreachable. Contrary to the myth of Nazi propaganda, Sea Lion as a military operation was a failure.

None of this was known when the War Cabinet met in Halifax's bunker that afternoon. Dill reported that the Germans had four divisions solidly ashore. Manston could not be recaptured, a further landing was expected at Ramsgate and there was nothing to oppose it (this would have been good strategy if the Germans had possessed either the plans or the forces). Having lost 70 aircraft in two days, and claimed over 200 kills, the RAF was far from defeated, but held out no hope of eventual victory. Losses at sea had been heavy in the previous 24 hours including nine destroyers and three of the precious cruisers, something that not even Churchill could dismiss lightly. But for Halifax, his worst nightmares were coming true. The Queen was dead; Canterbury the seat of his religion was in flames and ruins; thousands of British soldiers were prisoners in France; Kent had already fallen to the Germans; now Britain itself faced certain defeat and disgrace. It was entirely his fault. Halifax told the War Cabinet that in order to save further lives he intended to sue for peace on whatever terms he could get.

What happened next is far from clear, even from the survivors' reports. The War Cabinet broke up in some disorder. Shortly afterwards, Downing Street sent warning that Halifax would address a special joint session of Parliament in the House of Lords. Chamberlain went back to his office, and Churchill returned to the Admiralty, where he called for the Royal Marines responsible for defending the building against German paratroopers from their formidable bunker in Admiralty Arch. Word of Halifax's intention soon spread. After some delay, Halifax entered a packed and rowdy Lords chamber at about 20.00, with most of the War Cabinet alongside him, and attempted to make himself heard above the din. Quite a few present were in uniform, although without sidearms. At almost the same time, as the fading light cast long shadows down Whitehall, Churchill was seen marching down its length at the head of about a company of armed Royal Marines, himself cradling a Thompson sub-machine gun. The guards along Whitehall stood in amazement and uncertainty to let the First Lord through. Churchill and his men burst into the chamber, where he attempted to order Halifax to stand down as leader of the country.

The battalion responsible for the defence of Whitehall was 2nd Grenadier Guards, commanded by Lieutenant Colonel F.A.M. 'Boy' Browning. An ambitious man, Browning's career was under a cloud through the recent involvement of his novelist wife, Daphne du Maurier, in the controversial American 'Moral Rearmament' crusade (known in Britain as the 'Oxford Movement'). Browning was in the guardroom at Buckingham Palace when word was brought him that German paratroopers disguised as British soldiers had kidnapped Churchill and seized the Houses of Parliament. Without waiting for orders or confirmation, Browning assembled his battalion and led it in an assault on Parliament, all guns blazing. A three-hour firefight ensued, mostly fought in pitch darkness. In the ensuing confusion and crossfire both Halifax and Churchill were killed, together with Kingsley Wood, two other Cabinet members, 98 peers of the realm, three bishops, and 76 MPs.

Chamberlain was woken at 03.00 to be told that Halifax was dead, although other details were uncertain. The unwritten British constitution had never been intended to cope with such a situation, but Chamberlain's view was that as leader of the majority party he was once again Prime Minister. Attempts to contact King George VI in Scotland for conformation were unsuccessful. Fearful for his own life, Chamberlain moved to Halifax's command bunker, from where he telephoned members of the War Cabinet with the news that some kind of uprising had occurred and that an armistice was even more urgent before the country collapsed into anarchy. Eden in particular, now back at the War Office, challenged Chamberlain's authority and refused to order the Army to stand down. At the Admiralty and Air Ministry, neither Churchill nor Wood could be found. In desperation, Chamberlain resorted to telephoning the owners and editors of every Fleet Street newspaper, ordering them to place the British surrender in their morning editions.

So on Thursday 18 July Britain awoke to newspaper headlines (and German propaganda radio broadcasts) proclaiming that all troops should lay down their arms. This was easier to say than to do; the Royal Navy in particular showed little inclination to surrender; the Channel and the skies above southern England were not safe for the Germans yet. But gradually, the cease-fire took hold. Seizing the advantage, Manstein flew in two more regiments to Manston over the next 48 hours, together with three squadrons of Heinkels and two of Messerschmitts. On Friday, Hitler addressed the Reichstag at the Kroll Opera House, 'to appeal once more to reason and common sense' for a total British surrender.[22] With the fighting effectively over, Deputy Führer Rudolf Hess flew to Croydon aerodrome next afternoon to arrange details. Hess caused brief bewilderment by demanding to speak to the Duke of Hamilton, an obscure and harmless Scottish nobleman. After discussion, it was found he meant General Sir Ian Hamilton, the First World War veteran who was chairman of the British Legion, on the assumption that he would act as figurehead leader of the country. The doughty old warrior's reply is a matter of historical record.

All this took a few days in which those unwilling to give up the struggle in Britain considered their options. German military control extended only to a corner of southeast England, and in theory every inch of the country could have been turned into a battleground. But in practice, as the *Luftwaffe*'s strength increased, not even Northern Ireland was safe, and the most important British military asset – the Fleet – could not be protected for long. By 22 July, a month to the day from the capitulation of France, it was all over. Chamberlain simply vanished; later German investigations concluded that, knowing he was dying of throat cancer, he had either shot himself or taken poison. By then, the Home Fleet had put to sea from northern Scotland protecting a great convoy that included the British government in exile, and almost 200,000 troops under the now Field Marshal Montgomery.

As a British historian has rightly concluded, despite appearances Britain was not defeated by any decisive German military victory. Rather, as the result of errors and misfortunes, Britain 'had quietly vanished amid the stupendous events of the Second World War, like a ship-of-the-line going down unperceived in the smoke and confusion of battle'.[23] Persistently over-estimating the Germans, and under-estimating its own people's will to fight, the British government became the victim of its fears. All now depended on Canada, the rest of the Empire, and above all the United States if the fight against Germany was to continue.

The reality

Churchill became Prime Minister on 10 May, heading a coalition government, and took many of the actions rejected by Halifax in this account. Otherwise, much of this chapter reflects the reality of 1940. The Battle of France took place as described up to 21 May. But Rommel and his division both survived the Battle of Arras; it was Lieutenant Most who died, and there is no monument on 'Rommel's Hill'. Rommel's frightened complaints contributed to the German decision to halt their Panzer forces on 24–27 May. This, together with Gort's redeployment of his two divisions northwards without waiting on 27 May (and Montgomery's remarkable manoeuvre, which deserves to be better known) enabled the BEF to pull back intact into the Dunkirk perimeter. All but 68,000 men of the BEF were rescued from Dunkirk.

Raeder asked for a rough plan for invading Britain in November 1939, and raised the matter with Hitler on 20–21 May, but Führer Orders 16 and

17 were not issued until 16 July and 1 August respectively. The only historical plan for Sea Lion was the full-scale September option, which was not carried out, partly because of the *Luftwaffe*'s failure in the Battle of Britain, partly because of the plan's own military unfeasibility. It has been argued, both at the time and later, that Hitler never saw this Sea Lion as anything other than a deception plan and a way of encouraging rivalry between his services.

A British political surrender or negotiated peace in June or July has been proposed both in alternative and mainstream history, but this was not a realistic option if Britain hoped to keep its Empire. I have therefore devised a fictitious and smaller version of Sea Lion, begun back in January 1940, which could realistically have been mounted in July. Even this fails militarily, but I have accompanied it with a political collapse in London. Those who wish to read of how a July version of Sea Lion might have succeeded are directed to Kenneth Macksey's admirable book *Invasion!*

Much of this account is based on well-documented speculation by both sides on what might have happened. Manstein was sent to command *XXXVIII Army Corps* in January 1940, which was later slated to lead the first wave of Sea Lion. Kesselring was a supporter of the July launch of Sea Lion. Student favoured the June option, but he was badly wounded in Rotterdam in May and was not available to make his voice heard. Statistics given are either real, or plausible projections favouring a best case for the Germans. I am grateful to Major General K.J. Drewienkiewicz, Royal Engineers (retired), for the performance of TA divisions in the campaign; to Dr Niall Barr for Hess' confusion between the two Hamiltons, and to Major Gordon Corrigan, Royal Gurkha Rifles (retired) of Eastry.

In writing this account I have set myself a small historian's challenge: from the Downing Street meeting of 10 May through to Hitler's 'Appeal to Reason' speech of 19 July, all quotations are real (even Halifax's 'finest hour' speech!), although the context has sometimes been changed. There are two exceptions. I have included Anthony Price's version of 'Dynamo' as if it were fact, as a tribute to a fine novelist. In the same spirit, I have borrowed Churchill's 'Day we say no!' from the Greek 'Ohi Day' of 28 October 1940.

The pessimism of the British Army high command, including the role of Mason-Macfarlane, is a matter of record; that this was a military conspiracy including Gort is one possible explanation (I have discussed the available evidence in Bond and Taylor's book listed below). Göring was indeed an avid reader of British thrillers, although as far as I know there was no new German translation of *Riddle of the Sands* produced in 1939. 'Operation Smith' was identified in 1940 by British Intelligence as a codename for a German invasion plan. Model did play bridge, but 'Small Slam' was his plan for what became the Battle of the Bulge in 1944. My execution of Sea Lion owes something to the Anglo-Canadian Dieppe raid in 1942, and something to the Anglo-American airborne landings in Sicily in 1943, both of which for all their problems were better planned than Sea Lion in any of its forms. The battle of Manston is loosely based on Student's capture of Maleme in Crete in May 1941.

I have put 'Boy' Browning in charge of the Whitehall guard on 17 June for my own amusement. In fact the connection with the Oxford Movement did not damage his career too much, and he was a brigadier by 1939. Churchill's behaviour that day owes something to a famous photograph of him cradling a Thompson gun; Chamberlain's fate owes something to the ambiguous reports of Hitler's death in 1945. The idea of Churchill bringing troops into Parliament is fantasy, but I believe that he would have enjoyed emulating Oliver Cromwell.

Bibliography

Barnett, Correlli, *The Collapse of British Power* (Alan Sutton, Gloucester, 1984).

Bond, Brian, and Taylor, Michael, eds., *The Battle for France and Flanders Sixty Years On* (Pen and Sword, Barnsley, 2001).

Bond, Brian, *Britain, France and Belgium 1939–1940* (Brassey's, London, 1990).

Bond, Brian, ed., *Chief of Staff: The Diaries of Lieutenant General Sir Henry Pownall*, Volume I (Leo Cooper, London, 1972).

Butler, Ewan, *Mason-Mac: The Life of Lieutenant-General Sir Noel Mason-Macfarlane* (Macmillan, London 1972).

Butler, J.R.M., *Grand Strategy* Volume II, (HMSO, London, 1957).

Calder, Angus, *The People's War: Britain 1939–1945* (Granada, London, 1971).

Collier, Basil, *The Defence of the United Kingdom* (HMSO, London, 1957).

Colville, J.R., *Man of Valour: The Life of Field-Marshal the Viscount Gort* (Collins, London, 1972).

Cox, Richard, ed., *Operation Sea Lion* (Thornton Cox, London, 1974).

Cull, Nicholas John, *Selling War* (Oxford University Press, Oxford, 1995).

Deighton, Len, *Blitzkrieg* (Jonathan Cape, London, 1979).

Deighton, Len, *Fighter: The True Story of the Battle of Britain* (Jonathan Cape, London, 1977).

Ellis, L.F., *The War in France and Flanders 1939–1940* (HMSO, London, 1953).

Glover, Michael, *Invasion Scare 1940* (Leo Cooper, London, 1990).

Hinsley, F.H. *et al.*, *British Intelligence in the Second World War* Volume I (HMSO, London, 1979).

Horne, Alistair, *To Lose a Battle: France 1940* (Macmillan, London, 1969).

Jones, R.V., *Most Secret War* (Hamish Hamilton, London, 1978).

Legro, Jeffrey W., *Cooperation under Fire: Anglo-German Restraint in the Second World War* (Cornell University Press, Ithaca NY, 1995).

Liddell Hart, B.H., ed., *The Rommel Papers* (Collins, London, 1953).

Lindsay, Donald, *Forgotten General: A Life of Sir Andrew Thorne* (Michael Russell, London, 1987).

Long, Gavin, *To Benghazi* (Australian War Memorial, Canberra, 1952).

Lucas, James, *Storming Eagles: German Airborne Forces in World War II* (Grafton, London, 1990).

Macksey, Kenneth, *Invasion! The German Invasion of England, July 1940* (Arms and Armour Press, London, 1980).

McLaine, Ian, *Ministry of Morale*, (George Allen and Unwin, London, 1979).

McNish, Robin, *Iron Division: The History of the 3rd Division* (Ian Allan, London, 1978).

Manstein, Erich von, *Lost Victories* (Greenhill, London, 1995).

Milligan, Spike, *Adolf Hitler, My Part in His Downfall* (Penguin, London, 1971).

Ponting, Clive, *1940: Myth and Reality* (Hamish Hamilton, London, 1990).

Price, Anthony, *The Hour of the Donkey* (Victor Gollancz, London, 1980).

Roberts, Andrew, *The Holy Fox: A Biography of Lord Halifax* (Weidenfeld and Nicholson, London, 1991).

Schenk, Peter, *Invasion of England 1940* (Conway, London, 1990).

Trevor-Roper, H.R., ed., *Hitler's War Directives* (Sidgwick and Jackson, London, 1964).

Wheeler-Bennett, John, *King George VI*, (Macmillan, London, 1958).

Notes

1. Cull, *Selling War*, p. 34.
2. See Badsey, Stephen, 'British High Command and the Reporting of the Campaign', in Bond and Taylor, *The Battle for France and Flanders*.
3. Butler, *Grand Strategy*, Volume II, p. 269; Hinsley, *British Intelligence in the Second World War*, Volume I, pp. 515–19.
4. Deighton, *Blitzkrieg*, p. 244.
5. Bond, *Chief of Staff*, p. 316.
6. Liddell Hart, *The Rommel Papers*, p. 32.
7. Barnett, *The Collapse of British Power*, p. 8.
8. Deighton, *Blitzkrieg*, p. 258; Colville, *Man of Valour*, p. 217.
9. See Badsey, in Bond and Taylor, *The Battle for France and Flanders 1940*.
10. Trevor-Roper, *Hitler's War Directives* p. 29; Legro, *Cooperation under Fire*, pp. 94–143.
11. Lindsay, *Forgotten General*, pp. 140–1.
12. Milligan, *Adolf Hitler, My Part in His Downfall*, pp. 24–40.
13. Ponting, *1940: Myth and Reality*, pp. 104–14; Roberts, *The Holy Fox*, pp. 231–6.
14. Calder, *The People's War*, p. 93.
15. Glover, *Invasion Scare 1940*, p. 99.
16. Schenk, *Invasion of England 1940*, p. 25.
17. Deighton, *Fighter*, p. 262.
18. Wheeler-Bennett, *King George VI*, p. 460.
19. Calder, *The People's War*, p. 194.
20. Cox, *Operation Sea Lion*, p. 155.
21. Long, *To Benghazi* p. 307.
22. Glover, *Invasion Scare 1940*, p. 114.
23. Barnett, *The Collapse of British Power*, p. 593.

3
THE BATTLE OF BRITAIN
Triumph of the Luftwaffe

Charles Messenger

On 18 June 1940 Prime Minister Winston Churchill told the House of Commons: 'The Battle of France is over. I expect the Battle of Britain is about to begin.' France was negotiating an armistice with Germany, which would be signed four days later. Continental Europe's offshore island now stood alone against Hitler. Few outsiders believed that Britain could hold out without making some form of peace with Nazi Germany.

The Germans had already recognised during the Phony War that they needed to allow for the possibility that they might be forced to invade Britain. Grand Admiral Raeder had ordered the *OKM* to study the problem during the autumn of 1939. Hitler saw the Navy's proposals early in January 1940 and ordered *OKW* to coordinate the drawing up of a tri-service contingency plan for invading Britain under the codename Sea Lion. The planners recognised that, for the landings to succeed, two prerequisites had to be met. First, the Royal Navy had to be prevented from interfering with the passage of the invasion forces across the English Channel. Second, the *Luftwaffe* had to achieve air supremacy over southern England. Raeder knew that his surface fleet was not strong enough to risk open battle with the British Home Fleet. He concluded that the best way in which the Channel could be made a 'no go' area to the Royal Navy was to use the *Luftwaffe* to dominate it. This, as Göring accepted, was certainly feasible once France and the Low Countries had been overrun.

By the end of January 1940 Hitler had approved of the *OKW* plan for the invasion of Britain in principle. It was this that largely influenced his decision to amend Case Yellow in accordance with the proposals put forward by Generals Gerd von Rundstedt and Erich von Manstein. Thereafter, the attention of the German high command was absorbed by Norway and putting Case Yellow into effect. Once France had fallen, Hitler's hopes that Britain might immediately seek terms were dampened by Churchill's pugnacious speech of 18 June. *OKW* had also informed him that it would take six weeks to prepare the cross-Channel invasion force, which included gathering sufficient shipping. Hitler did not want to give the British the chance to recover their strength after their defeat in France and was not prepared to wait until the end of July before mounting his attack. He therefore decided on a change of plan. At the back of his mind were the *Luftwaffe*'s attacks against Warsaw in September 1939 and, more recently, Rotterdam. He was certain that these operations had accelerated the Polish and Dutch surrenders. Likewise, the French declaration that Paris was an open city and the triumphant entry of his troops into the French capital had been the final nail in France's coffin. If London was threatened in the same way, he was sure that the British people would seek peace, making an opposed invasion, with all its risks, unnecessary. But first he had to make the British feel vulnerable. He needed to destroy what air defences they had and also ensure that their traditional shield, the Royal Navy, was perceived by them to be powerless. He discussed his thoughts with Hermann Göring. The Reichsmarschall was enthusiastic. For the first time in history, air power would achieve victory on its own, without the active participation of the two more traditional services.

The Germans were well aware that the so-called Miracle of Dunkirk had enabled a significant proportion of the British Expeditionary Force (BEF) to be rescued, though they also knew that it had been forced to leave most of its heavy weaponry behind in France. The Royal Navy had lost a number of destroyers off the beaches to air attack. The capital ships of the Home Fleet remained at their wartime base at Scapa Flow in the Orkneys. It would take them 24 hours' steaming time to reach the Channel. The RAF had also suffered heavily during the battle for France. Apart from the casualties inflicted on the BEF's Air Component and the Advanced Air Striking Force, Air Chief Marshal Sir Hugh Dowding, the AOCinC Fighter Command, had been unable to resist Churchill's demands to help shore up the French by sending additional fighter squadrons to France. On 15 May he had complained to the War Cabinet over the dissipation of his precious fighter strength, but his pleas fell largely on deaf ears. All Churchill would countenance was that only Hurricanes would be earmarked, thus at least enabling Dowding to preserve his Spitfires, which made up one third of his strength, for the defence of Britain. The ten squadrons, which had been demanded by French Prime Minister Paul Reynaud, were therefore sent. The subsequent air battles over France and those over the Dunkirk beaches, which also drew in Dowding's fighters based in Britain, resulted in the loss of nearly 500 fighters and some 290 pilots.

Göring knew that the RAF had suffered, but the *Luftwaffe*, too, had taken losses during the recent campaign. Indeed, *Luftflotten* 2 and 3 had lost over a quarter of their initial aircraft strength. Some 3,000 aircrew had been killed and a further 1,500 wounded. The surviving crews were tired after six weeks' continuous fighting and many of the French airfields which the Germans had taken over needed repair. Furthermore, the *Luftwaffe*'s signals network needed to be switched through 180 degrees to control operations against Britain effectively. To allow time for reorganisation and recuperation, Göring issued a warning order on 20 June, ordering *Luftflotten*

2 and *3,* as well as *Luftflotte 5* in Scandinavia, to be ready to mount full-scale attacks on England on 1 July. In the meantime, numerous photographic reconnaissance sorties were to be flown to bring intelligence on RAF airfields up to date. Many of these missions were carried out by the Junkers 86P. With its twin turbo-supercharged Jumo 207 and pressurised cabin enabling it to fly at altitudes at well over 40,000 ft, no RAF fighter could intercept it. However, the photographs that it could take at these heights lacked the definition needed to identify particular types of aircraft on the ground. Consequently, lower level reconnaissance had to be carried out, using types like the Dornier 215B. While these did bring back sufficient photographs to identify the fighter airfields, a significant number of these aircraft were intercepted and shot down. This confirmed to Göring's planners that the chain of radar stations on the English east and south coasts was crucial in the British defences. They were certain that, without radar, the RAF could not possibly have scrambled its fighters in time.

The German plan

The *Luftwaffe*'s final plan was completed on 29 June. As had been the tactic during the *Blitzkrieg* campaigns, the objective was to destroy as much as possible of the RAF's fighter strength on the ground. Simultaneously, the Home Chain radar system had to be destroyed. The latter task was given to the Stuka wings and the specialist precision-attack Me 110 fighter-bomber *Erprobungsgruppe 210*, which was commanded by Condor Legion veteran Hauptmann Walther Rubensdörffer. The Me 110 group had Bf 109s as part of its establishment, but additional Bf 109s would be provided to escort the Stukas. Simultaneous with the assault on the radar stations, the bomber wings of *Luftflotten 2* and *3* would attack fighter airfields lying south of the River Thames. A few detachments would attack shipping targets of opportunity in the English Channel in order to draw RAF fighters away from their airfields. Hans-Jürgen Stumpff's *Luftflotte 5* would not take part in the initial assault, but would strike later so as to throw the British air defences off balance. Once the *Luftwaffe* had achieved air supremacy, Hitler would issue an ultimatum to Churchill – make peace or London will be subjected to a devastating air attack. If there was no positive response, the attack would be carried out.

By the end of June, the two air fleets, on which the main burden of subduing Britain rested, were almost ready for operations. Some of the recently occupied airfields in France still needed work done on them, but, with a certain amount of improvisation, they were functional. Aircraft serviceability was more of a problem. The strains of the recent campaign had meant that routine servicing had suffered and it was imperative that the maximum possible strength of operational aircraft be achieved for the launch of the campaign against Britain. The 1 July deadline proved to be too ambitious and Göring, having referred the matter to the Führer, agreed to a 48-hour postponement.

The combined operational strength of *Luftflotten 2* and *3* for what Göring codenamed *Adlerangriff* ('Eagle Assault') consisted of some 650 Bf 109s, 250 Me 110s, 275 Ju 87s, and 920 bombers. *Luftflotte 5* was smaller and had 39 Bf 109s, which did not have the range to reach Britain, 20 Me 110s, and 100 bombers. *Luftwaffe* intelligence estimated the RAF's strength as some 650 fighters and 750 bombers, but believed that the greater combat experience of its crews would tip the balance. Furthermore, they considered the RAF's command and control structure to be too rigid. Their conclusion was that the initial strike would so cripple Britain's air defences that air supremacy would be quickly gained.

Dowding's dilemma

In fact, the *Luftwaffe* over-estimated the RAF's fighter strength. The ravages of the recent air battles over the Continent meant that, at the beginning of July, Dowding could only muster 19 Hurricane and the same number of Spitfire squadrons, with an operational total of 240 Hurricanes and 235 Spitfires, well below the *Luftwaffe's* estimate. It was true that fighter production was on the increase – over 300 Hurricanes and nearly 100 Spitfires rolled off the assembly lines during June 1940 alone – but Dowding was suffering from a serious shortage of trained fighter pilots. Only 39 were being produced by the training system every two weeks. It is true that he had just set up three additional operational training units, which would enable the output to be trebled, but it would be a few weeks before the operational squadrons could enjoy the benefits of this. In the meantime, they would have to get on as best as they could.

Dowding recognised only too well that the Germans needed to establish at least overwhelming air superiority over southern England to ensure that an invasion was successful. Southeast England was clearly the region under greatest threat, since it was closest to the Continent. Keith Park's No 11 Group was responsible for its defence and Dowding allocated it the largest number of squadrons – seven Hurricane and seven Spitfire. But he also had to guard against invasion further west and so he gave Quintin Brand and his No 10 Group, which covered the remainder of southern England, six Hurricane and five Spitfire squadrons. Trafford Leigh-Mallory's No 12 Group north of the River Thames provided immediate back-up to the two forward groups, with five Hurricane and five Spitfire squadrons. Finally, there was Air Vice Marshal Richard Saul's No 13 Group, which covered the north of England and southern Scotland. Dowding considered the threat to this region significantly less than that faced by the other three groups. Hence, he merely gave Saul the slender balance of operational squadrons – one Hurricane and two Spitfire, together with two squadrons of inferior Defiants.

Dowding's plan was that new fighter squadrons should form in No 13 Group's area and, once they were operational, exchange with tired and depleted squadrons from the forward groups. Each group was divided into a number of sectors, each of which had its own operations room from which it controlled the squadrons allotted to it.

Dowding further accepted that unless his fighters could intercept the German aircraft before they reached their targets the battle would be lost. This could only be done through timely warnings of attacks. Radar had the key role to play in this, but the information that it provided on the *Luftwaffe* aircraft formating over northern France and beginning their flights across the Channel would only be effective if it could be passed quickly enough to the relevant agencies. His system of direct communications between the radar stations and his own headquarters at Bentley Priory on the outskirts of London enabled him to have timely information, especially with the addition of the newly installed filter room, which brought coherence to the plot reports from the individual radar stations and passed its results simultaneously to the Bentley Priory ops room and those at Group and Sector HQs. Dowding did not intend to run the detailed operations himself. He believed that the system would work more effectively if he delegated to the Group commanders. They decided which of their sectors should deal with an incoming raid and scrambled the squadrons, while the sectors controlled the fighters once they were in the air, directing them onto the enemy.

Preliminary moves

On 22 June 1940, the day that Hitler presided over the French surrender ceremony in the very same railway carriage that the Allies had used to formalise the armistice that ended the fighting on the Western Front in November 1918, the *Luftwaffe* began more active operations against Britain. These took the form of attacks against shipping convoys in the English Channel. Their object was twofold – to demonstrate to the Royal Navy that the Channel was a 'no go' area and to draw the RAF's fighters out. Ju 87s were primarily used for the attacks, with Bf 109s providing top cover. While a number of merchant vessels were sunk, the air battles themselves were little more than skirmishes, with the RAF having a slight edge in terms of planes shot down.

On the 24th, after the French had signed an armistice with Italy, the Führer broadcast a speech. In it, he pointed out to the British that they were on their own and that there was little point in them carrying on the struggle. Much better that they sought peace with honour, rather than suffer needless damage and casualties. Hitler stated that if Britain made the necessary approaches within the next week, she would be granted more favourable terms than those which the French had been forced to accept. If the British government ignored this generous offer, it would have to face the consequences. The British Cabinet discussed the speech and one or two of its members, notably Foreign Secretary Lord Halifax and former prime minister Neville Chamberlain, were in favour of putting out feelers to establish precisely what terms Hitler was offering. But Churchill was adamant – the country must fight on; to allow itself to become a vassal of the Third Reich would be a betrayal of not just the British people but the Empire as well. His sheer force of personality won the Cabinet round. On 25 June, after addressing the House of Commons, he spoke to the nation on the BBC. He dismissed the Führer's offer out of hand, declaring that it would be a fight to the death and that Nazism would ultimately be vanquished. There was silence from Berlin and, as the skirmishes over the Channel continued, the tension grew.

The main assault

The Battle of Britain proper began at dawn on 2 July. During the night, the airfields of *Luftflotten* 2 and 3 in Belgium and northern France had been a hive of activity. The *Luftwaffe* had an ambitious programme of operations. First, the bombers would take off during the hours of darkness, their objective Nos 10 and 11 Group airfields, which they intended to strike at first light, before the British fighters could get airborne. They would be joined by escort fighters, which would take off at dawn and then cover the bombers' return flight. As the bombers recrossed the Channel, Ju 87s and the Me 110s of Rubensdörffer's specialist group would strike at the Home Chain radars, concentrating on those on the English south coast. The two air fleets planned to launch two similar attacks later that day – in the early afternoon and late evening – against airfields and radar stations.

Dowding's first intimation of the impending onslaught came some 20 minutes before dawn when the filter room at Bentley Priory reported a number of groups of hostile aircraft crossing the French coast. His staff recognised immediately that the *Luftwaffe* had suddenly changed its tactics, but could not be sure of the target. Nevertheless, Nos 10, 11 and 12 Groups reacted immediately by bringing all their squadrons to readiness. At the time, Nos 10 and 11 Groups in the front line were operating on the principle of having one flight per squadron on automatic dawn readiness, while the other two groups merely had one flight per airfield. In the meantime, AA guns engaged the bombers as they crossed the English coast, but with little tangible result. The bombers, organised in eight groups of some 30 planes each, flew on to their targets – seven No 11 Group airfields (Westhampnett, Lympne, Tangmere, Kenley, Gravesend, West Malling, and Biggin Hill) and Middle Wallop in No 10 Group's area. They reached them as dawn broke. Simultaneously the RAF readiness flights began to take off, but it was too late. During the next ten minutes the *Luftwaffe* aircraft bombed with impunity, dropping down to as low as 5,000 feet to ensure accuracy. They then turned for home, gaining altitude as they did so. The RAF readiness flights which did manage to get airborne set off in pursuit, but, as they closed in, they were attacked by the freshly arrived Bf 109 escorts, which had the advantage of both height and sun. In the battle that followed, the RAF came off much worse, losing 20 Spitfires and Hurricanes shot down as against four Bf 109s, three He 111s, and a single Do 17.

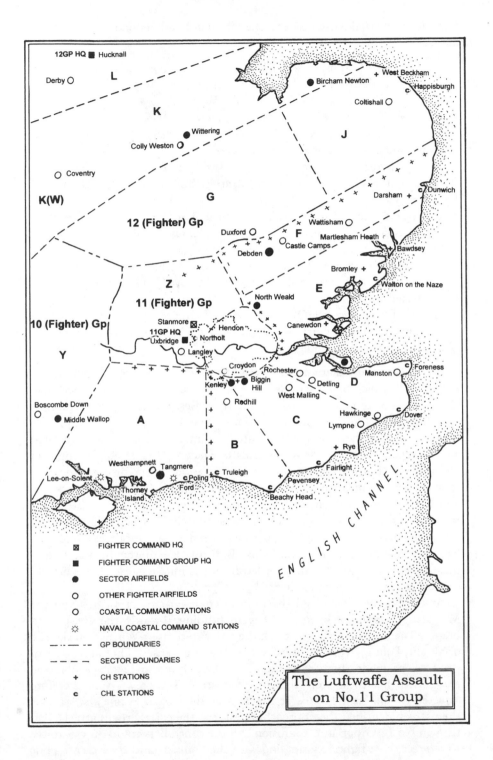

12GP HQ ■ Hucknall

Derby ○   L

K

K(W)

Wittering ●
Colly Weston ○

○ Coventry

G

12 (Fighter) Gp

Z

11 (Fighter) Gp

10 (Fighter) Gp

Y

Stanmore ⊠
11GP HQ
Uxbridge ■
Hendon ●
c Northolt

○ Langley

Boscombe Down
○
● Middle Wallop

A

B

Westhampnett
Tangmere ○
Lee-on-Solent ☼
Thorney
Island
☼ Poling
Ford
c Truleigh

West Beckham
+ West Beckham
● Bircham Newton
c Happisburgh

Coltishall ○

J

Darsham
c Dunwich

Wattisham ○
Duxford ○   F
Martlesham Heath c
Castle Camps
Debden ●

Bawdsey
+ Bawdsey

Bromley +

E
Walton on the Naze
c

North Weald ●

Canewdon +

Croydon
C
Rochester ○
Biggin
Hill
Kenley ● +
Detling
West Malling ○
D
Manston ●
Foreness
c

Redhill ○

Hawkinge ○
Lympne ○
c Dover

C

+ Rye

Fairlight
c Fairlight

Pevensey
+ Pevensey
Beachy Head
c

ENGLISH CHANNEL

FIGHTER COMMAND HQ
FIGHTER COMMAND GROUP HQ
SECTOR AIRFIELDS
OTHER FIGHTER AIRFIELDS
COASTAL COMMAND STATIONS
NAVAL COASTAL COMMAND STATIONS
GP BOUNDARIES
SECTOR BOUNDARIES
CH STATIONS
CHL STATIONS

The Luftwaffe Assault
on No.11 Group

As for the airfields themselves, the German bombers had caused serious damage:

Westhampnett – runway severely cratered, one hangar destroyed, five Hurricanes destroyed on the ground (including two under repair).

Lympne – runway damaged, huts badly damaged.

Tangmere (sector HQ) – runway rendered unusable, one hangar destroyed and one seriously damaged, six Hurricanes written off, ops room and other buildings badly damaged.

Kenley (sector HQ) – runway partially damaged, one hangar damaged, two Spitfires destroyed, administrative buildings damaged and destroyed.

Gravesend – one hangar badly damaged, two Hurricanes and two Spitfires destroyed, ops room and other buildings damaged.

West Malling – huts destroyed, much cratering.

Biggin Hill (sector HQ) – extensive damage, including to ops room, runway unusable, four Spitfires totally destroyed and several others damaged.

Middle Wallop (sector HQ) – One hangar destroyed, together with four Spitfires and three Hurricanes, some cratering to runway, and damage to administrative buildings.

Of greatest immediate concern was the damage done to Tangmere and Biggin Hill, which had a serious affect on command and control. Both had alternative ops rooms, situated outside the bases, but these were cramped and had only limited communications. The damage to runways also revealed another shortcoming in Fighter Command's organisation – limited airfield repair resources. Some airfields did have specialist Royal Engineer repair teams, but others had to rely on civilian labour. Worse, there was a serious shortage of plant equipment – three airfields (Manston, Hawkinge and Lympne) had just one bulldozer among them. A further problem was the number of unexploded bombs. Consequently, it would take time to repair the damage and the aircraft at bases rendered temporarily unusable had to redeploy to satellite airfields. But this lay in the future. In the meantime, while No 11 Group reeled from the initial shock of this attack, it was about to be struck again.

As the bombers recrossed the English coast, groups of Ju 87s and the Me 110s of *Erprobungsgruppe 210* were heading towards the coast from France. Their mission was to attack the radar stations at Ventnor on the Isle of Wight, Poling, Truleigh, Beachy Head, and Pevensey. The tall towers of the stations made them easy targets to find, but the *Luftwaffe* planners recognised that these were difficult to destroy. The crews were therefore directed to aim their bombs at the huts at their base. While the stations themselves identified the approaching raiders, the early airfield attacks had thrown No 11 Group into confusion. All the controllers could do was to try to redirect those fighters grappling with the bombers and their escorts, but only a few heeded the call. As a result, the Ju 87s and Me 110s were able to launch their attacks without interference. *Erprobungsgruppe 210* was tasked with taking on Ventnor and Poling and put its specialist training to good effect. Both were extensively damaged and went off the air. The Ju 87s also succeeded in blinding the station at Beachy Head, but, while they damaged the remaining two radars, these continued to function. Four Ju 87s were lost – two to anti-aircraft fire and two shot down by fighters on their return flight – and one Me 110 also fell victim to the AA guns.

As the *Luftwaffe* crews landed back at their bases and the initial debriefs took place, it soon became clear that the first major German attack in the Battle of Britain had been highly successful. Hermann Göring, who had established a temporary headquarters in his personal train on the outskirts of Paris, was elated by the reports he received. He issued a special order of the day, congratulating his aircrews and exhorting them to maintain the pressure – 'just a few more blows like those of this morning will fatally cripple the RAF and bring Britain to its knees!'

On the airfields themselves, the ground crews set to with a will to rearm and refuel the aircraft for the second strike of the day. The aircrews had an alfresco meal near their planes. While they ate it, they were briefed for the second attack. Having begun to clear a defence-free path to London, it was the *Luftwaffe*'s intention both to widen it and to build on the damage already inflicted. In the meantime, small groups of Bf 109s and 110s trailed their coats over the Channel to distract the RAF.

Dowding's most pressing immediate concerns were the gaps that now existed in his radar coverage. He ordered the deployment of mobile radar units (MRU) to cover these, but it would take some hours for these to become fully operational and they lacked the range of the static Chain Home stations. Realising the aircraft casualties suffered by No 11 Group, he decided to move one Spitfire and one Hurricane squadron from No 10 Group.

As for Park, he put priority on re-establishing the communications at Tangmere and Biggin Hill. Certain that the *Luftwaffe* would shortly strike again, neither he nor Dowding was tempted by the German activities over the Channel.

The next wave of German attacks began to develop shortly after 13.00. In spite of the holes in the radar coverage, the Bentley Priory filter room did manage to establish that the main effort was again being directed at No 11 Group. Park immediately scrambled his squadrons, not wanting them to be caught on the ground, but they were unable to intercept the bombers before they struck. Kenley, Biggin Hill, and Gravesend suffered further damage, while Manston, on the extreme eastern tip of Kent, and Croydon suffered for the first time. Further Stuka and Me 110 attacks were made against the radar system, adding to the damage at Ventnor and Poling, and virtually destroying that at Foreness, close to Manston. Nevertheless, the RAF fighters did enjoy slightly more success than they had in the morning. Four

He 111s and three Do 17s were destroyed, together with six Ju 87s, whose relatively low speed made them vulnerable to fighter attack, four Bf 109s and three Me 110s. But the Bf 109 escorts still enjoyed the advantage of height, enabling them to shoot down eight Hurricanes and six Spitfires. Apart from further disrupting Fighter Command's command, control, and communications, and creating additional holes in the radar coverage, this second wave of attacks caused the civilian airfield repair teams to stop work. They declared that it was too dangerous to continue. Efforts to persuade them to change their minds proved fruitless. The attack also further disrupted vital maintenance work on the RAF aircraft. The final main attack of the day took place an hour before sunset. The targets were again much the same and the casualties to both sides of the same order as the previous raid.

That night both sides took stock of the situation. The *Luftwaffe* leaders could be well satisfied over how the day had gone. They knew that they had weakened Fighter Command both in the air and on the ground. A clear indication of this was the inability of the British fighters to intercept the bombers before they reached their targets. It was also noticeable that during the final attacks there were fewer fighters in the air than during the lunchtime raids. While it had been a long day for the crews, both air and ground, their morale was high. Göring, Sperrle and Kesselring were all agreed that, if the pressure was maintained, the British air defences would soon crumble. In the meantime, in order to play on the nerves of the RAF, random attacks by small groups of bombers would continue throughout the hours of darkness against the airfields.

At Bentley Priory a grim-faced Dowding spoke to each of his group commanders on the telephone. Not surprisingly, his longest conversation was with Park. The situation that AOC No 11 Group painted was a gloomy one. Almost all his airfields were damaged to a greater or lesser extent. Repairs were being hampered by the lack of plant and the refusal of the civilian work teams to endanger themselves. His communications had also been seriously degraded and it was becoming difficult to communicate with the fighters in the air. Brand, who had already handed over two squadrons to Park, remained bullish, confident that he could hold his own as long as he was not forced to hand over more squadrons. Leigh-Mallory, on the other hand, was frustrated. Since all the *Luftwaffe* attacks had been to the south of London, No 12 Group had been little more than a bystander. As for Saul, there was not much that he could add. He needed all of his slender fighter strength to face the threat posed by *Luftflotte 5*.

Dowding next spoke to Marshal of the Royal Air Force Sir Cyril Newall, Chief of the Air Staff. To sustain No 11 Group in its desperate fight, Dowding needed help from the other RAF commands, as well as from the Royal Navy and Army. He asked Newall to arrange for Park to use the Coastal Command bases at Eastchurch and Gosport, and the Fleet Air Arm airfields at Ford in Sussex and Lee-on-Solent. Dowding also requested Army manpower to fill the vacuum created by the civilian airfield repair teams. The AOCinC also stated that he needed Bomber Command to launch retaliatory attacks on *Luftwaffe* bases in France and the Low Countries.

Newall asked Dowding how he intended to fight off the inevitable German attacks which would come on the morrow. The reply was that No 11 Group would battle on as best it could and that No 12 Group would provide standing patrols over London which could be sent to reinforce Park as the attacks materialised. In the meantime, RAF technicians were working throughout the night to make good the damage to the Chain Home stations. Newall was satisfied and came back to Dowding within the hour, telling him that Park had permission to use the Coastal Command and Fleet Air Arm bases and that the Army would co-operate over airfield repairs. Bomber Command would attack *Luftwaffe* bases the following night. Its AOCinC, 'Peter' Portal, was, however, loathe to mount attacks by day without a fighter escort, which he knew would be difficult to provide. Newall told Dowding that he had warned Portal that he might well have to do this. It was not the end of Dowding's day. At midnight he had a personal telephone call from the Prime Minister, who needed reassurance that Fighter Command could hold out against the German onslaught. Dowding put a brave face on the day's events and Churchill appeared to be satisfied.

Wartime censorship ensured that the BBC put out non-committal reports on the day's fighting. It merely reported that there had been fierce air battles over southern England and claimed that 50 German aircraft had been shot down. In contrast, the German radio stations adopted a triumphal tone to their reports, claiming that the final battle in the West was now being fought and that peace would soon return to Europe. William Joyce (whom the British nicknamed Lord Haw Haw) made a propaganda broadcast to the British people warning them that worse was to come and blaming Churchill for the continuation of the war. On the evening of 2 July, Adolf Hitler received a telephone call from his fellow Axis leader, Benito Mussolini, offering the services of the *Regia Aeronautica* to assist in the destruction of Britain. Hitler told him that he would bear this in mind.

Throughout the night the nuisance attacks by the German bombers forced many on the airfields of No 11 Group to spend much of their time in the air raid shelters, robbing them of much-needed sleep. At dawn the squadrons went over to instant readiness, while No 12 Group set up its standing patrols over the capital. But not until mid-morning did the expected German attack materialise. The *Luftwaffe* commanders had sensibly given priority to allowing their men some rest. Besides which, delaying the first attack of the day also helped to encourage uncertainty among the British. Sperrle and Kesselring also altered their tactics. Instead of trying to attack groups of airfields and radar stations simultaneously, they staggered their strikes, drawing out the assault to over two hours in the hope that the RAF fighters would run low on fuel. The initial strikes did suffer casualties because the British planes were able to concentrate to a degree against them. An attack against Hornchurch resulted in eight out of 40 German bombers shot down, some of them falling victim to the No 12 Group standing patrols. But, as the attacks built up, they began to swamp the defences and, as the *Luftwaffe* had planned, the RAF planes had to pull out of the battle to refuel. In one or two cases they did so too late and were either shot down or crash-landed. Two major assaults took place during the day, the second during the early evening. The *Luftwaffe* lost a total of 35 aircraft, while the RAF had 45 destroyed in the air and on the ground. Further airfield damage was inflicted and Home Chain received another battering. Indeed, such were the gaps in its coverage by the end of the day, that some *Luftwaffe* groups were slipping through undetected.

While replacing his aircraft losses was not a problem, given the excellent rate of fighter manufacture, Dowding was now becoming worried by his pilot casualties. In two days of air fighting Fighter Command had lost 25 pilots killed and another 20 wounded. This equated to three squadrons' worth. Intense combat and little sleep during the past 36 hours were beginning to tell on the remaining pilots of No 11 Group. The only solution, as Dowding saw it, was to swap the more battered squadrons with fresher ones from Nos 10 and 12 Groups. He gave orders that night for four No 11 Group squadrons to interchange with two each from Nos 10 and 12 Groups at first light on the following day.

A telephone call from Newall added to his concerns. The Chief of the Air Staff told him that the War Cabinet was beginning to ask him searching questions over the RAF's ability to hold out. Furthermore, there were indications of people beginning to leave London for the countryside, as well as absenteeism from work places, especially factories, in southern England.

Convinced that the *Luftwaffe*'s road to London was almost clear of obstacles, the Führer made a radio broadcast on the evening of 3 July. He addressed his remarks to Britain, pointing out that the RAF was rapidly being destroyed, leaving London and other major cities defenceless. He reminded the British of what had befallen Warsaw in September 1939 and Rotterdam in May 1940. British cities would suffer the same punishment if the government did not come to its senses and accept that it was pointless attempting to continue the war. He was still prepared to offer generous terms, but only if the British government made an immediate response. No sooner had Churchill read the English transcript to the speech than he summoned his War Cabinet to a late night emergency meeting. He realised that he would have to make some reply, but needed the backing of his ministers. The meeting took place at No 10 Downing Street – Churchill could have held it in his underground war room, but believed that this would indicate defeatism. Again, Chamberlain and Halifax intimated that the British people could not be allowed to endure unnecessary suffering. Churchill retorted that the results of standing up to Hitler would be nothing compared to the suffering that Britain would endure under the Nazi thrall. Once more he dominated the Cabinet by his strength of character. They agreed that Britain would fight on and Churchill would make this plain when he addressed Parliament the following day.

During the night of 3/4 July, Bomber Command mounted a series of attacks on airfields in northern France and Belgium. While most bombers found their targets, the bombing was inaccurate and caused little significant damage, although it did interrupt rest. *Luftwaffe* bombers continued their nuisance raids on RAF airfields.

The critical day

With the coming of daylight, the *Luftwaffe* resumed its offensive with dawn raids similar to those of 2 July. The RAF reaction was noticeably more sluggish than on previous days and it was clear that No 11 Group was beginning to buckle under the pressure. Now receiving little guidance from their ground controllers, the British fighter pilots were growing frustrated and desperate, especially since the radar system, now in tatters, was unable to provide much early warning. There were even two reported incidents of Hurricanes literally ramming German bombers. No 11 Group had also been forced to abandon its forward airfields – Manston, Lympne, Hawkinge, and Tangmere, as well as the Fleet Air Arm Station at Ford. None of its remaining bases was fully operational and Dowding was increasingly relying on No 12 Group. On the afternoon of the 4th, as Churchill addressed a subdued House of Commons, *Luftflotte* 5 made its first appearance. Fifty bombers, escorted by Me 110s, were picked up by radar approaching the River Humber. Their target was the port of Hull. The object of this raid was to distract the RAF from the main battle being waged in the south. Hull lay in the northern part of No 12 Group's area, but because the majority of its squadrons had been drawn towards London, it could only put up one Hurricane squadron to intercept the attack. No 13 Group, was able to get another airborne and these did meet the raiders as they reached the coast. They managed to shoot down five bombers and three of their escorts for the loss of three Hurricanes, but could not prevent the Germans from pressing home their attack, which caused damage to the docks and inflicted a number of civilian casualties.

Simultaneously, *Luftflotten* 2 and 3 made their second major attack of the day in the south.

Churchill's speech was full of defiance and optimism, but he failed to convince many of his listeners. After he concluded it, anxious groups of MPs gathered in the lobbies. There was talk of forming a fresh administration and many buttonholed Lord Halifax, whom they regarded as a natural successor to Churchill. The prime minister himself went back to Downing Street and made a transatlantic telephone call. It was to President Franklin Roosevelt. Churchill told him that only an immediate US declaration of war could save Britain. Roosevelt was sympathetic, but explained to Churchill that the American people would not countenance it. He pointed to recent opinion polls which showed that nearly 90 per cent of those questioned were firmly against entering the conflict. Churchill then went to Buckingham Palace to brief the King. He told the monarch that London was now virtually defenceless against air attack. The unthinkable might come to pass in that Britain might be forced to seek peace. If this was the case, the war would have to be continued by the British Empire. Churchill advised the King that this could only happen if the Royal Family raised its standard outside Britain. To this end, he had arranged for a cruiser to be stood by at the port of Liverpool to take the Royal Family to Canada. The King acquiesced and agreed to make preparations for a hurried flight from London. Churchill then chaired a meeting of the War Cabinet, which was attended by the Chiefs of Staff. Halifax warned Churchill that he was losing support in the Commons and that he should make some form of conciliatory reply to Hitler's speech of the previous evening. Churchill turned to Newall. What could the RAF do to prevent the situation from worsening still further? The Chief of the Air Staff gave a gloomy reply. Fighter Command had lost half its strength and many of its forward airfields were out of action. The radar coverage along the south coast was virtually non-existent. All he could suggest was a massive daylight strike by Bomber Command against the German airfields, which he proposed to mount the following day. Churchill agreed that this should take place and with that the meeting broke up.

In Berlin Hitler had summoned Göring to see him. They met that evening in the Reichs Chancellery. Hitler made it plain that the problem of British intransigence could not be allowed to drag on, especially after Churchill's speech. There must be a speedy resolution. Göring replied that the way to London was now open. He proposed an attack on the British capital the following day. Hitler agreed, but said that he would first give Britain one final ultimatum. It was broadcast late that same evening. Unless the British made peace overtures by noon on the following day, 5 July, the attack on their cities would begin.

During the night both the *Luftwaffe* and RAF Bomber Command carried out further nuisance raids against airfields. At 08.00 the first *Luftwaffe* attacks of the day began. It so happened that simultaneously RAF Bomber Command launched its assault against the German airfields. Some 150 bombers took part, principally the Blenheim day bombers of No 2 Group, but also Wellingtons, Hampdens, and Whitleys. They had been provided with an escort of three squadrons of Spitfires, drawn from Nos 10, 12, and 13 Groups, but these were diverted to deal with the latest German attacks. The British bombers flew on alone in what became known as the 'aerial charge of the Light Brigade' (an allusion to the disastrous action during the Battle of Balaclava in the Crimean War). While some reached their targets and did cause some damage, German fighters hacked many out of the sky. Others fell victim to the extensive flak defences around the airfields. All in all, 43 bombers were destroyed and many others damaged. Churchill had been pinning his hopes on this attack. Consequently, Hitler's noon deadline passed without any response from him. Göring therefore issued orders for the attack on London to be mounted later that afternoon.

The final blow

At 14.00 the British War Cabinet reconvened in Downing Street. They realised that the bomber attack had failed. A heated debate took place. Churchill found himself defending his position on his own. The remainder of the Cabinet members banded against him, reinforced by the knowledge that a motion of no confidence in Churchill was to be debated in the Commons later that afternoon. Britain had to seek peace. Churchill stated that he would defend himself in the House. The debate opened at 15.30. At that very moment the planes of *Luftflotten 2* and *3* were taking off from their airfields. Three-quarters of an hour later massed phalanxes of bombers, accompanied by Bf 109 and Me 110 escorts, were crossing the south coast, their target, the heart of London.

Brushing aside the few RAF fighters which rose to meet them as they approached the capital, the bombers flew on over the suburbs of the city. Further fighters tried to attack, but were kept at bay by the escorts. The bombers then began to release their bombs. In the House of Commons the no confidence debate was brought to an abrupt halt as the members sought shelter in the cellars. Half an hour later, the bombers set off for home leaving death and destruction in their wake. Some 700 Londoners had been killed and many others injured. Some of London's most famous streets and buildings were reduced to rubble. Two bombs had hit the Houses of Parliament. As the shaken members streamed out of their cellars, Churchill finally accepted that his time was up. In a few brief sentences he announced his resignation. He and Lord Halifax then made their way to the Palace for an audience with the King. Twenty minutes later, Lord Halifax reappeared as prime minister and went straightaway to the BBC at Bush House to make an emergency broadcast to the nation. At 17.30 he announced that he was about to instruct the British ambassadors to neutral Sweden and Switzerland to make approaches to their German opposite numbers with a view to making peace. In the meantime, he was instructing the Armed Forces to cease fire unless they were attacked.

Within 48 hours the war in Europe came to an end. On 7 July, Halifax flew to Berlin and signed an armistice. By this time the Royal Family, accompanied by Churchill, were on their way across the Atlantic to Canada. Britain was placed in much the same category as Vichy France, but foreign policy was now controlled by Berlin. The rest is history.

The four-day Battle of Britain marked airpower's coming of age. The dream of the air prophets like Guilio Douhet and Hugh Trenchard had been realised. For the first time in history, victory had been achieved by airpower alone.

The reality

The true story of the Battle of Britain was, of course, very different. For a start, prior to the fall of France, only the German Navy had given any consideration to the eventuality that it might become necessary to mount an invasion. Hitler himself assumed and, indeed, hoped that once France had been vanquished, the British would seek an honourable peace. It took him a month to decide that an invasion would have to be prepared and it was not until mid-August that the *Luftwaffe* mounted its concentrated offensive. This breathing space proved invaluable for RAF Fighter Command, enabling it to recover from the ravages of the Battle for France and to strengthen its defences. This was helped, in part, by Dowding's success in May in drastically limiting the number of fighters sent to France. The *Luftwaffe's* conduct of the Battle of Britain was fatally flawed for a number of reasons. First, its target list was too varied. Attacks on ports and the British aircraft industry stood little chance of achieving positive results in the short term. Göring failed to maintain his attacks on the Home Chain radar system, not appreciating that its ability to provide early warning of the *Luftwaffe* attacks was the cornerstone of Britain's defences. Furthermore, *Luftwaffe* intelligence was poor. Much effort was wasted in attacking airfields which did not belong to Fighter Command and which could have little influence on the battle. What is true is that the British organisation for airfield repair was lamentably weak, lacking plant and being too reliant on civilian labour.

Bibliography

Cooper, Matthew, *The German Air Force 1922–1945: An Anatomy of Failure* (Jane's, London, 1980).

Hooton, E.R., *Eagle in Flames: The Fall of the Luftwaffe* (Brockhampton Press, London, 1997).

Hough, Richard, and Richards, Denis, *The Battle of Britain: The Jubilee History* (Hodder & Stoughton, London, 1989).

James, T.C.G., *The Battle of Britain* (Frank Cass, London, 2000).

Macksey, Kenneth, *Invasion: The German Invasion of England July 1940* (Arms and Armour Press, London, 1980).

Overy, Richard, *The Battle* (Penguin Books, London, 2000).

Price, Alfred, *The Luftwaffe Data Book* (Greenhill Books, London, 1997).

Richards, Denis, *Royal Air Force 1939–1945*, Vol 1, (HMSO, London, 1993).

Wood, Derek, with Dempster, Derek, *The Narrow Margin: The Battle of Britain and the Rise of Air Power 1930–1940* (Tri-service Press, London, 1990).

Force H sorties against Lütjens' *Carrier Group III*, 12 September 1939. Note the antiquated Swordfish torpedo bomber circling over the fleet – Lütjens called them 'deathtraps'. *Author's collection*

Scapa Flow, 18.30 hours, 31 August 1939: Little did the crews of these British warships suspect that within 12 hours thick smoke would hide the horror of dying ships and dead men from watching eyes – the first of many harsh blows for the British Home Fleet. *Author's collection*

Kriegsmarine torpedo-boats, such as these of the *7th Flotilla*, escorted the *SS* invasion forces across the Channel in 1940. *US Army Art Collection*

(*Below left*) General Erich von Manstein, whose plans led to the defeat of both France and Britain. *Author's collection*

(*Below right*) Major General Bernard Montgomery, wearing his famous black beret with the two cap-badges. *Author's collection*

German troops and captured British equipment at Dunkirk. *Author's collection*

British garrison troops captured at Dover by the first wave of invading German troops. *Author's collection*

Adolf Hitler's victory in the east made him Germany's greatest warlord. *US Army Center for Military History*

(*Above left*) A photo of an RAF aircrew on the eve of the Battle of Britain. Their confidence was quickly shattered by the Luftwaffe onslaught. *Author's collection*

(*Left*) The results of the Luftwaffe's devastating attack on London on 5 July 1940. *Author's collection*

A sketch of Field Marshal Erwin Rommel made shortly after he received his baton. *US Army Center for Military History*

Troops of the (technically independent) Egyptian Army bring up a howitzer to help prop up Eighth Army HQ's position for the Alamein battle, around El Imayid.

Part of Brigadier Godfrey's 'motley force' hastily deployed to cover the sprawling camps around Amiriya on 6 July.

Benito Mussolini driving triumphantly eastwards down the Halfaya Pass in early July, on his way to yet another blazing row with his German allies.

A horse-drawn wagon delivering supplies to the *101st Jäger Division* in the Caucasus. Difficult terrain and weak logistical services limited operations by all the combatants in the Caucasus campaign. *US National Archives*

Machine-gunners of the Soviet 47th Mountain Division who died defending Batumi against the Turkish *8th Division* on 5 September 1942. *US Army Art Collection*

The commander of the Soviet 53rd Army visiting the 8th Indian Division during Operation Pluto. Co-operation between the Russians and their allies was hampered by language difficulties and pervasive mistrust. *US National Archives*

(*Left*) An Axis air attack on Allied ships off Gela, Sicily, July 1943. *Author's collection*

(*Right*) German night fighters catch and destroy a British bomber in a raid over Berlin. *US Army Art Collection*

(*Below*) Thousands of 88mm anti-aircraft guns played a vital role in the defence of the skies over the Reich. *US Army Art Collection*

(*Below left*) Right to left, Lieutenant-General George S. Patton (Seventh Army), Major-General Omar Bradley (II Corps), and Major-General Troy Middleton (45th Infantry Division), confer during the fighting in Sicily. *Author's collection*

Professor Werner Heisenberg, Germany's top atom-bomb physicist. *Author's collection*

Niels Bohr – world-renowned Danish physicist and early mentor for Heisenberg. *Author's collection*

(*Above*) Burning buildings in London, believed to be located 1.5 miles from the hypocentre of the atom bomb blast. *Author's collection*

(*Top left*) A B-17 being attacked by a Luftwaffe Fw 190 fighter. Even in the best of conditions in 1943, it required 10 sorties by German piston-engined fighters such as this to defeat a single B-17. *Author's collection*

(*Left*) An Me 262. Turbojet technology gave Germany an opportunity to achieve a qualitative lead over the Allies' quantitative superiority. *Author's collection*

Heinkel 177 bomber of the type used for the German atomic attacks on London and Moscow. *Author's collection*

Marshal G.K. Zhukov at the time of his assumption of duties as the Secretary General of the Communist Party of the Soviet Union. *Author's collection*

German infantry on the defensive – one of the most formidable obstacles in the world. Rebuilt and equipped with large numbers of antitank guns under Rommel's guidance, the German infantry divisions in their in-depth defences bled the Red Army to death in that awful winter of 1945. *US Army Art Collection*

German 88mm gun in action in central Poland. The suspension of the bomber campaign against Germany by the armistice in Normandy allowed thousands of guns to be moved from the Reich to the Eastern Front. *US Army Art Collection*

Burnt out Soviet T-34 tanks littered the flat farmlands of Central Poland after the destruction of four tank armies in Field Marshal von Manstein's classic replay of the Battle of Tannenberg on a vast scale in February 1945. *US Army Art Collection*

4
THE STORM AND THE WHIRLWIND
Zhukov Strikes First

Gilberto Villahermosa

'They know! They are ready!'

The period of Soviet inactivity and appeasement was over. By the end of May more than a dozen German reconnaissance and fighter aircraft had disappeared over the Soviet Union, bringing an end to overflights by the *Luftwaffe*. Moscow met Berlin's diplomatic inquiries with a wall of silence. A rupture in communications with the *Abwehr* (*Armed Forces High Command Foreign Intelligence Service*) teams operating in Russia only exacerbated the loss of the aircraft. German agents working in the Soviet Union reported that the groups had 'disappeared'. The agents themselves were next to drop off Berlin's intelligence net during the first week of June, the final transmission a brief 'They know! They are ready!' Scores of pro-German Russian citizens and infiltrated *Abwehr* operatives were arrested, tortured, interrogated, and then executed by an over zealous and unrestrained NKVD, the Soviet secret police. The German intelligence network in Russia was shattered. Finally, members of the German Embassy's staff were followed and harassed by the secret police before being restricted to their apartments and the embassy and then arrested for spying. Soon after, they were declared *persona non grata*, and ordered to leave the country immediately.

The German Foreign Ministry's protests were of no avail and the German Ambassador, Count Friedrich Werner von Schulenberg, was recalled to Berlin. Several flights of Stalin's newest Yak-1 and MiG-3 fighters escorted the count's aircraft to the border. The pair on either side of von Schulenberg's Ju 52 sported newly painted small German swastikas below their cockpits. Stalin wanted to make it quite clear what fate had befallen so many German reconnaissance aircraft. The Soviet pilots grinned and waved at the Ambassador, who simply nodded back. He looked down to see the highways running from Moscow to the Polish border choked with troops and equipment moving westward. Long lines of Soviet trains were carrying scores of clearly visible tanks and artillery pieces.

Major General Ernst August Köstring, the German Military Attaché to Moscow, noted that the vehicles appeared to be new types of heavy and medium tanks. He had heard a great deal about the Red Army's rapidly growing tank force and its newest armoured vehicles, but had not seen them before today. Köstring counted several dozen heavies and a like number of medium tanks, before realising that Stalin wanted the Ambassador to see all of this: the new aircraft, the tanks, the artillery, the trains, all moving west. Only a few weeks ago, these same trains had been loaded with Soviet grain, oil, manganese, chromium, and a host of other precious supplies bound for the Third Reich. Hundreds of thousands of tons of material, the price of a fragile and elusive peace, had been delivered to Germany as promised by Moscow, and then the flow, like every other manifestation of Soviet–German friendship, had abruptly stopped in the middle of May 1941. Perhaps it was all a bluff. If so, it was too late. For the next few days the world would hold its breath as Germany and the Soviet Union teetered on the brink of war.

Köstring reflected on the Führer's plans to end this uneasy peace along the German-Soviet frontier. In July 1940, the *OKH* (*Army High Command*) had begun preparing Operation Barbarossa, which called for the *Wehrmacht* to crush Russia in a lightning campaign. The objectives included the destruction of the Red Army, the seizure of enough territory to ensure the security of both Germany's armaments plans in the eastern portion of the country and Romanian oilfields, and the creation of an independent Ukraine and a confederation of Baltic States under German domination. The plan called for three army groups to attack along separate axes to destroy the Red Army while advancing deep into Russia. The 30 divisions of Field Marshal Wilhelm von Leeb's *Army Group North* had the mission of securing the Baltics, including the key city of Leningrad. The 51 divisions of Field Marshal Fedor von Bock's *Army Group Centre* were tasked with capturing Moscow. Finally, the 57 German and Romanian divisions of Field Marshal Gerd von Rundstedt's *Army Group South* would roll into the Ukraine toward Kiev. Four powerful Panzer groups, comprising 19 Panzer and 15 motorised divisions, would plunge deep into Soviet territory ahead of the army groups to facilitate their advances. The *Wehrmacht* massed more than 150 divisions for the operation, as well as 3,350 tanks, 7,200 artillery pieces, and 2,800 aircraft.[1] Another 14 Finnish divisions and a like number of brigade-sized Romanian divisions rounded off the German order of battle. Intelligence estimated that the Red Army could oppose the attack with 200 infantry, armour, and cavalry divisions as well as 50 brigades deployed in the western Soviet Union.[2] It was also believed that the Red Air Force could field 10,500 combat aircraft, including 7,500 in European Russia.[3]

Deployment for Barbarossa began in February 1941 and continued through May. Yet even as the *Wehrmacht* was moving into its final attack positions, Hitler and his generals still had an incomplete picture of the Red

Army and its deployments. High altitude missions, flown by Colonel Theodor Rowehl's special strategic reconnaissance squadron from bases in Germany, Poland, and the Balkans filled in some of the blanks. The squadron flew specially modified aircraft with pressurised cabins and an operational ceiling of 40,000 feet, making them impervious to Red Air Force interception.[4] The intelligence that was available confirmed that Stalin knew about the German attack on Russia and was preparing to meet it. Behind the cordon of Red Army aircraft, and air defence artillery and Border Troops were the unmistakable outlines of an army occupying positions near the border. But what type of positions – defensive or attacking? Hitler ordered a postponement of Barbarossa, the second since planning for the operation began. Initially scheduled for 15 May, it had first been deferred at the beginning of April after the start of the Balkans' campaign. The General Staff argued that, even if Stalin knew about Barbarossa, it was too late to push back the operation yet again and better to launch now. The Russians would be better prepared later that summer. But the Führer stood firm and the glint in his eyes as he studied the operations map told those around him that there was a method to his madness.[5]

The Zhukov plan

On 15 May 1941, with the armed peace between Germany and Russia coming to an end, General of the Army Georgi Zhukov met with Josef Stalin. After briefing the Soviet dictator on the *Wehrmacht*'s preparations for Barbarossa, the new Chief of the Soviet General Staff forcefully argued for a preemptive attack on enemy forces massing in eastern Poland. Zhukov presented the plan within the context of a justifiable preventive war with limited aims. He sought, however, nothing less than the complete destruction of what were believed to be 100 enemy divisions massing southeast of Warsaw. To accomplish this, the Red Army's Western and Southwestern Fronts would launch a double envelopment with 150 divisions from Byelorussia and the Ukraine deep into Poland. Having destroyed the forward echelon of the German Army, the two fronts would then swing north to the coast, acting as the anvil for an attack by the Northwestern Front to destroy follow-on German echelons remaining in East Prussia.[6]

When Zhukov had finished, Stalin, who had hoped to delay the beginning of war with Germany for at least a year, pointed out that the Red Army was not ready for such large-scale operations. He told Zhukov that in light of the German Army's brilliant performance against Poland and France, the plan amounted to a desperate gamble. Yet Stalin recognised that the Soviet Union might never again have such an opportunity. Even if the attack did not succeed entirely, the damage to the Germans might be heavy enough to cause Hitler to reconsider or at least delay his planned invasion of Russia. The Soviet Union would continue to mobilise its armed forces, as it had been doing since the beginning of May and would be ready to face the onslaught.[7]

Zhukov was the closest thing Stalin had to a protégé. This 44-year-old general had defeated the Japanese Army at Khalkhin Gol, Mongolia, in 1939 through the innovative use of armour and air power in a double envelopment similar to the one he now proposed. Made a Hero of the Soviet Union, Zhukov was next given command of the Kiev Special Military District. 'Bear in mind,' warned Stalin at the time, 'that in a fight with the probable enemy, your District is going to play the chief part.'[8] Six months later, he appointed this reluctant cavalry officer his Chief of the General Staff. Less than five months after that, Zhukov was urging a preemptive attack on Hitler. Stalin recognised the roots of the plan in the Red Army's victory in Mongolia, as well as its strategic deployment of October 1940 (when the General Staff considered invading East Prussia while the Germans were tied down in France) and the wargames of January 1941. During those exercises, Zhukov's invading Blue forces (representing the German Army) had decisively defeated General Dmitri Pavlov's defending Red forces (representing the Soviet Union). In this new proposal, however, the objectives were far bolder. 'Could he do it?' wondered Stalin. Could he catch Hitler and his vaunted *Wehrmacht* with their pants down in Poland? If he succeeded, the political advantages would be tremendous. 'It would be the beginning of the end for Hitler,' he thought. Having defeated the German Army, the Soviet Union would gain the respect of the entire world, but especially Britain and America. More importantly, it would have the peace it needed to finish rebuilding the Red Army. After that, all of Europe was Stalin's for the taking.

The only other alternative was to sit and wait for Hitler to attack first. Domestic and foreign intelligence sources had concluded that the Germans would indeed strike, probably in the third week of June. 'How long to defeat the Fascists?' the Soviet dictator asked. 'Thirty days,' replied Zhukov. 'Only 30 days to defeat 100 German divisions?' asked Stalin incredulously. 'And when would you attack?' he asked next. 'In June, before the Germans can launch Barbarossa,' replied Zhukov. 'Too early. We won't be ready until at least July. By then we will have more than five million men under arms, including an additional 50 divisions', observed Stalin. 'Fifty divisions to backstop you in case you fail,' he thought to himself. 'August would be better still,' he continued, 'allowing us to generate another 150 divisions,' although he recognised that arms and equipment for those divisions were another matter.

'Submit a plan within the next two weeks,' he ordered. 'Plan the attack for early or mid-July.' 'Comrade Stalin, a German attack may be only weeks away,' the protégé reminded his mentor. 'Yes, so our sources tell us,' repeated Stalin calmly. 'But we are simply not ready. As for the Germans, leave Hitler to me. He will give us the time we need. You have two weeks to plan, no more.' He was still looking at the map when the Chief of Staff turned to depart. 'And Zhukov!' he heard the Soviet leader call. 'Yes, Comrade Stalin?' he responded automatically as he turned. 'Thirty days, you say? I will give you everything you need. But do not fail me! Do you understand? We must bury them!' growled Stalin menacingly.

Zhukov returned to his own operations map depicting German units in blue and the Soviets in red. The detailed enemy deployment was a priceless gift from the Soviet spy ring, *Rote Kapelle* ('Red Orchestra'), operating out of Western Europe and Scandinavia. Operation Storm called for Lieutenant General M.P. Kirponos' Southwestern Front to attack across southern Poland to separate Germany from her southern allies. In the meantime, Lieutenant General D.G. Pavlov's Western Front would destroy the German main body and capture Warsaw.[9] The immediate mission of the Red Army during the first phase of the operation was to break up German forces east of the Vistula River and around Krakow, advance to the Narew and Vistula Rivers, and secure Katowice. The Southwestern Front would strike the main blow toward Krakow and Katowice, aimed at separating Germany from her Hungarian and Romanian allies. The secondary attack would be conducted by the left wing of the Western Front toward Warsaw and Deblin. Its missions were to fix German forces in and around Warsaw and to secure the Polish capital as well as destroy enemy forces in and around Lublin in cooperation with the Southwestern Front. General M.M. Popov's Northwestern Front was to conduct an active defence against Finland and East Prussia, while the left wing of the Southwestern Front would do the same against Hungary and Romania and be prepared to conduct offensive operations against Romania if favourable conditions arose there.[10]

Zhukov recognised the Red Army was not ready for war against Germany. Its performance during the 1939 Russo-Finnish War and its occupation of eastern Poland had been disastrous. The list of failures encompassed leadership, coordination, training, logistics, and maintenance. True, the Red Army's physical strength had grown dramatically as a result of the high output of the armaments industry. It now possessed some 24,000 tanks of all types, including more than 1,800 of the latest model tanks, almost 150,000 artillery pieces and mortars, and some 30,000 aircraft, including almost 18,000 produced in the last two years.[11] But the spiritual strength of the army had been shattered by Stalin's purges, which had eliminated the bulk of the army's corps, division, brigade, and regimental commanders. Of the 6,000 senior officers arrested, 1,500 were tortured and executed. The remainder disappeared into the concentration camps.[12] The purges decapitated the Red Army at all levels, stifled initiative, and ended all meaningful training. Zhukov faced the daunting task of taking on the legendary *Wehrmacht* with an army that was well equipped but lacked professional leadership and training. Still, it was better to strike first and hard, than to wait and be devoured piecemeal.

Zhukov was confident he could defeat or at least severely damage the

German Army. He sought to offset the army's shortcomings in four ways. First was surprise, both in the air and on the ground. Although tactical surprise had been lost, strategic surprise had not. The *Wehrmacht* neither expected nor was postured to receive a large-scale Russian attack, a fact confirmed by its shallow deployment. Next he would use mass to overwhelm the Germans, both in the air and on the ground. As Stalin was fond of saying: 'Quantity has a quality all of its own.' Intelligence reported that the *Luftwaffe* had deployed to the east short of fuel and spare parts. Zhukov planned on launching round the clock air operations as soon as possible to overwhelm the German air force while masking the movement of his troops and collecting intelligence on enemy deployments. The Chief of Staff hoped to desynchronise the German air-land battle combination.

On the ground, the Red Army would overwhelm the *Wehrmacht* by striking hard at the flanks of *Army Groups Centre* and *South*. Soviet intelligence had recently learned that almost half of the German divisions were equipped with captured Czechoslovakian and French equipment. These units were positioned in the gaps between the Panzer groups. What German propaganda portrayed as a homogeneous and powerful Panzer force was really a patchwork army. The Czech and French tanks, with their light armour and puny guns, were no match for any of their Soviet counterparts, from the light and fast BT-5s and BT-7s to the heavier T-34s and KV-1s. Even the bulk of German Panzers would be powerless to stop the Red Army's armoured onslaught. Superior technology and the correlation of forces dictated that the enemy line would break. The Red Army's initial echelons would undoubtedly suffer heavy losses, but so would the Germans. Zhukov planned on pounding them relentlessly with air strikes and artillery, and then dropping the bulk of two airborne corps into their rear to seize and hold crossings across the Vistula River until the arrival of the fronts' mobile groups. He counted on the first attacking waves to force the defenders to reveal their positions, expend their ammunition, and to wear them down. And then he would commit his breakthrough formations to drive deep into the enemy rear.

But Zhukov was counting on more than surprise, mass and superior technology to beat the Germans. He planned on concentrating the best commanders and equipment into select units and then holding them until a breakthrough had been achieved. Already, thousands of seasoned Soviet officers and NCOs were en route from the Far East to the country's western borders. They would man the elite mechanised corps of the first strategic echelon. At the heart of each mechanised corps were two tank and one motorised division. Each tank division consisted of two tank, a motorised rifle, and a howitzer regiment and deployed 375 tanks. Each motorised division consisted of two motorised rifle, a tank, and an artillery regiment and deployed 275 light tanks. Each mechanised corps was comprised of more than 36,000 men, 1,000 tanks, and 250 artillery pieces.[13] Zhukov also planned on massing almost 2,000 of his newest tanks in his leading breakthrough formations.[14]

There were, however, serious problems with the Red Army's most elite units. The mechanised corps had only half the tanks and tractors, and a third of the trucks they were authorised.[15] Furthermore, more than two-thirds of the older model tanks, which made up the vast bulk of the armour fleet, were down for maintenance.[16] Finally, although ammunition was plentiful, fuel and spare parts were not. Zhukov had less than two months to bring the mechanised corps to full strength and rectify these deficiencies. He planned on ruthlessly stripping the formations of the second and third strategic echelons to make up the shortages in the first and second. 'Robbing Tsar Peter to pay Tsar Paul,' the Chief of the Soviet General Staff thought to himself. 'What will Stalin say?' But Stalin did not interfere.

'A hell of a way to fight a war'

June 22 came and went without a German invasion. Reports indicated that the *Wehrmacht* would attack in mid-or late July. In the meantime, a steel curtain had descended over the Soviet border. NKVD Border Troops and the Red Army had thwarted attempts to infiltrate additional agents and even airdrop special operations forces into the Soviet Union. Meanwhile, the Red Air Force and Air Defence Forces had turned back growing efforts by the *Luftwaffe* to conduct armed reconnaissance. There had been heavy losses on both sides with 'Stalin's Falcons' coming out much the worse. Still, the Soviets, with their preponderance of aircraft, retained the upper hand. The Red Army High Command continued to reinforce the border region with anti-aircraft and air defence units and by the end of June, German pilots were reporting the heaviest concentration of anti-aircraft guns they had ever seen.

German low and medium altitude reconnaissance had failed to penetrate Soviet air space to any significant degree. More ominously, the Red Air Force had begun its own attempts to penetrate the skies over Poland. The attempts were clumsy affairs entailing the use of obsolete reconnaissance aircraft escorted by hundreds of fighters aimed at overwhelming the *Luftwaffe* at multiple points along the border. The Germans responded in kind and the race was on to see which side could throw more fighters and fighter-bombers into the air. Clumsy or not, the *Luftwaffe* was on the verge of being overwhelmed and calls went out to Berlin for additional units. The element of surprise and, with it, the hopes of destroying the Red Air Force on the ground had disappeared. The tempo and scale of air operations over the border region continued to grow. Huge air battles, involving hundreds of German and Soviet fighters, began to take place on a regular basis over the skies of eastern Poland and the western Soviet Union, with the Russian pilots coming out the worse.

The German pilots, who had only recently been chasing and dodging British fighters over the English Channel, had initially called it the 'Battle of Russia' or more simply *Das Tontaubenschiessen* ('The Pigeon Shoot'). They soon recognised, however, that it was no joking matter. Ivan did not shy away from aerial combat. Franze Schiess of *Stab/JG.53* later recalled: 'They would let us get almost into aiming position, and then bring their machines around a full 180 degrees, till both aircraft were firing at each other from head-on!'[17] What Ivan lacked in finesse, he made up in sheer doggedness. On 22 June three pilots of the Western Military District's 123rd Fighter Regiment, 43rd Fighter Division, sacrificed themselves in ramming attacks, destroying or damaging three Bf 109s.[18] In the meantime, the Soviet High Command continued to rotate fresh fighter regiments into the fray. Losses were high, but the *Luftwaffe* was being worn away, albeit gradually, and the Germans were left wondering where all these infernal machines were coming from and how long the Red Air Force could continue losing aircraft at this rate.

Soviet pilots had succeeded in downing several dozen German fighters in air-to-air combat. Still others were lost to the concentrated air defence forces, even though these tended to blast away at friend and foe indiscriminately. But it was the high operations tempo that was taking the heaviest toll of German aircraft, leaving scores of fighters down for maintenance. In June alone Soviet pilots flew more than 7,000 sorties, the bulk against *Army Group Centre*.[19] The *Luftwaffe*, which had to respond to these incursions, paid the price. By 28 June the Germans had only 1,213 of an authorised 1,401 Bf 109s on hand, and only 858 of these were operational.[20] Parts and fuel, already insufficient for the planned invasion of Russia, were becoming scarce, forcing units to cannibalise inoperable aircraft, ensuring they would never fly again. *OKL* (*Luftwaffe High Command*) was forced to fly in aircraft and spares directly from factories in the Reich as well as from France and Italy. 'It is,' reported a perturbed Feldmarschall Albert Kesselring, commander of *Luftflotte 2*, to Reichsmarschall Hermann Göring, the head of the *Luftwaffe*, 'a hell of a way to fight a war.' Still, German pilots managed to hold their own, shooting down Russians in droves and adding to their tally. By the end of June air ace Werner Mölders had exceeded Richthofen's First World War score of 80 victories and was well on his way to 100 kills.[21]

By the end of June the Red Air Force had accomplished only one of its three missions, that of wearing down the *Luftwaffe*, albeit at a heavy price. Almost 1,500 Soviet aircraft, including a large number of newer model Yak-1s and MiG-3s, had already been lost in the fighting. This had not been part of the initial plan. The Red Air Force had been attrited at an alarming rate. Zhukov, however, considered the price well worth the effort for he mistakenly believed that the Soviet pilots had not only succeeded in wearing down the *Luftwaffe* by some 500 machines, but had also denied the Germans intelligence on the deployment of the Red Army.[22]

Operation Storm

More than 4,000,000 Russian soldiers awaited the final order which would set Operation Storm into motion in the early morning hours of Sunday 6 July 1941. Two hours earlier, at 03.00, 35,000 artillery pieces and mortars had begun delivering their preparatory fires, lighting up the border from one end to the other. Stretching from the Baltic Sea to the Black Sea, the Red Army was organised into 200 divisions and supported by more than 15,000 tanks and 10,000 combat aircraft.[23] In the north, the Western Front's 11th and 10th Armies would attack southwest toward Warsaw to envelop German forces from the north. The 13th Army constituted the second echelon, while the Northwestern Front's 27th Army and the Western Front's 22nd and 20th Armies constituted the third. In the south, the Southwestern Front's 6th and 26th Armies would attack west and northwest toward Kielce to envelop German forces from the south. The 16th Army constituted the second echelon, the 21st and 19th Armies constituted the third. The strategic reserve consisted of 17 divisions located around the Pripet Marshes. Operation Storm called for an attack force of 149 divisions, with another 48 conducting defensive operations in support of the attack.[24]

Zhukov planned on opening the land campaign by dropping two airborne corps behind the German lines to seize vital crossings across the Vistula River. In the north the 4th Airborne Corps' 7th and 8th Airborne Brigades would seize crossings near Modlin, northwest of Warsaw, in support of the Western Front. In the south, the 1st Airborne Corps' 204th and 211th Airborne Brigades would seize crossings in the vicinity of Deblin, northwest of Lublin, in support of the Southwestern Front. A second lift would bring in the 214th Airborne Brigade in the north and the 1st Airborne Brigade in the south, completing the delivery of 21,000 Red Army paratroopers and 72 artillery pieces and anti-tank guns. Both objectives were 45 miles behind the front lines and the General Staff had allocated one to two days for the fronts' mobile groups to break through the German line and link up with the paratroopers.[25]

At first all went well. The bulk of the aircraft had taken off and formed up without incident in the darkness. As both formations began to cross the Soviet-Polish border, however, several Red Army anti-aircraft batteries opened up on the transport squadrons overhead. These opening bursts triggered a crescendo of sympathetic fire from other inexperienced and fatigued Soviet gunners all along the line. Within minutes every Red Army anti-aircraft weapon along the border had joined in. Russian air defence officers could do nothing to stop the massacre. They watched horrified as dozens of troop transports, savaged by the intense fire, broke into flames and spiralled out of control, crashing to the earth. Alerted by their opponents, the German gunners joined the slaughter. The Soviet transport pilots broke formation, careening into each other and dumping paratroopers everywhere. A number attempted to turn around and return to their bases, convinced that it was suicidal to proceed.[26] Some were 'persuaded' to press on, however, by pistol-wielding airborne officers who threatened to shoot them if they did not continue with their mission.

Fully a third of the airborne force, however, had been lost before even crossing the border. The rest were hopelessly scattered, and easy pickings for the eagles of the *Luftwaffe*. The operation in shambles, Zhukov ordered the commanders and crews of the responsible air defence divisions shot, along with any pilots that returned to their bases without dropping their men. He also postponed the launching of the second wave. 'To make an omelette you must break some eggs,' remarked Stalin matter-of-factly, when notified. 'Keep me informed.'

At 06.00, after almost three hours of preparatory artillery fires, Zhukov gave the order to begin the attack, sending in four armies of the first echelon. Reconnaissance elements and forward detachments from each army, corps, and division crossed the Bug River against surprisingly light resistance. Swarms of amphibious and light tanks were spreading out on the opposite bank and pushing rapidly westward, while engineers struggled to repair and rebuild damaged bridges for the heavier tanks. Behind them came the first wave of BT-5 and BT-7 fast tanks. '*Vperyod!*' ('Forward!') was the order of the day, as the red horde raced toward the Vistula. The first reports indicated that the left bank was clear, the Germans having abandoned their positions along the Bug River some time before the beginning of the Soviet artillery barrage. '*Nemsti ushli! My Pobedali!*' ('The Germans have left! We have won!') echoed over every radio, and the tank commanders, throwing caution to the wind, ordered the units onward at even greater speed.

'Find them!' demanded an angry and not so confident Zhukov of his front commanders. 'Get your forces across the river and to the Vistula as quickly as possible! And watch out for tricks!' It was, however, easier said than done. At that moment *Luftwaffe* attacks along the entire front caught the Red Army divisions massing on the east bank, savaging the struggling engineers and their bridges as well as the trucks and artillery of the first infantry and motorised formations waiting to cross. Hitler's eagles had caught Zhukov by surprise. The bulk of the Red Air Force units, returning from their first missions, were refuelling and rearming at their own air bases. By the time the first squadrons responded, the Germans had already inflicted significant damage on the Red Army's lead echelons.

Travelling at top speed, the forward elements of both fronts covered 15 miles in the first hour, leaving dozens of broken-down vehicles behind them. They found the enemy, or rather the enemy found them, in another hour. The light tanks began to explode, one after the other in rapid succession. First to go were the Soviet command tanks, with their radios and tell-tale multiple antennas. Having outrun their artillery and with no air support, frustrated commanders ordered their units forward in a mass rush to seize the hills and villages from which the fire was coming. More often than not, the Russians would take their objectives after the loss of dozens of vehicles, only to find the Germans had fallen back to engage them from another

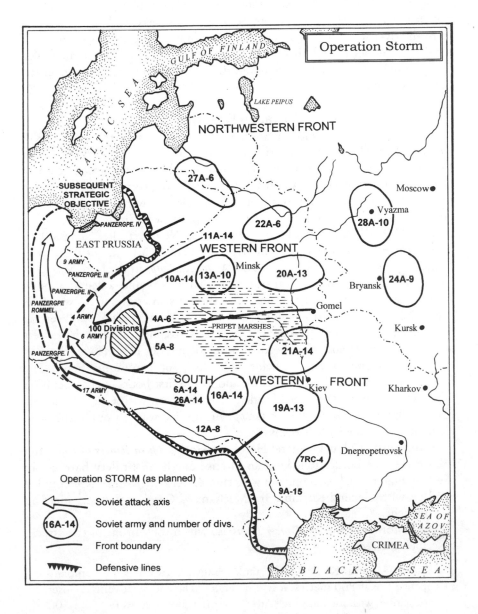

Operation Storm

Operation STORM (as planned)

Soviet attack axis

16A-14 Soviet army and number of divs.

Front boundary

Defensive lines

village or group of hills a thousand or so yards away. The fire was devastating and the advance began to slow and then to stall. Reports to the rear only brought admonitions and the same order: 'Keep moving! Find the German main defensive line!' And so they had kept moving slowly and warily toward the Vistula, losing tanks to the deadly enemy fire throughout the day. The greatly depleted Soviet formations were still some distance from the river when they found the German line. Heavy anti-tank and anti-aircraft guns decimated their ranks repeatedly. Roaming German tanks, firing from both flanks, finished off all those that tried to run away over the next several hours.

Operation Whirlwind

'Stalin has sown the wind,' announced Hitler, assessing the latest *OKW* (*Armed Forces High Command*) situation map at his headquarters in East Prussia. 'Let him reap the whirlwind.' He nodded to Keitel, a worn copy of the 1936 edition of Count Alfred von Schlieffen's *Cannae* tightly clutched in his hands.[27] Within minutes the necessary orders were flying over the airwaves to the commanders in the field: 'Commence Whirlwind.'

Field Marshal Ritter von Leeb's *Army Group North* attacked at 09.00 on 6 July, three hours after the beginning of the Soviet attack, with a heavily reinforced *Fourth Panzer Group* and *XLI Motorised Corps* in the lead. Von Leeb was confident that his six corps and 30 divisions would advance rapidly toward Estonia and Leningrad, smashing the Russian armies in his way. The preparatory artillery strike along a 140-mile front lasted only several minutes. Then the infantrymen and engineers rose up out of their shelters and began their assault. Overhead, almost 400 aircraft of *Luftflotte 1* headed for Soviet strong points, airfields, and lines of communications. The Russians had been caught off balance and in the first hours of the operation von Leeb's forces reached deep inside Soviet territory, with Colonel General Erich Höppner's *Fourth Panzer Group* slicing its way through the lead elements of the Soviet 8th Army.[28]

In the centre Colonel General Hermann Hoth's *Third Panzer Group* flung itself across the border following an intense one-hour artillery barrage. In the first major tank battle of the war, the *XXXIV Motorised Corps* collided head on with General Kurkin's 3rd Mechanised Corps in a classic meeting engagement.

The historian of the *7th Panzer Division*, which took brunt of the attack, described the scene:

'The KV-1 and KV-2 46-ton tanks, raged forward! Our company opened fire at 800 metres: it had no effect. The enemy advanced closer and closer without flagging. After a short time, they were 50 to 100 metres in front of us. A furious fight ensued without any noticeable German success. The Russian tanks advanced further. All of our anti-tank shells bounced off them... The Russian tanks rolled through the ranks of the 25th Panzer Regiment and into our rear. The Panzer regiment turned about and moved to high ground.'[29]

The tankers of Kurkin's corps advanced unhindered by the German fire, slowing only long enough to crush the anti-tank guns and their gunners beneath their tracks before speeding off to wreak havoc on the artillery positions farther to the rear. Joint action by the Panzer IIIs and IVs of the *27th Panzer Division* and the *20th Motorised Division*, reinforced with 88mm guns, stopped the Russians dead in their tracks, inflicting heavy losses. The remainder of the German corps deployed to encircle the Soviet corps and complete its destruction. The first phase of the operation thus opened well for the Germans.

The brainchild of Adolf Hitler, Whirlwind sought the complete destruction of the Red Army in Poland and the western Soviet Union. 'Let us show Stalin how the German Army conducts a real Cannae,' he had remarked to his staff, ordering the drafting of a Barbarossa variant. High-altitude reconnaissance photographs had revealed a concentration of mechanised corps to the north and south of *Army Groups Centre* and *South* and Hitler had correctly surmised that the Red Army sought to destroy *Wehrmacht* forces in Poland. Whirlwind called for *Army Group North* to attack on the morning of 6 July to desynchronise Stalin's plan by shattering the Russian Northwestern and threatening the northern flank of the Western Military District. In the meantime, the rest of the Germany Army would fall back to more defensible terrain near the Vistula River, luring the Red Army into eastern Poland, where it would first be ground down by defensive fires and then annihilated by a counter-stroke.

In the north, *Army Group Centre*'s *Ninth Army*, commanded by Colonel General Adolf Strauss, defended from Allenstein to the northern bank of the Vistula near Warsaw, while *Third Panzer Group* conducted a spoiling attack against the Soviet 11th Army. In the centre Field Marshal Günther von Kluge's *Fourth Army* held a sector from Warsaw to Deblin with Colonel General Heinz Guderian's *Second Panzer Group* in reserve. At the same time, *Army Group South*'s *Sixth Army*, commanded by Field Marshal Walter von Reichenau, defended from Deblin to Sandomierz with Colonel General Ewald von Kleist's *First Panzer Group* in reserve. Finally, General Karl Heinrich von Stülpnagel's *Seventeenth Army* guarded a sector stretching from Sandomierz to Gorlice.

The Germans had organised their defences in depth with three main belts. The advanced position was intended to wear down the Russians and delay their attempts to seize key terrain which might assist them in launching attacks against the main line of resistance. Anticipating the storm that was to follow and unwilling to sacrifice any troops to a static defence, the two front commanders had agreed to use Panzer formations all the way to the Bug in order to inflict greater casualties. A battle outpost line, intended to wear down the Russians further, canalise their attacks, and

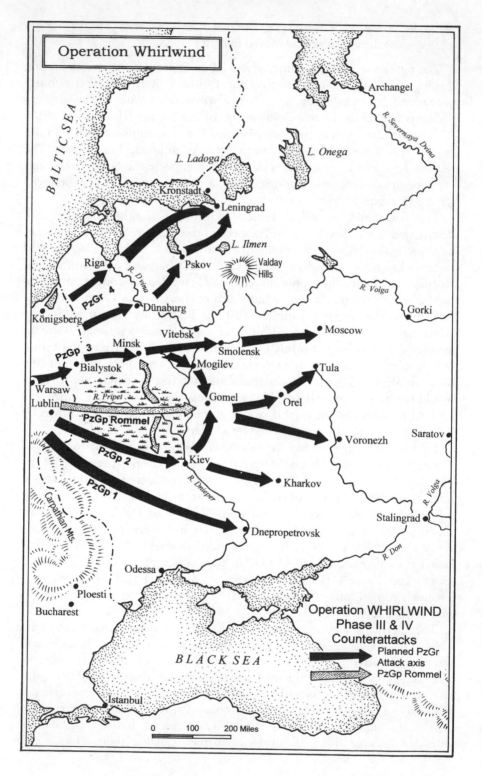

deceive them as to the exact location of the main defensive line, ran from roughly Ostrotchka in the north to Siedlice and Lublin in the centre and Przemysl in the south. This was manned by well-entrenched motorised infantry battalions fighting from high ground and villages. They were well supported by anti-tank guns and heavy anti-aircraft guns operating in the anti-tank role. Finally the main line of resistance was organised in depth behind the Vistula. Strong mobile units from the Panzer groups were placed on the flanks and in reserve.

To assist the army groups in their defensive mission, the Führer had ordered hundreds of heavy and mixed air defence batteries, with their high velocity 88mm and 105mm guns, sent from the Reich to Poland. These weapons could destroy any tank in the Soviet inventory, while the lighter guns were ideal for use against infantry and soft targets. They would also provide additional protection for *Wehrmacht* and *Luftwaffe* units against Russian air attacks. The German Army had positioned the bulk of the anti-aircraft guns with their heavy anti-tank guns along the main line of resistance. Finally, each division had laid thousands of anti-tank mines between the main line of resistance and the battle outpost line.

Once the *Wehrmacht* had eroded the strength of the Red Army sufficiently, the entire German Army would counter-attack to trap the remaining Russian armies in and around the Pripet Marshes. The German Army would then advance in its own right to take Leningrad, Moscow, and Stalingrad. Hitler envisioned four weeks for the entire operation. In order to accomplish this better, Whirlwind added a fifth Panzer group to the original Barbarossa plan. A formidable force, it consisted of four Panzer divisions, three motorised divisions, one infantry division, one cavalry division, and three independent Panzer battalions. The *2nd* and *5th Panzer Divisions* were both veterans of Yugoslavia and Greece, while the *22nd* and *23rd Panzer Divisions* were newly constituted formations. The *52nd Infantry Division* was joined by three motorised divisions; the *60th*, the *1st SS 'Leibstandarte Adolf Hitler'*, and the *3rd SS 'Totenkopf'*. As for the *1st Cavalry Division*, it was the only formation of its kind in the German Army. Last were three independent light Panzer battalions, a conglomeration of Czech and German tanks, including a large number of flame tanks. The new Panzer group was thus a mixture of the new and the old. It was equipped with more than 900 tanks in its Panzer divisions – and almost 4,500 horses and sabres in its cavalry division![30]

In May, Lieutenant General Erwin Rommel, one of the Panzertruppe's most audacious commanders, had returned to Germany, after a brief and successful spell in Africa, at the personal request of Hitler. Upon being briefed on Operation Whirlwind and the creation of the new Panzer group, the ambitious general had asked for command of the unit. Hitler had agreed immediately. The German leader had, in fact, not considered anyone else for the command. Rommel had long been one of the Führer's favourites. Indeed, the German leader had already designated the formation

Panzergruppe 'Rommel' in honour of his young protégé.

Rommel had worked with his usual zeal and energy in transforming his paper group into a formidable fighting force. His first priority was ensuring that his armour units had as many tanks as possible. He and his staff begged, borrowed, and stole tanks, trucks, anti-tank guns, artillery, ammunition, and mobile communications equipment from anyone and everyone. No garrison unit in France or Germany was safe from the unit's predatory practices. Officers and NCOs who had served with the general in France and Northern Africa flocked to his headquarters, which usually found a position for them without first informing their commands. Nor did the antics stop there. Units reporting for gunnery training at ranges throughout Germany arrived to find Rommel's units had arrived first and were firing their ammunition, burning their fuel, and eating their food. Complaints poured in to Hitler's office, but the Führer was content to turn a blind eye. 'Genius must be nurtured,' explained Hitler to a fuming General Staff. By the end of June, *Panzergruppe 'Rommel'* was much more than a paper tiger, although it was still not the formidable fighting force its commander desired. Training thus continued in the group's assembly areas near Lodz, where Rommel's group acted as *OKW* reserve.

The experience with the Red Army's reconnaissance elements and forward detachments had validated the German defensive scheme. The Soviets had advanced only as far as the outpost line before being annihilated. But the respite was short, for the bulk of four Soviet armies had entered Poland in strength.

'Ponderous in the attack, steadfast in the defence'

Army Group North's offensive and *Third Panzer Group*'s spoiling attack had desynchronised Operation Storm by savaging the 11th Army and preventing its participation in the Soviet offensive. The commanders of the Northwestern Front and the Western Front's 11th Army were reeling from the unexpected German assault and screaming for air support to halt its advance. Zhukov responded by dispatching additional Red Air Force units and the 22nd Reserve Army to stop *Army Group North*. In the meantime, the 28th Reserve Army was ordered to Smolensk for commitment in either the north or the west. With the 11th Army out of the picture, he ordered the 13th Army to take its place. As it would take some time for that formation to catch up with Major General Golikov's attacking 10th Army, Zhukov also attached the 14th Mechanised Corps from Major General A.A. Korobkov's 4th Army to the 10th Army.

The rest of the operation had started just as badly. It had taken the front commanders almost four hours to recover from the German air attacks and begin crossing the border in strength. To make up for lost time, Golikov attacked with his two mechanised corps in the lead, followed by two tank-reinforced infantry corps and a cavalry corps. In the south, the 6th Army, responsible for the close envelopment, attacked with two rifle corps abreast, followed by two mechanised corps, while the 26th Army, responsible for the deep envelopment, attacked with its mechanised and cavalry corps in the first echelon followed by its infantry corps.

In the north, *Third Panzer Group*'s *LVII Motorised Corps* had the mission of slowing the Western Front's advance without becoming decisively engaged. It would be joined by the *XXXIX Motorised Corps* once that formation had finished with its spoiling attack against the 11th Army. *Second Panzer Group*'s *XLVI* and *XLVII Motorised Corps* and *First Panzer Group*'s *XLVIII Motorised Corps* were charged with the same mission against the Southwestern Front in the centre and south. The German commanders were told to give priority to the destruction of the Soviet mechanised corps. Their corps began to engage the heads and flanks of the three Russian armies soon after they crossed the border, knocking out scores of Soviet tanks from a range of 1,000 yards and greater. Now and then the Red Army tanks responded, but their fire proved generally ineffective. The Russians, however, continued advancing ponderously, a thick screen of light tanks to their front and flanks, foiling German efforts to slow the momentum of the main body. 'They moved like Cossacks,' remembered one Panzer officer, as he watched the swarms of enemy tanks flow toward any threatening Panzer formations before ebbing back to the main body. The armour screen was well supported by Soviet artillery, which fired at the Germans whenever they appeared in strength.

After two hours of this game, the commander of the *LVII Motorised Corps* decided to attack in an attempt to penetrate the 10th Army's screen, knock out the artillery and engage the main body. It was a mistake. Russian heavy anti-tank guns backed by detachments of T-34s and more artillery awaited the two Panzer divisions. The Germans encountered a withering fire which mauled the lead regiments and sent both formations reeling northward. 'Ponderous in the attack, steadfast in the defence,' reported the chastened corps commander to General Hoth.

By 18.00 the Southwestern Front armies had almost reached the outpost line. At about the same time, 500 aircraft of *Luftflotte 4* came screaming over the battlefield at tree-top level, wreaking havoc on the massed tanks, artillery, trucks, and horses strung out along the highway to Przemysl. Wave after wave of Bf 109s, Me 110s, and Ju 87s pummelled Russian units on the highway for almost two hours, scattering them everywhere. In the meantime, elements of the *XLVIII Motorised Corps* finally penetrated the Soviet tank screen and battered the 8th Mechanised Corps. In the *Army Group Centre* sector, *Luftflotte 1* and the *XXXIV Motorised Corps* pulverised the 10th Army in much the same way. By the time the much diminished Red Air Force reached the battlefield, the rear elements of three Russian armies were in shambles.

In the meantime, the Russian forward corps had continued moving, reaching the German outpost line in strength at 20.00. Although they had already lost hundreds of tanks each, the army commanders decided to attack without waiting for the remainder of their infantry and artillery far to the rear. The Western Front's 6th, 13th, and 14th Mechanised Corps attempted to steamroller the German line, assaulting in deep columns. A dense wall of tank and anti-tank fire from the front and flanks crushed the first Russian attempt, transforming hundreds of KV-1s and T-34s into flaming obstacles and breaking the momentum of the attack within the hour. Another two assaults in the next two hours were repulsed in a similar manner with heavy Soviet losses and little gain. Only the intervention of nightfall prevented the Red Army from making another attempt. Zhukov, boiling with rage, ordered the two front commanders to dig in for the night and continue the fight in the morning. 'Lead with your infantry and artillery!' he admonished. He ordered Pavlov and Kirponos to reorganise their shattered infantry corps and supporting artillery and to integrate them into the next morning's attacks. In the meantime, the Chief of the General Staff would coordinate Red Air Force support, which had been disappointingly ineffective to date. He also planned on pushing the 13th and 16th Armies forward under the cover of darkness, followed by the 19th and 20th Armies. 'We will break them in the morning,' he told his staff.

Both sides used the night to move up or reposition units, as well as to refuel and rearm their vehicles. The men of the two armies sensed that the fate of the war could be decided the following day. For the majority, sleep was out of the question. Not that it had ever been a viable option. German and Russian fighter-bombers attempted to bomb each other's armies, running the gauntlet of improvised night fighters and heavy air defence fire, which shook the entire battlefield even as it illuminated the skies overhead. Scores of Soviet reconnaissance and cavalry units took advantage of the darkness to probe German positions, while engineers attempted to clear lanes through the minefields. At the same time, strong Panzer formations roamed along the flanks of the Russian armies and well to their rear, moving toward the Bug River to reconnoitre future attack routes and interdict supplies and reinforcements. A meeting engagement between the *XXXIX Motorised Corps* and the forward detachments of the advancing 13th Army set off a series of brief but intense battles that stopped both formations in their tracks. Zhukov demanded that his army commanders continue moving through the night, but chance encounters ate away at the courage and forward momentum of the two Russian armies, bringing their advance to a crawl. Illumination lit up the battlefield constantly, sending soldiers and vehicles scurrying for cover in the shadows like ants.

At 04.00 on 7 July 1941 Soviet artillery opened up on the *Wehrmacht*'s battle outpost line with high explosive and smoke rounds, reducing Ostow, Lublin, and Przemysl to rubble. The barrage tore the German defensive positions to pieces, neutralising their fires and forcing many of the defenders to fall back to the main defensive line. Thirty minutes later, some 400 Red Army fighters and fighter-bombers began their attacks on both the strong points and the motorised corps which had caused Zhukov's plan such grief.

The *Luftwaffe*, on its way to punish the Red Army yet again, entered the fray only minutes later and a free-for-all soon developed, with both sides diverted from their ground support mission.

At 06.00 the Russian ground attack began. Soviet engineers had done their work well and the forward detachments were through the cleared and marked lanes, advancing on the German defensive line within an hour. Behind them came a wave of engineers, infantry, artillery, and cavalry pouring through the gaps under the cover of smoke to deal with the minefields and strong points ahead. Finally came the tank and motorised divisions of the mechanised corps, which had been reconstituted during the night by merging depleted units. By noon, the lead elements of both fronts had reached the German main defensive line, running along the Ostrotchka–Deblin highway, then south along the Vistula River to Sandomierz, and finally to Gorlice and the Hungarian border.

At 16.00 both fronts launched a concerted attack on the forward edge of the final German line. The 10th Army's artillery barrage preceding the attack lasted only a few minutes, due to a shortage of ammunition. Even before it ended, General Golubev's mechanised corps was racing for Warsaw at top speed, his tanks laden with infantry. The first salvo from the waiting *Fourth Army* tank, anti-tank, and anti-aircraft guns devastated the lead battalions in minutes before they ever reached the outskirts of the Polish capital. The following echelons continued pushing down the highway, while an infantry regiment attempted to storm the heights at Ostrotchka overlooking the main east–west road to the Polish capital. The Red Army enveloping detachment was decimated by rapid firing 20mm anti-aircraft guns. A second assault by a mounted cavalry regiment, attempting to take advantage of the wooded terrain ended in similar failure, as did a third attack by a combination of infantry, light armour, and artillery.

On the ridge, waiting Panzers began slowly to move forward, enveloping the road from the north and concentrating their fires on the medium and heavy tanks of the mechanised corps. The Soviets returned an ineffectual fire. After several hours of this uneven fight, the surviving Russians began to flee back up the highway toward Bialystok. Golubev next committed two rifle corps supported by what remained of the 14th Mechanised Corps to renew the attempted breakthrough to Warsaw. Within hours, however, they too had been routed. Fearing an envelopment from the north and worried about his supply situation, he ordered his depleted mechanised corps and cavalry corps to cover the withdrawal of broken rifle units. He planned on falling back on the advancing 13th and 20th Armies before rejoining the Western Front's offensive in the morning.

To the south, the Southwestern Front fared noticeably better. The weight of its artillery hammered General Stülpnagel's *Seventeenth Army* unmercifully. The Russian 6th and 26th Armies, advancing under the cover of smoke, closed quickly with the defenders. Although the Soviet 6th Army was thrown back by the German *Sixth Army* in a bitter struggle that lasted all day, the badly battered and reconstituted 8th Mechanised Corps and the 8th Rifle Corps broke through the *Wehrmacht*'s *XLIX Mountain Corps* at Rzeszow by the end of the day. The 24th and 7th Motorised Divisions surged through the breach, heading west toward Krakow, while the 8th Rifle Corps, and the 4th Cavalry Corps struck out toward the northwest of Kielce. '*Proryv!*' ('Breakthrough!') shouted an ecstatic Kirponos to Zhukov, who, in turn, reported this first bit of good luck to Stalin. By early in the night the lead elements of the 26th Army were advancing on Tarnow and Mielec. Before they could reach either destination, however, the advance ground to a halt, the Russian tank commanders weeping and pounding their tanks in frustration. The Red Army had run out of fuel!

The second day of Operation Storm ended with mixed results. In the north Pavlov was falling back, while in the south Kirponos had broken through and advanced. The two front commanders reported they were short of fuel and ammunition and that hundreds of tanks were down for maintenance. They could not mount another major attack until they were supplied. But resupply would be difficult, for the Red Army was in the midst of a logistics' nightmare. The *Luftwaffe*'s bombers had hammered Soviet support units and supply depots repeatedly throughout the first two days of the operation, resulting in a major shortage of fuel and ammunition, as well as trucks to deliver them forward. To add insult to injury, the Red Air Force had proved unable to challenge the *Luftwaffe* seriously.

Still, Zhukov believed the morning held great promise. Depots in the Pripet Marshes had escaped relatively unscathed, and transportation units from Strategic Reserve's 24th and 28th Armies were expect to arrive within the next day. Also, the commanders of the 13th and 16th Armies, battered throughout the day from the air, had finally linked up with their colleagues in the front lines, although too late to be committed into battle. With them came much-needed fuel and ammunition, albeit not enough to meet everyone's needs. Zhukov had also committed the under-strength 4th and 5th Armies to fix the German centre along the Vistula. Both were already advancing under the cover of darkness. Finally, staff officers were hastening the movement of the 19th, 20th, and 21st Armies toward the border. The Soviets thus had five armies on the front lines, two more expected to join them within the next 24 hours, and three more within another 48 hours.

'Dig in and hold your positions. There will be no falling back!' Zhukov ordered Pavlov and Kirponos. 'With a little time and a bit of luck, we can still win this war,' he thought. But the Russians had run out of both.

'Release your hounds before the bear can recover!'

Hitler studied the overhead photos taken by his strategic reconnaissance squadron and developed during the night. The *Luftwaffe* had succeeded in separating the advancing Russian armies into distinct echelons almost too far apart to be mutually supporting. Furthermore, the army group commanders were all reporting tremendous Soviet losses on the ground and in the air. Finally, signals intelligence indicated that the Red Army was experiencing a major fuel shortage. 'They are dead in their tracks,' reported Rommel from the front. 'Release your hounds before the bear can recover!'[31] Hitler would have preferred to wait another day until the Red Army was well within the bag. Despite the Soviet breakthrough in the south, the confidence of his commanders convinced the Führer that now was the time to start his counter-stroke.

At 03.00 on 8 July 1941, the guns of *Army Groups Centre* and *South* erupted in a concentrated and sustained artillery barrage, tearing huge gaps in the first echelon Russian armies massed in front of them. The *Luftwaffe* joined the attack minutes later, pounding the second echelon armies of the two Russian fronts. Two hours later, *OKW* unleashed its Panzer groups, which had moved forward during the night. In the north, *Third Panzer Group* attacked across the Narew from Warsaw toward Bialystok, ripping through Pavlov's 10th Army and into the advancing 13th Army. In the centre, *Second Panzer Group* pushed across the Vistula from Warsaw southeast toward Lublin, slashing through the already battered 6th Army. In the meantime, *Panzer Group 'Rommel'*, its flame tanks in the lead spewing fire in every direction, sent the 26th Army's 8th Rifle and 8th Cavalry Corps running for their lives as it attacked toward Lublin. In the south, *First Panzer Group* attacked from Krakow to Przemysl, overrunning the stalled 8th Mechanised Corps' 24th and 7th Motorised Divisions before crashing into the 16th Army. The concerted German ground and air attack was too much for the exhausted and depleted Russian units, and the Red Army's front echelons disintegrated under the German onslaught.

On the flanks, however, the Soviet 13th and 16th Armies responded well with intense tank and anti-tank fire backed up by plenty of artillery, slowing *Third Panzer Group*'s advance in the north and stopping *First Panzer Group* dead in its tracks. The *Luftwaffe* moved to intervene but was effectively countered by scores of Russian fighters. The Panzers attempted to circumvent the pockets of resistance, while the infantry and artillery moved forward to eliminate the threat. *'Flak Vorwärts!'* ('Flak Forward!') shouted a regimental commander in *First Panzer Group*'s *16th Motorised Division*. Minutes later intense rapid fire from 20mm, 88mm, and 105mm anti-aircraft guns ravaged the Russian 109th Motorised Division, while the Panzer divisions slugged it out with the Russian 13th and 17th Tank Divisions.

Rommel's *1st Cavalry Division* broke the impasse by charging south and striking the Russians a surprise blow, scattering first the artillery and then the anti-tank guns. Behind them came wave after wave of flame tanks, sowing panic in the enemy ranks and breaking his will to resist. The cries of *'Kamerad'* or *'Tovaritch'* (German and Russian for 'Comrade') rang out from tens of thousands of Red Army soldiers as they began to surrender. *Third Panzer Group*, without the luxury of either cavalry or flame tanks, had to resort to more conventional methods, battering its way through the 13th

Army with heavy artillery and air support.

In the meantime, Guderian and Rommel were racing for the Bug River and scattering the Russians, when they collided with the newly arrived Soviet 4th and 5th Armies. Rommel's units replied with a barrage of high explosive and smoke rounds from his self-propelled artillery following the first wave. His lead Panzer regiments then advanced under the cover of smoke supported by infantry and a battalion of flame tanks. This time, however, the flame tanks failed to have any effect on the Russians, who quickly hit a dozen of the vulnerable vehicles, forcing the others to retire. The catastrophic explosions that ensued, however, drew the attention of the *Luftwaffe*, which tore into the Soviet formations. The air and artillery strikes, in combination with accurate tank fire, were too much for the Red Army soldiers and they grudgingly began to give way to the Germans.

Both Guderian and Rommel had dispatched strong mobile corps to conduct a deep envelopment at the beginning of the engagement and this additional pressure proved decisive. The Russians began to fall apart, slowly as first, but their disintegration accelerated noticeably as the Germans tore into their flanks with a vengeance. A frontal attack by the massed Panzers of the two groups finally broke the front echelons of the two Soviet armies, sending them dashing against the follow-on Red Army formations with the Germans in hot pursuit. The cry *'Kamerad'* was everywhere, as the Russians began to throw down their arms and abandon their heavy equipment. 'No time to stop for prisoners!' Rommel told his commanders. 'Point them toward the west and keep moving.' By nightfall the lead elements of *Panzer Group 'Rommel'* had reached the Bug River, opposite Brest Litovsk. The remainder of his command continued arriving throughout the night, as Rommel planned his next move. As soon as all his commanders were assembled he informed them matter-of-factly: 'We are going through the Pripet Marshes.'

'Rommel has gone to Gomel!'

Phase III of Whirlwind called for the Panzer groups to drive deep into the Soviet Union, while the remainder of *Army Groups Centre* and *South* completed the destruction of the Russian armies in Poland. In the centre, *Third Panzer Group* and *Panzer Group 'Rommel'* would attack north of the Pripet Marshes toward Minsk, smashing the remaining Russian armies in Byelorussia and seizing the city. *Third Panzer Group* would then continue its attack northeast toward Smolensk, while Rommel attacked southeast toward Gomel to close the northern pincer of the German encirclement.

In the meantime, *Army Group Centre*'s *Second Panzer Group* would attack south of the Pripet Marshes toward Kiev, and then swing northeast toward Gomel, destroying the remaining Russian armies in the northern Ukraine and linking up with Rommel. It would thus close the southern pincer of the German encirclement.

Simultaneously, *First Panzer Group* would attack from Przyemysl southwest toward Dnepropetrovsk to destroy the remaining Russian armies positioned in the southern Ukraine. Farther south, a Hungarian motorised corps, two Romanian armies, and the German *Eleventh Army* would attack across Soviet Bessarabia toward Odessa to destroy the Russian 12th and 9th Armies.

Rommel, however, had other ideas. Well aware that the Russian armies were probably converging to the north and south of the Pripet Marshes, he believed the quickest road to victory was also the straightest. German Panzers had pierced the impenetrable Ardennes in 1940 and he was confident they could do it again here in the Soviet Union in 1941. Besides, where were all these Russian armies coming from? Instinct told him that the Soviet High Command was probably using a road network through the marshes to expedite the deployment of the Red Army to the border. Experience told him that Russians did not expect an attack from that direction. His mind made up, Rommel dispatched reconnaissance battalions across the river under cover of darkness to reconnoitre Brest-Litovsk and the road to Pinsk. The remainder of the night was spent planning the advance.

When Phase III of Whirlwind kicked off at 03.00 on 9 July, Rommel's lead elements had already crossed the Bug River and seized Brest-Litovsk against almost light Soviet resistance. The German units immediately set off for Pinsk, 110 miles to the east, the first day's objective. The reconnaissance battalions reported that the road was open and being used only by Red Army support units. Rommel's Panzers moved swiftly through the countryside, entering Kobrin, where the German motorcycles and armoured cars had already shot up various headquarters and support units as they moved through, leaving the city in flames. The Panzers and motorised infantry moved all day and night without stopping. Outside of Pinsk, they overran an inattentive Russian rifle division in its assembly area. They continued moving until they reached the edge of the marshes on the far side of the city. There they refuelled and briefly rested, while awaiting the remainder of the command. A messenger met Rommel with the latest report. Two parallel corduroy roads, running east–west, bisected the marshes. The reconnaissance battalions had proceeded along both roads, shooting up Russian traffic police, support units, radio and relay stations, and ammunition and fuel depots. The bad news was that the marshy ground tended to absorb radio signals, making it impossible for the lead units to communicate with the Panzer group. There was thus no way for the main body to know where the roads led and what lay ahead. 'Perfect!' responded Rommel, ordering his command to advance. 'If we can't communicate then neither can the Russians!'

They continued moving during the early morning darkness and throughout the next day, the Panzers always in the lead. By midnight of the second day, they had reached firm ground. Another messenger informed Rommel that they had reached a major intersection with a second corduroy road running generally north–south. Looking at his map, the Panzer leader estimated that they were about two-thirds of the way through the marshes and concluded that the northern route led to Minsk while the southern route led to Zhitomir. Rommel sent two Panzer and two motorised infantry divisions north under his chief of staff to facilitate the capture of the Byelorussian capital by Hoth's *Third Panzer Group* and pave the way for a future advance to Moscow. He himself proceeded toward Gomel with two Panzer divisions, a motorised division and an infantry division, sending the *1st Cavalry Division* to screen to the south along with the three battalions of light tanks.

Panzer Group 'Rommel' had been on the move for two days, stopping only to refuel. '*Wo ist Rommel?*' ('Where is Rommel?') ran the standing joke in the unit. '*Rommel hat nach Gommel gegangen!*' ('Rommel has gone to Gommel!') The exhausted German soldiers laughed as they continued advancing, past burning fuel dumps and ammo depots, dead Russian soldiers and horses, abandoned field hospitals, kitchens, and unit headquarters. By midnight of the third day they were through the Pripet Marshes, having marched almost 250 miles in 72 hours. They were met by the reconnaissance battalions, which escorted them into a series of assembly areas where they refuelled their vehicles before collapsing on the ground in exhaustion.

The respite was brief. Hours later they were on the move again, racing the advanced guard of the Soviet 24th Reserve Army, which was approaching Gomel from the east. The city was held by the reconnaissance battalions, which had been reinforced with two Panzer battalions dispatched earlier in the morning. Rommel's tanks closed the distance first, emerging on the far edge to deliver a withering fire on the Russians advancing in almost textbook formation. 'They come on in the same old way!' marvelled the Panzer leader's driver. 'And we shall beat them in the same old way!' responded a tired but ecstatic Rommel. Within minutes the *Luftwaffe* had joined the fray, tearing into the neat Russian ranks. A counter-attack by the lead battalions of the Panzer divisions finished the job, shattering the Soviet regiments and sending the entire formation into retreat, hotly pursued by Hitler's eagles. In the meantime, the arriving infantry and Panzer battalions occupied positions around the city. With communications restored shortly thereafter, Rommel personally informed a jubilant Hitler that *Panzer Group 'Rommel'* had taken Gomel.

On the roads to Moscow

Zhukov had spun the wheel of destiny and lost. From eastern Poland to the Soviet Union, the Red Army lay shattered. Little stood between the Germans and Moscow, except a few undermanned, unequipped, and scattered rifle corps. The Chief of the Soviet General Staff had underestimated the 'patchwork' German Army and overestimated the Red Army. He had front-loaded his attack, gambled, and lost. He was ready when the NKVD officers came to take him away. He smiled to himself and thought with a hint of humour: 'In war there are no great and indispensable generals, only great and indispensable leaders.' Perhaps, if he had had the luxury of learning from his mistakes he might have developed into a first-rate military figure, a great captain of Russia, perhaps even of the world. But in Stalin's Russia, mistakes were not tolerated in the summer of 1941, not even by favourites. The general's driver retrieved the small suitcase every Soviet officer kept for such a contingency. It contained a change of underwear, a pair of socks, a metal cup and spoon, a bag of biscuits, some tea, and a picture of his wife. It was one of the bitter lessons Russian officers had learned from the purges. The NKVD officers treated him with a certain deference as they invited him into the car. A curt nod to his staff and the car was on its way.

The Brest-Litovsk Treaty

Panzer Group 'Rommel''s daring march through the Pripet Marshes won the war for Germany. The destruction of the ammunition and fuel depots deprived the Red Army of critical supplies in its greatest hour of need. The eradication of command posts and radio stations prevented the Soviet High Command from moving reinforcements through the marshes. *Panzer Group 'Rommel'* had split the Russian fronts. More importantly, lead elements of the four divisions dispatched to Minsk emerged from the darkness, like ghosts, on the flanks of the defending Soviet 20th Army. These 13 Russian divisions, augmented by another five reserve divisions north of the Pripet Marshes, were all that stood between *Third Panzer Group* and the Byelorussian capital.

An audacious early morning attack by Rommel's troops demolished the Soviet left flank, forcing the Red Army soldiers to abandon their strongly entrenched positions. Seeing the Russians in disarray, Hoth, whose earlier assaults had stalled, attacked again behind a heavy artillery barrage. This time, his Panzers broke through, annihilating the enemy formations and entering Minsk. Likewise, the *1st Cavalry Division* emerged from the marshes in the early morning hours behind 12 reserve Russian divisions blocking Guderian's *Second Panzer Group* along with the Soviet 21st Army. Leading with flame tanks, the German cavalrymen boldly charged the panic-stricken Red Army reserve, shattering it and causing the fleeing Russian soldiers to retreat into the 21st Army, which also broke and ran. Guderian's Panzers sliced through both formations and headed for a defenceless Kiev, which they entered later that day. Within another three weeks German forces were in possession of Leningrad, Smolensk, Bryansk, Kursk, and Stalingrad.

On 6 August 1941 Stalin sued for a beggar's peace. The Second Treaty of Brest-Litovsk was signed in the same city where Lenin and Trotsky had capitulated to the German Army in World War I. Like the First Treaty of Brest-Litovsk of 1918, it was a harsh, one-sided peace, dictated by Germany, and which emasculated Russia economically and militarily. Gone, at the stroke of the pen, were the Soviet republics of Latvia, Lithuania, Estonia, the

Ukraine and Byelorussia. All would become Reich Commissariats and be ruthlessly exploited as sources of labour, food, and raw materials. Anti-Soviet uprisings throughout the Caucasus and Central Asia indicated those republics might not remain under Stalin for too much longer. Soviet borders were thus pushed back to the boundaries of Ivan the Terrible.

The treaty was also accompanied by a range of protocols which confirmed German supremacy. The Diplomatic Protocol called for the immediate resumption of the Non-Aggression Pact between the two sides as well as for the opening or reopening of all German embassies and consulates in all the major cities of the Soviet Union. The Economic Protocol dictated an immediate resumption of shipments of oil, gas, metal ores, and grain to Germany. Under the Technical Protocol, Moscow would send samples of all the Red Army's latest tanks, armoured cars, and artillery and the Red Air Force's aircraft to the Third Reich along with blueprints and technicians for discussions. The Factories Protocol, which ensured open access to all factories for special teams of German civilian and military inspectors on demand, was intended to deny the Soviets the ability to hide any new technology. The Open Skies Protocol allowed the *Luftwaffe* unhindered access to Soviet airspace, while the Open Waters Protocol did the same for the *Kreigsmarine*.

Moscow had asked for a repatriation clause, but Hitler had refused to make any concessions to Stalin. Besides, he was seriously considering making use of the millions of Soviet POWs who had surrendered to the *Wehrmacht*.[32] 'A Slavic Legion to fight Bolshevism under Nazi Germany,' he thought to himself. 'What an irony!'

It was only the battered condition of the armed forces that had caused Hitler to agree to peace. About half the *Wehrmacht*'s Panzers and the *Luftwaffe*'s aircraft had either been destroyed or damaged and many of the rest were out of service for maintenance. Furthermore, the German armed forces were seriously short of spare parts, fuel, and ammunition. This short war had been much more intense than anyone expected. Hitler thought he would use the next year to rebuild his victorious but dilapidated army. He was intent on finishing this business with Stalin after that. For the moment he was persuaded by Rommel, the Reich's newest field marshal, to turn his attention to the West. 'Let Stalin wait,' he had advised Hitler, 'There are bigger fish to fry!' The Führer was now planning to dispatch a new Panzer group to North Africa to settle the score with Churchill once and for all. Hitler was confident that the Third Reich would, once again, emerge victorious.

The reality

In the spring of 1941 Zhukov tried to persuade Stalin of the need for a preemptive attack on Germany. The new Chief of the General Staff wrote a 'Report on the Plan of Strategic Deployment of the Armed Forces of the Soviet Union to the Chairman of the Council of People's Commissar's on 15

May 1941.' In this hand-written proposal, Zhukov argued for an immediate offensive using 152 divisions to destroy the estimated 100 German divisions assembling in Poland. Given the many problems the Red Army was experiencing at the time, Stalin ignored Zhukov's proposal, believing such an attack would have been a desperate gamble. On 22 June 1941 Germany invaded the Soviet Union. Despite devastating losses, the Red Army survived to fight another day and defeat the *Wehrmacht*, entering Berlin four years later.

Bibliography

Andreev, V.A., *et al*, *Istoriya Velikoi Otechestvenoi Voiny Sovetskogo Soyuza 1941–1945 [History of the Great Patriotic War of the Soviet Union 1941–1945]*, Volume 1 (Moscow: Voenizdat, 1961).

Blair, Clay, *Ridgway's Paratroopers. The American Airborne in World War II* (The Dial Press, Garden City, New York, 1985).

Boog, Horst, ed., *Germany and the Second World War*, Volume IV, *The Attack on the Soviet Union* (Research Institute for Military History, Potsdam, Germany, 1996, translated by Dean S. McMurry, *et al.*, Clarendon Press, New York, 1998).

Glantz, David, *The Military Strategy of the Soviet Union. A History* (Frank Cass, London, 1992).

Glantz, David, and House, Jonathan, *When Titans Clashed. How the Red Army Stopped Hitler* (University of Kansas Press, 1995).

Haupt, Werner, *Army Group Center. The Wehrmacht in Russia 1941–1945* (Schiffer Military History, Atglen, Pennsylvania, 1997).

Jentz, Thomas J., *Panzer Truppen. The Complete Guide to the Creation and Combat Employment of Germany's Tank Force 1933–1942*, 2 volumes (Schiffer Military History, Atglen, Pennsylvania, 1996).

Krupchenko, I.P., *Sovetskie Tankovye Voiska 1941–1945 [Soviet Tank Forces 1941–1945]* (Moscow: Voenizdat, 1973).

Piekalkiewicz, Janusz, *The Cavalry 1939–1945* (Historical Times, Harrisburg, Pennsylvania, 1987).

Radzievskiy, General of the Army A.I., *Tankovyi Udar. Tankovaya Armiya v Nastupatel'noi Operatsii Fronta po opytu Velikoi Otechestvenoi Voiny [Tank Strike. The Tank Army in Front Offensive Operations from the Experience of the Great Patriotic War]* (Voenizdat, Moscow, 1977).

Schlieffen, General Field Marshal Count Alfred von, *Cannae* (The Command and General Staff College, Fort Leavenworth, Kansas, 1936).

Shukman, Harold, ed., *Stalin's Generals* (Grove Press, New York, 1993).

The Soviet Air Force in World War II (Doubleday, Garden City, New York, 1973). This is a translation of the Soviet Ministry of Defence official history of the Soviet Air Force in World War II.

Spick, Mike, *Luftwaffe Fighter Aces. The Jagdflieger and their Combat Tactics and Techniques* (Greenhill Books, London, 1996).

Stoves, Rolf O., *1st Panzer Division History, 1939–1945* (Podzun, Bad Nauheim, 1962).

Suvorov, Viktor, *Ledokol. Kto Nachal Vtoraya Mirovaya Voina? [Icebreaker. Who Started the Second World War?]* (ACT, London, 1999)

Suvorov, Viktor, *Den' 'M'. Logda Nachalas Vtoraya Mirovaya Voina? [D-Day. When Did the Second World War Begin?]* (ACT, London, 1999).

Notes

1. Boog, *Germany and the Second World War*, Volume IV, *The Attack on the Soviet Union*, p. 318.
2. *Ibid.*, p. 325. Estimate as of 20 June 1941.
3. *Ibid.*, p. 343.
4. *Ibid.*, p. 340; Haupt, *Army Group Center*, pp. 18–19.
*5. Hitler, Adolf, *Germany's Supreme Warlord*, 22 volumes (Das Reich, Berlin, 1950), Vol. 2, p. 228. Unless otherwise cited, all references to Hitler are from this work.
6. Glantz, *The Military Strategy of the Soviet Union*, pp. 88–91. See also Suvorov, *Ledokol* and *Den' 'M'*.
*7. Taken from Zhukov, General of the Army Georgi K., *Operation Storm*, 2 volumes (Voenizdat, Moscow, 1954), Vol I, pp. 102–22. Unless otherwise cited all references to Zhukov are from this work. Zhukov survived twelve years in a Soviet prison camp before being released and allowed to publish this account.
8. Viktor Anfilov, 'Georgy Konstantinovich Zhukov,' in Shukman, *Stalin's Generals*, p. 343.
9. Glantz & House, *When Titans Clashed*, p. 41.
10. Glantz, *The Military Strategy of the Soviet Union*, pp. 88–91.
11. Hoffmann, Joachim, 'The Soviet Union up to the Eve of the German Attack', in Boog, *The Attack on the Soviet Union*, pp. 78–81 and Boog, Horst, 'Military Concepts of the War with Russia', in Boog, *The Attack on the Soviet Union*, p. 352.
12. Hoffman, *op. cit.*, p. 66.
13. Radzievskiy, *Tankovyi Udar*, p. 8.
14. *Ibid.*, p. 9.
15. *Ibid.*, p. 22. *Sovetskie Tankovye Voiska 1941–1945*, p. 22.
16. Andreev, *Istoriya Velikoi Otechestvennoi Voiny Sovetskogo Soyuza 1941–1945*, Volume 1, p. 475.
17. Spick, *Luftwaffe Fighter Aces*, p. 78. Schiess scored 67 air victories during the war.
18. *The Soviet Air Force in World War II*, p. 38; See also Horst Boog *et al.*, Volume IV, Maps.
19. *The Soviet Air Force in World War II*, p. 39.
20. 'Single Engine Fighters 28.06.41', in *German Order of Battle – Statistics as of Quarter Years 1938–1945*, HRA 137.306-14 on microfilm roll A1128, US Strategic Bombing Survey, Military Analysis Division, USAF Historical Research Agency, Maxwell Air Force Base, Alabama.
21. Spick, *op. cit.*, pp. 78–9.
*22. Danilov, General of the Army V.I., *Official History of the Soviet Armed Forces in World War II*, 12 volumes (Voenizdat, Moscow, 2000), Vol. 2, p. 114. Unless otherwise cited all references to Red Army operations are from this work.
23. Boog, p. 93.
24. *Ibid.*
25. For the organisation and order of battle of Soviet airborne forces on the eve of the German invasion, see Glantz, David M., *Research Survey No. 4 The Soviet Airborne Experience* (Fort Leavenworth, Kansas: Combat Studies Institute, November 1984), pp. 21–2, 26.
26. Based on an actual experience of the US Army's 82nd Airborne Division during World War II. See Blair, *Ridgway's Paratroopers*, 101–03.
27. For an English translation, see the edition of Schlieffen's *Cannae* cited in the bibliography above.
*28. Rommel, General Field Marshal Erwin, ed., *Official History of the German Armed Forces in World War II*, 10 volumes (Das Reich, Berlin, 1960), Vol. 3, p. 98. Unless otherwise cited, all references to German armed forces operations are from this work.

29. Stoves, *1st Panzer Division History, 1939–1945*, p. 882.
30. This is the actual number of tanks in the four Panzer formations, which, in reality, arrived in the Eastern Front after the beginning of Barbarossa. See Jentz, *Panzer Truppen*, Vol. I, pp. 212–3 'Panzer Units Sent to the Eastern Front After the Start of the Campaign'. For the number of horses in the 1st Cavalry Division, see Piekalkiewicz, *The Cavalry 1939–1945*, pp. 238–40.
*31. Extracted from Rommel, General Field Marshal Erwin, *Rommel hat nach Gomel gegangen!* (Das Reich, Berlin, 1942), pp. 99–224. Unless otherwise cited all references to Rommel or the operations of his Panzer group are from this work.
*32. Extracted from Schulenberg, Count Friedrich Werner von, *Victory in the East: The Second Treaty of Brest-Litovsk* (Das Reich, Berlin, 1942), p. 302.

5
THE HINGE[1]
Alamein to Basra, 1942

Paddy Griffith

'So that every man understands, the objective is the Suez Canal.'
Erwin Rommel, 10 April 1941.

The White House, Washington

When President Franklin D. Roosevelt passed the telegram announcing the fall of Tobruk to his distinguished guest in the Oval Office, he was taken somewhat aback by the depth of feeling with which the information was greeted. 'Defeat is one thing; disgrace is another', gloomily intoned Winston S. Churchill, the British prime minister, who was visibly shaken by the news. He went on to compare the loss of the desert fortress – together with some 33,000 prisoners of war and immeasurable logistic resources – with the equally bitter humiliation of Singapore a mere four months earlier. Even more than Singapore, perhaps, Tobruk had been held up as a symbol of determined resistance, since it had successfully withstood an eight-month siege all through the summer of 1941, effectively halting a brilliant German offensive dead in its tracks. Now on 20–21 June 1942, the same fortress had fallen within the space of just 36 hours, almost before anyone had noticed that it was again being attacked. From symbolising the British bulldog spirit, it had instantly been transformed into a telling icon of unfocussed British ineffectiveness; of feebleness, congenital bumbling and apparently unending defeat. The general public reaction in Britain would be demonstrated within a week, when the government lost the Maldon by-election, after which a vote of no confidence was moved in the House of Commons.

It was no consolation to Churchill that Erwin Rommel, the tireless 'Desert Fox', was promoted field marshal (the youngest in the German Army) just one day after he had accepted Tobruk's surrender. Nor did it help the British prime minister that his generals had repeatedly warned him that they never had any intention of holding Tobruk once the main Gazala position, further to the west, had been broken. A series of military experts had carefully itemised all the gaping deficiencies in the Tobruk defences, which had been comprehensively pillaged to strengthen the front line.

Finally, it was very cold comfort to be told that 2nd South African Division, assigned as the Tobruk garrison, had been raw, inexperienced and far from the high fighting efficiency of the veteran Australians who had performed the same duty so staunchly in the previous year. The division lost in Tobruk represented no less than one third of the total manpower contributed to the war by the Dominion of South Africa, and its capture dealt a shattering blow to the already shaky solidarity of the Commonwealth worldwide.

Far from lessening the force of the blow, the many preparatory warnings about Tobruk made its dramatic but obviously inevitable fall all the more difficult for Churchill to swallow. He was only too well aware that he was personally very directly responsible for the scale of the debacle. In his heart of hearts he well knew that he had almost unilaterally decided to ignore all the warnings, in the interest only of personal pride and a misguided view of press relations. From Washington, some 4,000 miles distant, he had tried to will the success of Tobruk's defenders, as if he could somehow create minefields, ditches, anti-tank guns and high fighting morale solely by the prodigious charismatic force of his thought-waves. In the case of Tobruk this technique had failed in the most signal and public manner possible, with the result that within himself Churchill knew that he should never have attempted it at all. It was he who had almost unilaterally overruled his military experts, and had thrown a major spanner into their plans by his last-minute insistence that Tobruk should be defended. He must secretly have seen himself as a man who demanded bricks to be made without straw, and who caused Eighth Army's smooth evacuation eastwards to be fatally disrupted by a politically-motivated attempt to hold an untenable town merely because its name was known to the public.

When President Roosevelt tried to probe the inner mood of his distinguished guest a little further, he was nevertheless quickly met with an outward wall of optimism and reassurance. Churchill may have been suffering from personal turmoil and even guilt, but he had been active in public life for long enough to cover over such setbacks with the minimum of detectable consternation. Having made his acid observations on how closely Tobruk reminded him of Singapore, he moved back swiftly to the central business that had brought him to the Second Washington Conference in the first place, namely the vital plans for an early US amphibious landing somewhere within the German area of operations. The Americans and the Russians both wanted this to be in France, but to Churchill such an attempt appeared both premature and highly dangerous. His preference was for the landing to be made in Morocco and Algeria, as a means of hastening the complete conquest of North Africa. Once that had been achieved the whole 'soft underbelly' of southern Europe, east as well as west, would lie open to allied attack. Indeed, if it were not achieved, the awful news from Tobruk suggested that the whole British position in Egypt might itself be in dire jeopardy.

With considerable difficulty Churchill would eventually manage to secure American agreement for the landing in Algeria, but he was always acutely aware that his more urgent business had to be to stop the rot in the desert, and sooner rather than later. The developing news was far from reassuring. As early as 23 June the proposed Sollum position to cover the Egyptian frontier had been outflanked and abandoned without a fight, as General Neil Ritchie's battered Eighth Army determined instead to make its all-out stand at Mersa Matruh, some 120 waterless miles further to the rear. It was on this same day that Ritchie's immediate superior, General Claude Auchinleck, the Commander in Chief, Middle East (CinC ME), offered his resignation to General Sir Alan Brooke, the Chief of the Imperial General Staff. 'The Auk' by now had little confidence in either Ritchie or the Matruh plan, and he was acutely aware that this supposed 'coastal fortress' was no more than a dangerous cul-de-sac which could easily be bypassed on the landward side, and in which a large force could all too easily be imprisoned. It could boast a number of aging minefields and a plentiful infantry garrison, but its essential armoured back-up was hastily-assembled, badly-coordinated and – perhaps most importantly – weighed down by a crushing awareness of defeat at Gazala and the vast distances that had subsequently been covered in the retreat. Auchinleck knew that the responsibility for all the recent defeats ultimately rested on his own shoulders, and so he felt he should now ask for either an official endorsement of his position, or a replacement.

Auchinleck's letter arrived on Churchill's desk during the trickiest part of the American negotiations, so it was not perhaps accorded the full reflection that it deserved. What Churchill did know was that he had been mightily disappointed by the fall of Tobruk, and so he was psychologically ready to accept the offer of a new broom in the Middle East. Auchinleck's resignation was therefore duly accepted and General Sir Harold Alexander, who fortuitously happened to be on his way through Cairo on his way to the UK from India, was made CinC ME in his place. Alexander in turn dismissed Ritchie on 26 June, replacing him in the Eighth Army command by General W.H.E. 'Strafer' Gott, a veteran desert hand who was currently commanding XIII Corps outside Matruh.

The 'Alamein Line', Egypt

'Strafer' had an enviable and a bellicose fighting record – as indeed his nickname suggested – which extended back through the whole of the Libyan campaigning since the start of the war. He was in many ways the ideal saviour for the flagging Eighth Army and even, in his own solid British way, a warrior who sprang from much the same mould as Rommel himself. But by late June 1942 even his friends found Gott tired and mentally oppressed by defeat and by the scale of his responsibilities – he had, after all, risen from command of a brigade to that of an army corps within a short eight months. As a corps commander he had perhaps been promoted one rank above his competence, or at least above the arena in which his sense of aggressive manoeuvre could operate freely. Maybe it was simply that he had always enjoyed a certain brand of intermittent success when commanding a brigade or a division, but no such result had been accorded to him in the bruising Gazala battle, when he had commanded a corps.

In these circumstances Churchill's high hopes for his radical hand-over of command were not, alas, destined to be gratified. Alexander was still very new to the theatre, and essentially an infantry general coming from the relatively slow moving and tank-free warfare in the Burmese jungle, so he was still very much feeling his way in this totally novel mechanised environment. By contrast Gott, who had previously been holding the XIII Corps armour ready to strike from the inland flank, was a true armoured warrior, but he was fatally distracted at the critical moment in the battle. He found himself brusquely called into the coastal town of Matruh, introduced to a whole new staff and *modus operandi*, and in particular he was suddenly and disorientatingly invited to share in all the anxieties of W.G. Holmes's inexperienced, infantry-heavy X Corps. No good could possibly come from this mixture, and in the event Rommel's first spearhead of just 20 tanks in *21st Panzer Division* almost effortlessly managed to bluff the British (who had a total of over 150 tanks in the area) into a most precipitate and undignified withdrawal from the Matruh area. By the morning of 29 June, after 'a night of chaos', Gott's totally disorganised command had escaped eastwards out of the clutches of its heavily-outnumbered attackers, leaving behind some 6,000 prisoners and over 40 tanks. In strictly military terms this actually represented a far more shameful and humiliating outcome than the far bigger loss of Tobruk, which had been a politically-designed battle, fought against the advice of the soldiers.

The next supposedly 'impregnable' position east of Matruh was the El Alamein line, which was also the final defensible line before Cairo, Alexandria and the delta. It extended some 38 miles southwards from the railway station of Alamein, and it was noteworthy because – unlike all its predecessors at Gazala, Sollum or Matruh – it could not be turned by the inland, or desert, flank. The vast Quattara Depression prohibited the movement of armies south of the line, thereby giving the British a rare opportunity to stand firm and consolidate on a narrow front. It was known that Rommel was by now very short of fuel, water and armoured striking power, with a greatly extended line of communication that was under constant bombardment by the RAF. His men were exhausted, and driven forward solely by his own single-minded willpower. In essence Rommel knew that he would get only one honest shot at the Alamein position, after which – if he failed to break through – he would be doomed to an everlasting logistic deficiency in the face of a rapidly escalating British build-up. If he did succeed in carrying off the coup, by contrast, he would win through to the fabulously supply-rich Nile delta base area, and all his replenishment problems would be solved. Absolutely everything therefore depended on the speed with which the Germans could mount their assault, as compared to the skill with which Alexander and Gott could patch together their last-minute defences.

Unfortunately for the British, very little had been prepared on the ground at Alamein, where the famous 'line' existed only on maps, and the ground itself was often too rocky to allow the rapid digging of trenches. The position rested primarily on a fortified, well mined and partially-wired 'box', manned by 3rd South African Brigade with the battered remainder of 1st South African Division in rear. The box was anchored firmly on the coast and covered a radius of about four miles around the Alamein rail station. 6th New Zealand Brigade held a smaller box at Bab el Quattara, some 13 miles further south, although it had no minefield; and finally 9th Indian Brigade held a very poorly fortified position at Naqb Abu Dweis, perched on the rim of the Quattara Depression on the extreme left flank. In the wide gaps between these three firm points there was little more than a shifting population of disorganised units still coming in from the west, mixed with a mobile screen of light forces, including all that remained of the once mighty 7th Armoured Division. Also 18th Indian Brigade, newly-arrived from Iraq, was now digging in at Deir el Shein, half way between the Alamein and Bab el Quattara boxes. In the rear there was little more than the remainder of the New Zealand Division, the two demoralised tank brigades of 1st Armoured Division commanded by the (equally demoralised) Herbert Lumsden and then, scattered around Gott's new HQ at El Imayid, some hastily-assembling columns made up from the very numerous defeated and unorganised men whom Alexander did not want to continue their retreat any further back towards the delta. The new CinC ME was no less well aware than Rommel himself that the coming battle would be decisive for the whole theatre, and in order to help him win it, Alexander was particularly anxious to restore morale both at the front and in the rear areas, where rumours were spreading fast that further withdrawals were already being planned. His personal experience in both France and Burma had been in the management of humiliating retreats, and he was determined not to preside over yet another one now. He therefore cancelled all movement towards the rear, as well as all building of defences behind the front line, and issued a famously stark general order on the evening of 30 June which decreed that 'Alamein will be defended to the last. There will be no further retreat.'[2]

For his part Rommel instinctively, albeit recklessly, opted not to spend time in careful preparations or reconnaissance, but began his attack as soon as he could, at 03.00 on Wednesday 1 July – perhaps the most ominous of all anniversaries for the British Army.[3] He hoped to encircle the Alamein box with *90th Light Division*, while the main striking force, with 55 tanks, would advance level with it at first, but would then turn south to drive through the whole centre and rear of the British positions. It was an essentially sound and typically aggressive plan, but it soon became bogged

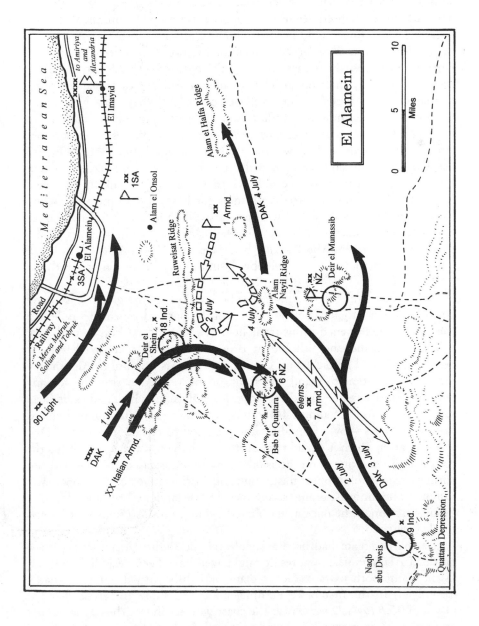

down by poor going and the unexpected discovery of 18th Indian Brigade directly in the path of the advancing *Deutsches Afrika Korps* (*DAK*) whose commander, General Walther Nehring, decided to make a frontal assault. This led to a fierce battle which continued throughout the day until the brave but inexperienced defence eventually succumbed before the Germans' overwhelming force and incomparable familiarity with desert combat tactics. Meanwhile *90th Light Division*, further north, received a rude shock when it encountered the massed fire of the entire South African divisional artillery and was pinned down. Then, while the Axis forces were attempting to maintain and replenish their vehicles overnight, they and their supply echelons were illuminated by flares and subjected to almost continuous bombing. On the credit side, however, Rommel was interested to note not only that the 'Alamein line' was not really a line at all, but that the British 1st Armoured Division had remained apparently supine and inactive all day. He was also gratified to receive news that the Mediterranean Fleet had shown prudence, not unmixed with indecent haste, by abruptly removing itself from Alexandria, which was now just 90 miles away from the most advanced Axis airstrips. Also on this day came news that the assault by *Second Panzer Army* in the Ukraine had caused the Russian front to break 'like glass under a hammer',[4] thereby posing a very major long term threat to the strategic rear of the British Middle East Command.

On his side Gott might admire and be grateful for the gallant last stand of 18th Indian Brigade, but he was seriously alarmed by the 13-mile gap that its fall had opened in his front line. His staff urged him to pull back 6th New Zealand and 9th Indian Brigades from the exposed left flank before they could be picked off in turn, but he was mindful of Alexander's firm determination to stand and fight, so he refused permission for any withdrawal. Instead he urged 1st Armoured Division, which had again been made up to a total of almost 150 tanks, to smash the *DAK* – now reduced to just 37 tanks – by a frontal assault designed to re-take the area of Deir el Shein, after which it would turn north to cut the coast road which fed the Axis rear. In making these decisions Gott demonstrated that he had not entirely lost his old opportunistic fighting instincts; yet by his apparently resigned and unquestioning acceptance of Alexander's brutally simplistic 'stand firm' order, he once again offered evidence to historians that he was tired. Very tired.

If a sharper team had been available to tide Eighth Army through the battle of Alamein, the final result might well have been very different, but in the event both parts of Gott's plan for 2 July turned out to be badly misjudged. In the first place Rommel made the shrewd analysis that the plight of *90th Light Division* near the coast was not in fact the key issue that at first sight it seemed. He was prepared to leave it without fuel and unsupported (except by the Italian *'Trento' Division*) as a 'gambit' to absorb the main attentions of the British artillery and reserves. Meanwhile he correctly identified the more southerly allied boxes as the true *Schwerpunkt*, so he sent most of the *DAK* and the remaining Italian forces against them. At the same time, in order to cover his centre and the continuing mopping-up at Deir el Shein, he left a strong force of infantry, artillery and anti-tank guns to hold that position. It was this force which successfully absorbed the eventual attack by Lumsden's 1st Armoured Division, while the *DAK*'s own armour completed the investment of the two infantry boxes at Bab el Quattara and Naqb Abu Dweis.

Lumsden committed the classic Eighth Army error of sending the tanks of 22nd Armoured Brigade forward against unsuppressed anti-tank guns, while his preliminary artillery barrage fell in the wrong place. The tanks were badly mauled and made no progress against the enemy position. Meanwhile 4th Armoured Brigade suffered from all the usual problems of soft sand and poor radio communication, together with a certain unacknowledged 'combat shyness', with the final result that it penetrated only a little way into the notional enemy 'front line', and failed to find any significant enemy force to attack. By the end of the day 1st Armoured Division had achieved practically nothing, but had seen its 150 tanks fall to a total of about 90, of which only one squadron was still operating the famous American Grants.

Meanwhile Nehring's *DAK*, with Rommel motoring at its head, had failed to overrun 6th New Zealand Brigade by its first attack on Bab el Quattara, but it had succeeded in surrounding and masking it with what remained of the *'Brescia' Division* and the Italian *XX Armoured Corps*. The German armour then pushed on relentlessly further to the south, and by a felicitous mixture of speed, surprise and shock action managed to pull off a brilliant *coup de main* against 9th Indian Brigade at Naqb Abu Dweis, which was overrun in classic style. By nightfall the *DAK* was encamped on the lip of the Quattara Depression and had effectively turned the flank of the Eighth Army's supposedly 'flankless' position. It had also destroyed or neutralised almost 40 per cent of the effective allied fighting strength and – still more precious to the new German field marshal – it had captured a large convoy of fuel wagons intact.

On the morning of 3 July Rommel again had his men up and moving early, heading northeast directly towards the rear elements of the New Zealand Division and the remnants of 7th Armoured Division. He was relieved to note that ever since he had moved inland away from the distinctive coast road, he was able to enjoy the anonymity of the trackless desert and could therefore be located far less readily by allied air power. As for the concentrated artillery that had stymied *90th Light Division* on the Alamein perimeter, it had remained stolidly in place, and only small mobile artillery columns remained in contact with the *DAK* itself; more a nuisance than a serious threat. The only stiff resistance that the Germans encountered in the day came from the New Zealand Division box at Deir el Munassib, which had to be surrounded, masked and immobilised in the same manner that 6th New Zealand Brigade had been on the previous day.

A significant part of its essential transport was cut off and destroyed, leaving its infantry stranded until such time as it could be relieved by the main British armoured striking force.

On the 'firework day' of 4 July the Germans were poised and ready to beat off precisely such a relief attempt. They had reorganised themselves and had set up an anti-tank ambush along the line of the prominent Alam Nayil ridge, which ran east to west on a line some four miles north of the beleaguered New Zealanders. With a horrible predictability Lumsden's armour duly arrived from the north around noon, and attacked directly into the sun. The result was a turkey shoot in which the 20 remaining German tanks did not really need to participate at all. The lurking 50mm and 88mm guns were quite sufficient to pick off over half the attackers before they retired back to the Ruweisat Ridge from which they had started, leaving only a few medical Dingoes and tracked carriers to pick up the wounded. At 16.00 Rommel ordered the pursuit to start, but not due north into the heavily-defended Ruweisat area. Instead, he would use his last fuel reserves to drive east-northeast to seize the crucial Alam el Halfa feature, which dominated the deep rear of the British and from which a shrewd artilleryman could even lob a 105mm shell straight onto Gott's HQ caravan at El Imayid. By nightfall all this had indeed been achieved, and to all intents and purposes the decisive Battle of Alamein had been won.

Alexandria, Egypt

While General Alexander was busy laying down his inflexible policy for fighting and dying in the front line – a doctrine that was, alas, all too literally obeyed – the news of Rommel's advances was spreading far, wide and fast throughout the Nile delta. Many Commonwealth civilians hastened to make their way out of the area: to Palestine, Khartoum or, most popular of all, to find a ship to South Africa from Suez. Equally the military authorities took a hard look at their policy for demolitions and the preparation of the delta area for defence. In view of Alexander's determination to fight only at Alamein, however, the official policy remained one of outward calm and 'business as usual'. Nothing was done to build additional pontoon bridges to assist the army's retreat, to fire demolitions or flood the salt pans around Alexandria to delay the enemy, nor even to dig defensive trenches across the coast road in the area of Amiriya. Such measures were deemed to be bad for morale, and it was morale-building that Alexander still saw as his main task. He also ordered an effort to be made to halt the civilian evacuations, although that could never be applied in more than a half-hearted way, and little noticeable effect was observed. Nor could anything be done about the Egyptian government, which was technically neutral and apparently ready to make its own separate peace with the invader. Axis flags began to be seen in the streets; prices started to rise, and there was a marked increase in backstreet attacks on Europeans.

In the port of Alexandria the naval authorities had always demanded regular updates on the motoring time between Rommel and themselves.[5] When he had arrived in front of Alamein it was set at 12 hours, rising to 18 hours when he was thought to be bogged down inland, engaging the New Zealanders and the British armour. Towards the end of 4 July, however, the news that he was on the Alam el Halfa ridge caused a sudden downward revision of the estimated time to just four hours. It was at that point that Admiral Sir Henry Harwood, CinC Mediterranean Fleet, told Alexander bluntly that he could maintain the 'business as usual' policy no longer, and that a programme of demolitions would have to be activated, regardless of the effect on morale, in order to prevent the base facilities and dockyards falling into enemy hands. They represented the most important naval installations in the whole of the Eastern Mediterranean, and could potentially be decisively valuable to both the powerful Italian fleet and its vital convoys supplying the Axis ground forces at the front. General Alexander was not yet ready to accept that the situation was sufficiently desperate for the docks to be destroyed, and pointed out that they would take many months to restore to working order, but he discovered that his personal authority was insufficient to overrule the fixed will of the Royal Navy which was, after all, the 'senior service'.

Alexandria's harbour was closed by blockships and its dockyards were dynamited during the fire-filled night of 4/5 July, which unfortunately coincided with the first real flood of fugitives coming in from the desert battle. They represented the start of yet another Eighth Army 'flap', or 'gold rush', which were the names given to a particular type of informal manoeuvre when all shapes and sizes of vehicles drove rapidly eastwards without any sort of order or organisation. Such events had become depressingly common in recent weeks, although this was the first occasion on which one of them had arrived as far to the east as the delta base area. It was no longer a private operation taking place in the open desert, witnessed only by other front-line troops. This time it was a public display in a built-up area, of what to the uninitiated looked very much like a blind panic. The effect on the civilian population, and on the equally large population of rear echelon base personnel, was electric. Mechanics and fitters who had previously been repairing vehicles to send forward towards Alamein, now jumped into them and started to motor eastwards to Port Said or southwards towards Cairo. Wherever they went, they spread rumours of chaos and defeat. Many subordinate officers took their own decisions to burn sensitive documents, initiate demolitions, or open sluices to create inundations as obstacles in the path of *Panzerarmee Afrika*. These measures also, of course, created obstacles to the retreating fugitives, and a series of gigantic traffic jams had built up by dawn. They could not possibly be missed by the routine *Luftwaffe* reconnaissance patrols, which duly called in successive waves of Stukas and Savoia-Marchettis, adding death and mayhem to the existing self-imposed destruction and panic.

On 5 July the RAF was still able to mobilise a strong screen of defensive fighters, operating comfortably within their own airspace almost directly above their base airfields. They exacted a heavy toll on the lumbering enemy bombers, with claims amounting to 18 definites and 11 possibles; although five of their own number were shot down by the ever-dangerous Messerschmitt 109s. This stalwart defence could not be maintained for long, however, since the RAF was already reviewing the vulnerability of its landing grounds in just the same way as the navy had already looked at its port facilities. An air redeployment to the canal zone and Palestine was initiated at 13.30, although much of its transport rapidly became mired in the general confusion of traffic and refugees, with the overall result that very many sorties were lost.

As for the army, 5 July was a day of which the New Zealanders would be justly proud, since they doggedly beat off a series of ferocious attempts to reduce their two boxes. Further to the rear events went much less well. Gott's Eighth Army HQ had been disrupted by shelling at dusk on the 4th, and had hastily removed itself further to the east, losing contact with many of its vehicles in the dark. It was not until 03.00 on Sunday 5 July[6] that Gott was able to issue his next set of army orders, which necessarily arrived too late for units to launch counter-attacks at dawn. In essence he wanted to concentrate all available armour, mobile forces and reserve columns against the *DAK* on Alam el Halfa ridge, but when Rommel launched his own attack first, the British columns were committed piecemeal and defeated in detail. By noon the Germans were firmly astride the coast road well to the rear of El Imayid, where they found extensive supply dumps. Yet again their fuel shortage was solved in the nick of time by courtesy of the British Empire. They also found a large mass of invaluable motor transport, not to mention a large park of partially-repaired tanks which the tireless DAK maintenance teams would quickly be able to restore to fighting order.

All allied formations further to the west were now effectively cut off, and faced with an unpalatable choice between surrender and attempting to slip through the lines of their besiegers. In every case the second option was preferred, and a series of fighting breakouts was launched soon after darkness fell, but in many cases the attempt was unsuccessful. Many confused battles were fought during the night, with dawn on the 6th revealing that all the infantry boxes had been evacuated, but some 8,000 South Africans and New Zealanders had passed into captivity. The remainder were scattered all over the desert and moving in small groups, either on foot or on wheels, in the same general direction as the victorious German and Italian columns. At the head of the pack rode Rommel himself, now totally committed to a flat-out race to Alexandria, and safe in the knowledge that the RAF could no longer distinguish his ragged dust-caked vehicles from those of the Eighth Army. All were mixed together in an incoherent mass which normally seemed to be more worried by traffic congestion than with maintaining hostilities.

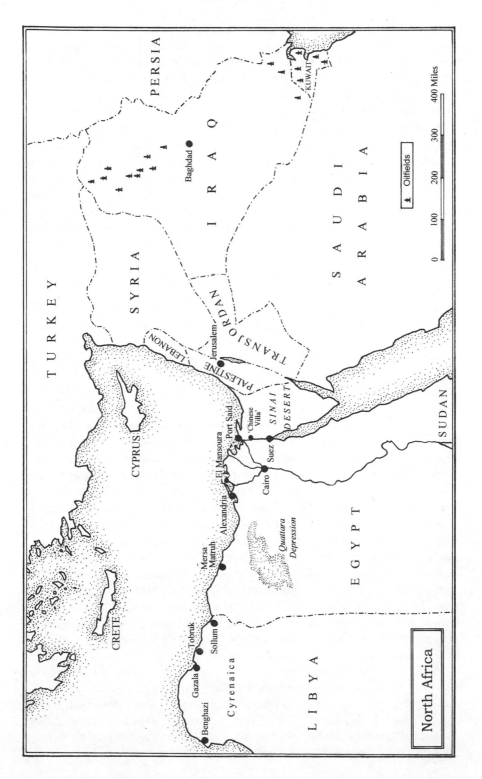

North Africa

The first truckloads of Panzergrenadiers entered the suburbs of Alexandria at 11.00, but encountered little organised opposition apart from what even the official history would call Brigadier A.H.L. Godfrey's 'motley force' around Amiriya. During the afternoon the Germans pushed on into the city centre, with a few sharp firefights but more normally a sullen acceptance of defeat by service personnel who had never really thought of themselves as front-line troops, let alone as cannon fodder. Beyond those there was an equally resigned acceptance among the local population, meticulously schooled by centuries of experience, of whichever rudely invading army happened to be passing through at the time. Meanwhile Gott was desperately trying to gather a coherent fighting force further inland, although he was seriously hampered by the catastrophic dispersion and confusion throughout his command. As for Alexander, he had returned to GHQ in Cairo to cope with a contingency that until then he had tried to deny was even a possibility.

Cairo, Egypt

Apart from Gott's remnants, what could still be rescued, now that Alexandria had fallen into enemy hands? There was actually a very substantial reserve scattered all around the area, with its more battle-worthy elements forming 'Delta Force', commanded by the same General Holmes who had failed to defend Mersa Matruh. Perhaps his most solid bastion was formed by General Sir Leslie Morshead's 9th Australian Division blocking the approaches to Cairo – ably reinforced by such distinguished warrior bands as an up-gunned Greek police battalion left over from Crete, a Basuto artillery regiment, and the GHQ 'Officer Cadet Training Unit' which was delighted to be excused lectures for the duration of the crisis. Also refitting in the same area were 50th Division and 10th Indian Division, both of which had been badly battered at Matruh. Behind these were many more units located in various camps along the canal, especially towards its southern end where new arrivals from overseas were groggily finding their bearings after disembarkation at the port of Suez. Among the more experienced combat elements were 2nd and 8th Armoured Brigades, which were in the process of being composited from a number of shattered tank regiments; 161st Indian Motor Brigade, just in from Iraq, and a skeleton 2nd Free French Brigade Group. On paper there should have been the best part of 1,100 tanks, although only a very small percentage of these were in any state to fight, even if they had not already fallen into enemy hands around Alexandria.

Against all this Rommel was also receiving reinforcements of his own, not least in the shape of captured British fuel, guns, tanks, and an esoteric variety of specialist equipments ranging from experimental mine flails to the much-admired 'Mammoth' armoured command vehicles. Some 2,000 individual German reinforcements were airlifted in from Crete by 5 July, soon to be followed by *164th Light 'Afrika' Division* and then, towards the end of the month, the *'Ramcke' Paratroop Brigade* – which was surely as happy to have been spared the dangerous task of jumping onto Malta as Rommel was happy to add them to his own order of battle in Egypt. All these were accompanied by an even greater number of Italian reinforcements, not least the *'Folgore' Parachute Division*, also relieved from duty in Malta, as well as the pre-eminent figure of Il Duce himself. Benito Mussolini had been hovering in Cyrenaica since 29 June, complete with a handsome white horse and appropriately imperial trappings, and he now came forward to El Imayid in readiness for the final triumphal entry into Cairo. However, he quickly fell into a blazing argument with Rommel when the Desert Fox let slip that he had no intention of going to Cairo at all, but was going to let it 'wither on the vine' while he pushed on eastwards to Port Said. The German staff analysis was that the British had concentrated their strongest defensive position around the militarily irrelevant capital city, thereby leaving proportionally less to cover the vital high road into Asia. There would thus be no new 'battle of the Pyramids', but a far more telling strategic thrust across the canal and then – who could tell? – onwards to link hands with the victorious German armies coming through southern Russia. As always the Italian objections were quickly overruled by reference back to Hitler, and Mussolini had to rest content with an almost-triumphant parade through Alexandria, after which he took himself away to Rome in a very angry mood.

Not even Rommel, however, was ready to continue his eastwards thrust immediately after such a breathless gallop from Gazala to the Nile. He was now ready for a logistic pause to digest his prizes, gather his forces and study his next move. In particular he needed to bring forward the infrastructure of his air force, in the hope of regaining local parity with the RAF and hence a greater level of security for the vital sea supply lanes from Italy. He also now found a need for one item that had been distinctly unnecessary in the arid wastes of the western desert, namely a pontoon train for crossing the branches of the Nile, and the Suez Canal itself. His engineers set about collecting small boats that could be put to this use, and won an unexpected golden bonus when they discovered a large store of British bridging material hidden amidst the almost endless warren of base facilities in the region of Amiriya.

Meanwhile General Alexander had at last abandoned his reluctance to contemplate further retreats, and had ordered hasty staff studies for a double withdrawal: northeastwards into Palestine, and southwards up the Nile towards the Sudan. A major difficulty was that the two routes were divergent and would split the army in the face of a centrally-positioned enemy, but it had to be accepted that the basic geography of Egypt nevertheless made such an outcome inevitable. The really awkward political dilemma was to know which of the two lines of retreat should be given the main priority. In the Mehemet Ali Club in Cairo the overwhelming opinion was naturally strongly in favour of concentrating maximum effort on the defence of Cairo itself, which was considered to be the real jewel in the crown of the British Empire in the Middle East. By contrast, in Alexander's HQ, and beyond that in Whitehall and Downing Street, the main concern was centred on the oilfields of Iraq. Not only was the oil vital to the British war effort, but the Axis powers were known to be suffering badly from an acute oil shortage. It would therefore not be too much to predict that the side which ended in possession of Iraq would also be the side which won the war.

In the event Alexander believed he could fight on both fronts equally, especially since Churchill kept reminding him that he had two thirds of a million men and '1,100 tanks' under his command, whereas the Axis troops in Alexandria could not have numbered many more than 10,000 men and were last seen running only the proverbial '20 tanks'. Everyone at GHQ was confident that a solid defence on all fronts was perfectly feasible, especially since it was estimated that Rommel could not resume his advance before mid-August at the earliest. Signals intercepts revealed that his scheduled reinforcements would not all have arrived until about that time, and so it was assumed that he would not dare to attack until they had all been fully incorporated in his force. Plans were duly made for a pre-emptive counter-attack upon him with four armoured brigades, to be launched on 5 August, under the codename 'Operation Locust'.[7] It was only a troublesome group of pessimistic desert veterans, led by Gott himself, who rocked the boat by pointing out how often in the past GHQ had made bad overestimates of the time Rommel would need to regroup. Alexander, who had not personally experienced those occasions, replied that optimism and belief in victory were the key requirements at this delicate phase. The preparations continued according to the GHQ timetable, regardless of Gott's objections.

Sure enough, however, Rommel did strike first, on the night of 27–28 July, in Operation *Zauberteppich* ('Magic Carpet'). Parties of *'Ramcke'* and *'Folgore'* paratroops took the lead, in what was the first major operational night drop of the war. They unrolled an 'airborne carpet' eastwards across the various waterways and branches of the Nile, similar to the one that had been unrolled in Holland in 1940 over the Maas, Waal and Lek. This concept involved seizing key bridges before they could be blown, or key crossing points where they had been, and then holding onto them tenaciously until a heavy spearhead of *15th Panzer Division*, with combat engineers well forward, could arrive overland and either cross directly or lay a pontoon bridge. It was judged too ambitious to attempt a drive all the way through to the Suez Canal itself, 100 miles distant, which might have been 'a bridge too far'. Even without that the operation was already very ambitious, and frankly lucky to succeed as well as it did. All key objectives were secured by the paratroops soon after dawn; the British were visibly taken by surprise; and the remainder of the airborne carpet had been fully unrolled by the evening of 28 July. Then came the battle of the bridgehead (officially known as 'The Battle of the Nile Delta'), as Rommel hastened to consolidate his winnings against counter-attacks and also, still more important, to rush forward the main body of the *DAK*, now respectably rebuilt to a tank strength of 190. Almost half of the tanks were captured Matildas, Grants and Valentines, which were the only British types considered worth running. Meanwhile, Rommel had strengthened his defences south and west of Alexandria with a line of Italian infantry positions stiffened by *Luftwaffe* anti-aircraft units manning the remarkably large total of 36 British 3.7-inch anti-aircraft guns that had been captured. These guns were actually ballistically superior to the equivalent German 88mm piece, but it had always been a tenet of British belief that they were best used to protect the Alexandria naval base and airfields against air attack, rather than to go out hunting Panzers in the desert. Now that he had captured Alexandria's stock of 3.7s, however, Rommel was easily able to convert them for use against tank attack, in the habitual German manner.

July 29 was a day of heavy battle, but the unexpected timing, direction and speed of the attack had caught the British armour dispersed and unprepared. As so often in the past, it came in uncoordinated and piecemeal, suffering all the disadvantages of being forced into a tactical offensive after the Germans had grabbed the operational initiative. The newly-arrived 23rd Armoured Brigade put up a particularly disappointing performance when it attempted to attack Alexandria from the west, and fell foul of a well organised *Pakfront*. The Australian infantry and artillery which tried to follow up by seizing Amiriya during the following night fared considerably better, but were eventually pinned down and forced to withdraw next morning, when the *'Ariete' Armoured Division* threatened a counter-attack. Nearer to the *Schwerpunkt* around El Mansoura, some 60 miles further to the east, rather better results were achieved by 2nd and 8th Armoured Brigades, supported by the Free French Brigade. They too were eventually ground down by the concentrated might of the *DAK*, but not without a hard fight during which Rommel twice believed he would have to retreat. As for 1st Armoured Division, it scarcely managed to engage at all, and scatological opinions over who should take the blame varied colourfully between 'badly trained junior officers', Lumsden, Gott and even Alexander himself.

Into Asia

After the battle of the Nile Delta, Rommel paused briefly to reassemble his forces and bridging pontoons, before he was ready to strike onwards across the Suez Canal. He always had to guard against fresh attacks from the Cairo flank to his south, which absorbed a large proportion of his available infantry and artillery, but this still left him with the core of the *DAK* available for mobile operations towards the east. He selected a suitable bridging point about 35 miles south of Port Said, between El Quantara and Ismailia, and prepared a formal 'river-crossing' operation according to all the classical rules of military science. Nevertheless he now believed that he had finally broken the backbone of the opposition, and resistance would gradually but inevitably collapse, provided that he could continue to maintain a high level of onward pressure.

The crossing went ahead smoothly on the night of 7/8 August, following an extensive bombardment from artillery, tank guns and bombers. The front line troops established their bridgehead without difficulty on the Asian side, but they were fascinated to find that the 'opposition' had (perhaps appropriately) consisted of no more than a colony of unarmed Chinese labourers employed by the canal company, whose distinctively-decorated barrack block was immediately nicknamed 'Chinese Villa' – a name that has subsequently come to designate the battle as a whole.

Once the Germans were across the canal, they immediately sensed that the military threat to them had dramatically lightened. They were loose in a new continent, and free to roam north and south, to surround the naval base at Port Said from the east, and pick off the many dispersed outposts of canal defence troops at will. Provoking particular amusement was the discovery of a squadron of tracked and armoured 'canal defence lights' which had apparently been designed by the respected British tank expert (and friend of Adolf Hitler) J.F.C. Fuller, but which on close inspection turned out to be militarily useless, and actually laughable. Their chassis were immediately stripped of their innocuous searchlights, and converted to carry more lethal cargoes such as mortars and anti-tank guns instead.

By this time the level of moral supremacy enjoyed by the Germans had risen by several vital pegs. The trickle of civilian refugees hastening out of Cairo had grown to a flood. The docks at Suez had become permanently choked with traffic, and the Egyptian population was increasingly releasing its hitherto repressed hostility to the British. In the air the RAF was still capable of winning some spectacular victories, but in general its fighting efficiency was wilting away, day by day. The loss of the Alexandria base area had been a fatal blow to the continuity and coherence of air operations, and the atmosphere of crisis around Cairo had produced many further problems. It is true that all the military HQs continued to operate calmly and professionally, but after the failure of so many of their battle plans, they could not avoid a deeply frustrating feeling that, although they always seemed to be getting something wrong, they were quite incapable of working out exactly what it was. The mood in GHQ was sombre, and even Alexander's confidence and the knowledge that major reinforcements were on the way – including 300 of the latest Sherman tanks from the USA – could not convince them that the best future plan was a successful offensive to the north rather than a humiliating retreat to the south.

In these circumstances Rommel found he was well able to hold Eighth Army and the Cairo command in check, at the same time as the *DAK* crossed the Sinai desert and made daring new thrusts deep into the effectively undefended Ninth Army area in Palestine. His armoured spearheads managed to enter Jerusalem as early as 15 August, despite a spirited (albeit incongruously multi-faith) resistance offered by compositied elements of the Arab Legion, the Jewish Haganah, a brigade of Indian infantry, and squads of the British Palestine Police Force, who hailed mainly from the Presbyterian quarters of central Belfast. However, all attempts at defence ultimately proved to be in vain, and the city had fallen entirely under Axis control by dusk the following day. Rommel was then able to make another logistic pause, consolidating his forces and extending his hold over the surrounding areas, during which he was gratified to receive additional air, infantry and logistic reinforcements from Germany – but considerably less amused to learn that a special *SS* detachment was also being sent to 'help him with Jewish relations'.

It was perhaps no accident that the Axis pause during late August coincided with some major Allied re-evaluations. In the first place Churchill's proposed visit to Moscow, intended to consolidate inter-allied relations, was brusquely cancelled by Stalin, who was disgusted that the British could apparently no longer guarantee his southern flank – nor even the flow of Lend-Lease supplies through Persia. Historians have often suggested that this was the decisive moment when to all intents and purposes the Second World War was lost by the allies.

Secondly the Anglo-American armada destined to arrive in Morocco and Algeria in November had to be radically re-jigged, since it was now obvious that North Africa had become a definitively Axis-controlled zone. Apart from anything else, it was known that the Germans had seized secret files in Alexandria which revealed the whole plan, with the result that any idea of surprise had been lost. Half of the invasion flotilla was therefore re-routed to Britain, to increase the invasion forces preparing to invade France in some indeterminate future; while the other half, including Eisenhower's and Patton's tactical HQs, was sent by the long sea route via South Africa to Suez. The intention was for these forces to turn the tide in Egypt – but alas by the time they arrived there the whole situation had taken a serious turn for the worse, and they had to be forwarded yet again – this time to Burma, where their arrival was mirthfully hailed as a near-circumnavigation of the globe.

The final act in the Middle Eastern drama began in early September, when the *DAK* again lunged forward, this time against General 'Jumbo' Maitland Wilson's Tenth Army in Iraq. Once again it encountered a defensive force that was morally enthusiastic but institutionally disorganised and badly co-ordinated. The 31st Indian Armoured Division, for example, ought to have put up a gallant resistance, except for the inconvenient fact that it possessed no actual tanks. Equally the individual infantry battalions of XXI Indian Corps each fought well, but there were no corps troops or central artillery reserve to support them, and no coherent defensive plan sufficient to cope with the scale and shock of the German onslaught. Even so it became a hard and gruelling campaign, concluded only on 23 October, when Field Marshal Erwin Rommel was finally able to send his decisive last telegram to Berlin that stated: 'Baghdad & all oil fields now in hands *Panzerarmee Afrika.*'

Within the hour he was at long long last free to relax, and to board a plane home for two months' well-earned leave with his dear wife Lu.

The reality

All the military events that I have recounted up to and including 1 July occurred exactly as described, with the single exception of the high command arrangements on the British side. Auchinleck's offer of resignation on 23 June was not in fact accepted, so Alexander was left free to continue his onward journey to Britain. Auchinleck then took personal command of Eighth Army and fought a highly flexible but ultimately successful defensive battle at Alamein, only to be sacked on 8 August after he had failed to convert that significant victory into a successful counter-offensive. Auchinleck's reputation was tainted by the suspicion that his 'flexibility' had meant he was ready to continue the retreat not only back to Cairo and even – and this was the particularly shocking thing to the lounge lizards at the Gezira tennis club – that he was ready to abandon Cairo itself. He had tolerated the mass burning of secret documents on 'Ash Wednesday', 1 July, in a way that suggested a readiness to evacuate, and it helped generate panic. Therefore when Alexander was made CinC ME in August, he had to make it clear that there would be 'no more retreats', and many regretted that this had not been spelled out much earlier. As for Strafer Gott, he was designated to take over Eighth Army at the same time, but his Bombay aircraft was shot down and he was killed before he could take up the post, which then fell to one of Brooke's self-important cronies from England.

From 2 July onwards the real First Battle of Alamein was fought very differently from my fictitious description. I have let Rommel win it by turning south against two exposed British brigade boxes, whereas in reality both of those brigades had already been withdrawn further to the east, as a result of Auchinleck's realism and readiness to manoeuvre. Rommel was actually defeated when he reinforced failure by turning to help *90th Light Division* in the north. However, if Alexander had been in charge, instead of the Auk, we may speculate that British tenure of the front line would have been rigid and unbending, out of a misplaced and potentially disastrous belief in the later revisionist Eighth Army propaganda line that Auchinleck's willingness to contemplate a further retreat was corrosive of morale throughout Egypt and all the military forces.

Bibliography

Agar-Hamilton, J.A.I., and Turner, L.C.F., *Crisis in the Desert, May–June 1942* (Oxford UP, Cape Town, 1952)

Barnett, Correlli, *The Desert Generals* (Kimber, London, 1960).

Greacen, Lavinia, *Chink, a Biography* (Macmillan, London, 1989). 'Chink' was the nickname of Gen Eric Dorman-Smith, one of Auchinleck's staff officers.

Mellenthin, F.W. von, *Panzer Battles* (trans Betzler, Cassell, London, 1955 and Oklahoma University 1956: Futura edn, London, 1977).

Neillands, Robin, *The Desert Rats, 7th Armoured Division 1940–45* (first published 1991, Orion edn., London, 1995).

Nicolson, N., *Alex, The life of Field Marshal Earl Alexander of Tunis* (Weidenfeld & Nicolson, London, 1973).

Playfair, I.S.O., *et al.*, *The Mediterranean and Middle East*, Volume 3, *British fortunes reach their lowest ebb* (UK Official History, HMSO, London, 1960).

Richardson, Charles, *Flashback, A soldier's story* (Kimber, London, 1985).

Rommel, E., *The Rommel Papers* (first published 1950 as *Krieg ohne Hass*: English translation ed. B.H. Liddell Hart, Collins, London, 1953).

Schmidt, H.W., *With Rommel in the Desert* (Harrap, London, 1951).

Notes

1. 'If Egypt had fallen, the hinge of three continents would have snapped', Nicolson, *Alex*, p. 152.
2. Quotation taken from Nicolson's summary of the Alexander/Montgomery view in late August, *ibid.*, p. 158.
3. On 1 July 1916 the British Fourth Army on the Somme had suffered 58,000 casualties killed and wounded in less than a day.
4. Barnett, *The Desert Generals*, p. 198.
5. The daily 'WC' reports, sent from 20 July onwards, Richardson, *Flashback*, p. 104.
*6. The day would become popularly known as 'Palm Sunday', from the many hands that began to be raised to the sky in surrender, although in statistical fact far more prisoners would be captured on the following day, Monday 6th.
*7. The codename 'Locust' was the inspiration of some bright spark from GHQ who had read his Bible around Exodus 10, shortly after dining well in Shepheard's Hotel.

6
INTO THE CAUCASUS
The Turkish Attack
on Russia, 1942

John H. Gill

East Prussia, early 1942

For many inhabitants of the *Wolfsschanze*, the military situation in early 1942 was as bleak as the view through the narrow windows of Hitler's East Prussian headquarters. Although Field Marshal Erwin Rommel had regained much lost ground in the Western Desert with his surprise offensive in January and U-boats were rampaging up and down the coast of the United States in Operation Drum Beat (*Paukenschlag*), the appalling developments on the Eastern Front cast an almost impenetrable gloom over the Führer's staff. The gargantuan undertaking had opened with high hopes – 'the world will hold its breath!' their leader had declared – and fabulous successes that had carried the *Wehrmacht* to the very gates of Moscow. The fighting over the winter of 1941–42, however, brought an abrupt crash from the heights of euphoria.

In addition to the dramatic retreats and the severe blows to the army's prestige and confidence, ten months of war with the Soviet Union had inflicted staggering losses in men and material. Among other problems, a March 1942 study prepared by the *Army High Command* (*OKH*), highlighted the loss of nearly 7,000 artillery pieces of all calibres, 75,000 motor transport vehicles and more than 179,000 horses, as well as the expenditure of huge amounts of motor fuel and ammunition. None of these deficits could be repaired in the weeks before the expected summer offensive.

The *Wehrmacht*'s manpower shortages were even more acute. In terms of numbers of divisions, the army hoped that its order of battle for June 1942 would exceed that of June 1941 by a count of 11 more infantry and three more Panzer divisions. But this represented only an illusion of improvement. Despite the provision of 1.1 million replacements to the Eastern Front since June 1941, the three army groups facing the Russians would still be short 625,000 men when May 1942 arrived. There would not be enough men to create reserves for the front and many of the new soldiers would be young recruits with less training than had previously been considered mandatory. Naturally, the losses during the winter also meant that experienced leadership in the commissioned and non-commissioned officer ranks would be far below the army's needs. Confronted with these daunting statistics, it is little wonder that many of Hitler's advisors regarded the coming summer with more foreboding than optimism.[1]

'The Russian is dead'

If some looked fearfully at the future, the Führer remained confident. Though aware of the *Wehrmacht*'s deficiencies and the limitations of German resources, Hitler was convinced that his foe was in even worse condition. Haranguing the German people on 15 March 1942, he told his listeners that 'the Bolshevik hordes, which were unable to defeat the German soldiers and their allies this winter, will be beaten by us into annihilation this coming summer!' These sentiments were not simply for public consumption. He related tales of starvation, even cannibalism, in the Soviet Union to Josef Goebbels on 26 April in private conversation and spoke of the miserable equipment found on captured Red Army troops as evidence of Russia's desperate condition.[2] He told his military advisors simply that 'the Russian is dead', and Germany's generals began to assume with Colonel General Franz Halder, the Chief of Staff at *OKH*, that 'although we are weak, the enemy is presently far worse off than we are.'[3]

Hitler fully intended to exploit this presumed Soviet weakness in the coming summer, but the *Wehrmacht*'s condition, and to a lesser extent the *Luftwaffe*'s, meant that German forces would only be able to strike in a few select sectors of the Eastern Front. There was never any serious consideration given to shifting the Reich's emphasis to another part of Europe. Psychological considerations alone demanded that Germany retain the initiative in the war and no one wanted to allow Russia a respite to recover its strength. Moreover, it was recognised that the entry of the United States into the war, though welcomed with cheers in the *Wolfsschanze*, would mean a second front somewhere on the continent no later than mid-1943. From a grand strategic perspective, therefore, the naval war against the 'Anglo-Saxon Powers' would continue to receive high priority, and defences on the European mainland would be built up to resist the eventual invasion, but the assault on Malta was deferred and Rommel would have to make do with little more than what he had on hand. The East would remain the principal focus of German attention and resources.

If the overwhelming importance of the war with Russia was blindingly obvious in Hitler's view, the strategic imperatives across that enormous front were no less clear. On the northern flank, a secondary offensive would capture Leningrad, establish a land route to Finland and threaten the Soviet link to the West through Murmansk. In the south, the *Schwerpunkt* of the 1942 summer offensive would be a drive across the Don to deny Russia the use of the Volga as a supply route and to seize the oil fields of the Caucasus.

With these facilities in hand by the autumn of 1942, Germany would secure its own access to vital oil supplies while simultaneously depriving the USSR of this key resource. In conjunction with the effort towards Murmansk, the thrust toward the Caucasus would also impede the flow of US and British supplies to the Soviets. German planners further hoped to cripple the Red Army during the course of the offensive, scooping up hundreds of thousands of prisoners as they swept toward the distant mountains. With Caucasus oil in hand, a secure connection to the Finns and the Russian Army in collapse, Germany could await the winter and Anglo-American attacks with confidence even if the USSR remained temporarily in the war. The great contest would thus be decided in the East, because, as Hitler himself admitted, 'If I don't get the oil of Maykop and Groznyy, then I must finish this war.' But he was confident as the summer approached, telling the Italian ambassador, 'it can therefore in no way become worse for us, but only better.'[4]

Hitler's vision, however, was not confined by the borders of the Soviet Union. Having conquered the Caucasus, German forces from Russia would be poised to deal a perhaps mortal blow to British and American hopes by combining with Rommel in a gigantic pincer movement designed to seize the Suez Canal as well as the oil fields of Iran and Iraq. This enticing prospect, already shimmering before his eyes in the heady days of 1941, became all the more alluring with Japan's entry into the war and its stunning victories in Malaya and Singapore. Underestimating Britain's resolve and overestimating Japan's capabilities, the Führer began to imagine a German triumph in the Middle East that would unhinge Allied strategy, pose a direct threat to India and, combined with the unrelenting pressure of the U-boat campaign, perhaps bring Britain to negotiate on Hitler's terms. 'At all costs we must descend into the Mesopotamian plains and take the oil of Mosul away from the English', he told his staff, 'then the entire war will end.'[5]

'The transition of Turkey into our camp'

The paucity of German resources, however, clearly meant that these ambitious goals could only be accomplished with the more or less willing cooperation of Berlin's allies. As German power secretly began to assemble in southern Russia for Operation Blue, the code name of the summer offensive, Hitler launched a diplomatic offensive to coerce his Axis partners into greater exertions on behalf of the supposedly common cause. He was surprisingly successful with Romania, Hungary and Italy, each of whom committed thousands of its soldiers to the great endeavour. Bulgaria, a Russophile state in German eyes, was able to evade any involvement at the front, but its army was usefully employed in guarding against Russian landings on the Black Sea coast and in a sizable proportion of the onerous occupation duties in Yugoslavia.

Though generally successful in his negotiations with his treaty allies,

Hitler faced a much greater challenge in convincing the other key 'flanking power', Turkey, to join the Axis. For the military planners in the *Wolfsschanze* and Foreign Minister Ribbentrop's diplomats, Turkey represented a potentially invaluable asset in the struggle for the Middle East. During the 1941 Balkans campaign, the *Armed Forces High Command* (*OKW*) had considered attacking Turkey as a launching pad for further operations against the British position in Palestine and Iraq. However, the prospect of assaulting a natural fortress defended by an army of renowned fighting qualities in what General Alfred Jodl was certain would be a 'protracted campaign' was decidedly unappealing. Instead, the Germans chose to respect Turkish neutrality while keeping a contingency occupation plan on the shelf and holding the Bulgarian Army in defensive readiness should Turkey join the Allies.[6]

The approach to Ankara was not new. While over-running the Balkans and preparing for Operation Barbarossa in 1941, Berlin began what proved to be an extended diplomatic effort to persuade Turkey to side with the Axis as an active belligerent. In the chaotic Nazi state, however, the actions of the various government organs were not always well coordinated. Ribbentrop's arrogance and crude threats, for instance, were seldom orchestrated with Ambassador Franz von Papen's smooth diplomacy or Goebbels' widespread pro-German, anti-Soviet propaganda. A member of Papen's staff, for example, defused a potential crisis by buying up Turkish phrase books for German soldiers (*Türkisches Soldaten-Wörterbuch für den Feldgebrauch*) which the propaganda minister had had distributed to Istanbul book stalls as an unsubtle reminder of German power.[7] Nonetheless, the combined effect favoured Berlin. In an especially well-received measure, the Führer wrote a personal letter to Turkish President Ismet Inönü recalling the comradeship of the First World War, the common interest in reducing British influence in the Mediterranean and the shared concerns about the USSR. These efforts culminated in a treaty of friendship signed by the unsuspecting Turks on 18 June 1941, only four days before the invasion of Russia.

Perhaps most important, however, was an autumn 1941 visit to the Russian Front arranged for Colonel General Ali Fuat Erden and a group of senior officers when the *Wehrmacht* was at the height of its apparently victorious progress. Returning with vivid impressions of Germany's military might and the swift violence of modern war, Erden met with Inönü and other national leaders for six hours to discuss his tour and Turkey's future.[8]

Ankara, however, remained noncommittal. Although the brightest mind in the Foreign Ministry, Numan Menemencioglu, was inclined toward Germany, the Foreign Minister, Sükrü Saracoglu, favoured the West and Marshal Fevzi Cakmak, the Chief of the Army Staff, feared that, after the Soviet Union, Turkey would be Nazi regime's next victim. With Inönü undecided, Hitler ordered preparation of a plan to rearrange the constellation of political power in Ankara to suit Berlin's purposes better.

In the spring of 1942, as thousands of Axis troops were assembling in southern Russia for Operation Blue, German pressure on the Turks increased. In addition to a 'leading place in the Axis new order', Papen broadly hinted at important 'territorial rectifications' in favour of the Turkey in the event of actual alliance. He specifically mentioned parts of northern Syria, Mosul in Iraq, and 'adjustments' in the Dodecanese Islands and Thrace.[9] The German proposals excluded the key oil centres in the Caucasus, but left open the possibility of some Turkish acquisitions in this direction and in the Crimea as well. Even Cakmak, his aversion to the Germans notwithstanding, found the expansion into the Caucasus attractive. Such a move appealed to the pan-Turkic sentiments he shared with many of his fellow officers and represented a first step toward uniting all Turkic peoples of Central Asia under Ankara's guidance. Germany also undertook to provide modern weapons and training for the antiquated if courageous Turkish military and offered a *Wehrmacht* expeditionary corps to fight alongside their prospective allies. In return, Berlin expected a Turkish advance into the Caucasus from the south, pressure toward Syria, Iraq and Iran to tie down British forces, U-boat access to the Black Sea and sole rights to Turkey's chromite ore, key to the German armaments industry.

The Turkish president balked at these proposals. Despite Papen's diplomatic skill and the stunning German victory against the Soviet Kharkov offensive in May, Inönü remained adamant as the late June deadline for the start of Operation Blue approached. Hitler, furious, decided to have him removed. Code-named Case Gertrud, the German plan sought to oust Inönü by exploiting his negative image inside the army and by building on the pro-German and anti-Soviet propaganda of the preceding year.[10] As General Emir Erkilet, one of Erden's companions during the 1941 tour, told von Papen, 'participation in the war against Russia would be very popular in the army and in many sectors of the population.'[11]

Those involved in the coming coup were still plotting, however, when Operation Blue opened with a tremendous crash of artillery at 02.15 on 28 June. As the *Wehrmacht* armoured columns raced across the steppes, fruitlessly endeavouring to repeat their dramatic *Kesselschlacht* ('encirclement') triumphs of the previous year, the Germans and their Turkish co-conspirators in Ankara were favoured with an enormous piece of luck when Prime Minister Refik Saydam died on 9 July. Although Saydam had been a figurehead in the government, the pro-German faction used the temporary disruption cleverly to put Erkilet, an ardent pan-Turkist, in his place. Saracoglu was forced into retirement ten days later under the pretext that his hesitant stance would invite German wrath and deny Turkey its share in the spoils of war. The lure of Berlin's blandishments, the evident success of Operation Blue, Rommel's capture of Tobruk and Hitler's dark threat that 'Constantinople could share the fate of Birmingham and Coventry' pushed Inönü toward allegiance with Germany, but Allied appeals and his recognition that his country was not ready for war held him back.[12] Although von Papen assured Hitler that 'we can definitely and also very quickly find a treaty instrument preparing the transition of Turkey into our camp', tension dominated Ankara through that hot, dusty July as Inönü's decision hung in the balance.[13]

In the end, the decision was taken out of the president's hands. On 23 July, Rostov fell to the advancing Germans. Over the next several days, the *Wehrmacht*'s *Army Group A* poured south in a seemingly unstoppable drive toward the Caucasus. Erden, Erkilet, Menemencioglu, now Foreign Minister in Saracoglu's stead, and even Cakmak attempted to sway the president, but 'Inönü did not appear at all convinced.'[14] In a desperate atmosphere of mingled hope and fear, the generals and the Foreign Minister eased Inönü from power on 30 July and had him respectfully escorted to a coastal villa to 'recover his health'. The following day, they signed a secret treaty with Germany and prepared to take their country into the war.

'Not a war but a crusade'
Foreign Minister Menemencioglu was exultant on signing the alliance agreement. 'This is not a war but a crusade,' he told Papen at the small, tense reception held after the ceremony.[15] Others among the coup plotters had their doubts. Indeed, Turkey was not in a position to enter the fray immediately. Nor, for that matter, was Germany postured to provide the support Hitler and Papen had lavishly promised. Both sides thus agreed to delay announcing their agreement until military preparations could be completed.

The Turkish armed forces in 1942 were both an asset and a liability to the Axis cause. The army in particular was large and enjoyed a proven reputation for ferocity and endurance in combat. After several weeks of mobilisation, the Turks could plan on fielding at least 41 infantry or mountain divisions, three cavalry divisions and a weak armoured division as well as fortress garrisons and headquarters units for a total of more than one million men in arms. The Germans assessed this formidable force as capable of putting up tenacious resistance in defensive missions, especially in the rugged terrain of their homeland.

Wehrmacht officers, however, were much less sanguine about the ability of their new Turkish allies to conduct effective offensive operations. They had good reason to be concerned. Bravery aside, the army suffered from numerous shortfalls in modern training and equipment. 'A new era had dawned in warfare, but we were still teaching the rules of the First World War', one Turkish officer ruefully recalled, 'Our arms, tactics and techniques dated from that time.' Another lamented that, 'we had guns which had served at Verdun in the First War: naturally these were not arms to be proud of compared to the Panzers.'[16] Logistical support was especially weak. With inadequate fuel for its limited pool of motor vehicles, the army relied almost exclusively on animal transport trains loosely organised in caravan fashion. The lack of vehicles and the poor roads also restricted strategic mobility, a situation compounded by the huge deficiencies in the nation's rail system.

The air force and navy had even greater problems. Of the 300 available aircraft, only half could be considered modern and the pilots to fly them 'could at best only be rated as moderately skilled and with little ability to fly in bad weather', according to the British air attaché. British observers had similar comments about the navy: 'Judged by the standards of modern navies, however small, the condition of the fleet is far from satisfactory.'[17] Despite its five submarines, the Turkish Navy, therefore would do little to bolster Axis maritime strength in the Mediterranean. Much worse, from the German perspective, were the deficiencies in the air force, as these could only be overcome by a substantial commitment of scarce *Luftwaffe* assets to this remote and primitive theatre of operations.

Indeed, the *Luftwaffe* had posed the greatest objections to providing support to the Turks. Reichsmarschall Hermann Göring, however, promised that all difficulties would be overcome and expressed his confidence that most of the *Luftwaffe*'s problems would melt away once the *Wehrmacht*'s final push secured the oil of the Caucasus. His subordinates were appalled, but scrambled and scraped to find a few combat squadrons to deploy to Turkey. However, support to Rommel, the bombardment of Malta, and the defence of the Reich against growing RAF raids, not to mention the colossal war in the East, left little for this new task. Despite the Reichsmarschall's promise, his staff ultimately failed to meet their goal and had to resort to the dubious assertion that *Luftwaffe* planes operating out of Russia with *Army Group A* would provide air support to the offensive from Turkey.

Wehrmacht assistance to the southern thrust into the Caucasus, now named Operation Dessau, was more substantial. This took the form of the *97th* and *101st Jäger Divisions* under General Maximilian de Angelis' *XLIV Corps* from *Army Group A*. Though not true mountain formations, these two divisions had been especially prepared for operations in difficult terrain with limited logistical support. They had both 'proved their mettle in heavy fighting' on the Eastern Front and, as Hitler had already committed the only available mountain divisions to the German arm of the offensive into the Caucasus, the *97th* and *101st* were assigned to the expeditionary force for Turkey.[18] Based on Papen's optimistic reportage following Saydam's death, the corps was withdrawn from Operation Blue in mid-July and transported to the Crimea as *Training Command South* (*Lehrkommando Süd*). *Army Group A*'s commander, Field Marshal Wilhelm List, protested bitterly over the loss, but his pleas were unavailing. *OKH* opined that the pressure *XLIV Corps* and the Turks would create from the south would more than compensate for the absence of the two divisions from List's command. Furthermore, *OKH* promised that List would receive the three divisions of the Italian *Alpini Corps* by mid-August when his army group was expected to reach the mountains. List was hardly mollified, but while he argued in vain, the trains carrying the thinly-disguised *XLIV Corps* rattled south. The divisions had only a few days to refit and train for their new mission (including distribution of the newly-reprinted *Türkisches Soldaten-Wörterbuch für den Feldgebrauch*) before boarding ships for transit to Samsun on the Turkish coast.

As *XLIV Corps* was steaming across the Black Sea, the Turks were mobilising, consulting with an *OKW* staff delegation on plans, and bombarding Papen with requests for equipment, ammunition and fuel. The mobilisation process, though hampered by innumerable obstacles, proved relatively successful. By the end of August, most of the army's regular and reserve divisions were up to strength and fairly well organised. There were serious deficiencies, however, in equipment and training. The paucity of useful field artillery caused the gravest concern among the Turkish officers and their increasingly sceptical German partner, but some units still lacked rifles, mortars, and other basic gear as they headed for the frontier. The Germans delivered some arms, but most of these items were captured French or Soviet weapons that only provided marginal increases in Turkish combat capability. Their poor state of repair did little to foster Turkish–German amity. Fuel was one of the most significant problems, but in this area, too, the Germans, facing major fuel shortfalls themselves, could provide little immediate assistance. Ammunition was also in short supply. Compounding all of these difficulties was the miserable state of the logistic and transportation system. Even in cases where the material was on hand, it often proved impossible to distribute it in a timely and efficient manner to the units which were in need. The priority attached to movement of *XLIV Corps* and its supplies only exacerbated the transportation challenge for the Turks.

While commanders, logisticians and railway officials wrestled with the raising, deployment and supply of the Turkish Army and the German expeditionary corps, Marshal Cakmak and his German counterparts outlined the strategy for the coming offensive. Both sides agreed that the main thrust would be launched from north-eastern Turkey into the southern Caucasus. Two Turkish armies (*Second* and *Third* with 21 divisions) and *XLIV Corps* would attack on this front. The Turkish *Fourth* and *Fifth Armies* were assembling 15 divisions on the country's southern and eastern borders to keep the British from interfering in the main effort and to occupy key pieces of territory scheduled to fall under Ankara's control. To the annoyance of the Germans, the Turks insisted on retaining their *First Army*, including their fledgling armoured division, in the west. Though willing to ally with the Germans, the Turks were viscerally suspicious of the Italians and Bulgarians. They had no intention of denuding the Thracian frontier or the Aegean coast. Similarly, Cakmak issued secret oral orders to the commanders of the *Fourth* and *Fifth Armies* to refrain from overly aggressive action against the British. The shrewdly cautious marshal wanted to avoid unnecessarily provocative action against the Western Allies in case Erden's and Erkilet's faith in the inevitable future triumphs of Germany proved unfounded.

The Allies assemble

The mid-summer of 1942 was a grim time for the Allies. Among other worries, threats to Middle Eastern oil and the tenuous link to Russia through Iran seemed to be compounding just when German air and sea attacks forced the closing of the convoy route to Murmansk. In the Western Desert, Rommel had reached the El Alamein position on 30 June and costly British attacks through late July failed to dislodge him, while German forces driving south from Rostov had reached the northern fringes of the Caucasus and raised the Nazi banner on the highest peak in the range, the 18,481-foot Mt Elbrus, on 21 August. Though Hitler railed against the 'stupid mountaineers who should have been court-martialled', the extent of the German advance caused grave concern in London, Washington and Moscow. News of Turkey's actions added to the gloom. Although intelligence had yet to confirm Ankara's entry into the Axis, Turkish mobilisation could not be hidden entirely, and the transfer of ten divisions from Thrace to the east was a clear indicator of looming peril to 'the northern bastion of our position in the Middle East'.[19]

British intelligence had become convinced of the German 'concern to reach the Caucasus' as early as the autumn of 1941. This fear abated during the winter, but 'by August 1942 Whitehall's anxiety about the German danger to the Middle East', this time with active Turkish support, 'was again acute'.[20] Having occupied Syria, Iraq and, in conjunction with the Russians, most of Iran in 1941, the British should have been well positioned to assist their Soviet allies and repulse any thrust toward the Suez Canal or Abadan. Combat troops, however, were in short supply. Some could be released from homeland defence as the threat of a German invasion receded, but the demands of the fronts in Egypt and India could not be ignored. Nonetheless, by late summer 1942, Great Britain had assembled a force of eight British, Indian and Polish divisions under Tenth Army, with headquarters in Baghdad. The United States, constrained by its commitments to Operation Torch, was reluctant to offer ground troops, but did provide several desperately-needed fighter and bomber squadrons as well as crucial logistical help. Judging that a German drive through Baku into Iran posed the greatest danger, British and American leaders decided to concentrate their true strength in Tenth Army, leaving Syria covered by a thin screen of real units and a welter of false formations under the imposing title of Ninth Army.[21]

The Russians were no less concerned than the Western Allies. With the Red Army crumbling before the *Wehrmacht*, Stalin issued a draconian order declaring 'Not One Step Back!' in an effort to stem the German onslaught before it reached the Caucasus. This order, combined with command changes and a wealth of reinforcements, bolstered Soviet resistance appreciably and the German advance slowed. The Panzers continued to press, however, and the imminent entry of Turkey into the war created a tremendous strain on Soviet forces. The Turkish Army was clearly massing for an offensive and Russian border troops were already reporting that 'black partisans' were slipping over the mountainous frontier to foment unrest among Stalin's Turkic subjects and to conduct 'diversionary-terrorist operations on USSR territory'.[22] Faced with this growing crisis, Stalin had no choice but to release additional formations from the General Staff (Stavka) Reserve and to redeploy units from the occupation force in Iran. By late August, the Soviets were in the awkward situation of having the eight armies of the North Caucasus Front facing north against the depredations of the Germans while the Transcaucasus Front was gathering its five armies only 75 or 80 miles to the south to face the anticipated Turkish onslaught.

The roads to Baku

While the Allies scrambled and scraped to find troops to defend the vital oil fields, the Germans were encountering problems of their own in the drive south from Rostov. Lead elements of *Seventeenth Army* were pressing towards Novorossiysk and *First Panzer Army*'s spearheads were slowly approaching Groznyy, but critical fuel shortages and stiffening resistance retarded the offensive. Moreover, there simply were not enough combat units to cover *Army Group A*'s expanding sector. By late August, its 20 divisions were advancing across a 500-mile front with its two main axes of attack separated by more than 200 miles. Indeed, instead of gaining reinforcements, the army group was losing troops. The *Fourth Panzer Army* and almost all of *Army Group A*'s air support had already been drawn north toward Stalingrad and, much to Field Marshal List's disgust, the three Italian *Alpini* divisions that were to replace *XLIV Corps* were likewise diverted to support the effort against Stalingrad. As early as 21 August, the *OKW* staff noted that 'the Führer is angry because of the slow progress made in the crossing of the Caucasus', but Stalingrad remained Hitler's priority and he increasingly looked to Operation Dessau as the solution that 'would kick open the door to Allied oil.'[23] Anxious veterans of the previous Russian winter noticed, however, that snow was already falling in the upper reaches of the mountains at the end of August

The plan for Dessau was straightforward. The Axis main effort would be in the centre, where the German *XLIV Corps* and Turkish *III Corps* were concentrated under General de Angelis. In the first phase of the operation, the two *Jäger* divisions were to break through along the line of the railroad from Erzurum and capture Tiflis (Tbilisi), thereby severing the rail and pipeline connection from Baku to the Black Sea. If the fall of Tiflis did not suffice to cause a complete collapse of the Soviet position in the Caucasus, *XLIV Corps* would leave a Turkish garrison in the city and march east toward Baku in conjunction with *First Panzer Army*'s push from the north. On *XLIV Corps*' left, Turkish *III* and *IV Corps* of General Orbay's *Third Army* were to pry back the Russian defenders and head for the rail line to seal off the Soviet forces on the Black Sea coast. As a secondary mission, *Third Army* was to capture the important port of Batumi. Orbay assigned this task to his *X* and *XI Corps*, but hoped that this city would fall into Axis hands without major fighting once Tiflis was taken. Turkish *Second Army* under General Gürman was to protect the right flank of *XLIV Corps'* attack with one corps (*VIII*) while two others (*XII* and *XIII Corps*) advanced on Baku along the Russian–Iranian border. Gürman's *XVII Corps* had a defensive mission east of Lake Van where it tied in with *VII Corps* of *Fifth Army*. Though constrained by Cakmak's instructions, *Fifth Army* was directed to seize Mosul in Iraq and *Fourth Army* had orders to take Aleppo. The Turkish General Staff recognised that it was beyond their power to conquer Iraq or Syria, and they had selected these objectives in the hopes of controlling the Baghdad–Beirut railway and influencing post-war territorial arrangements.

Orders written and briefed, Operation Dessau opened with a short, carefully-planned artillery barrage just before sunrise on 2 September. With few heavy guns and limited ammunition, the Turks and Germans could not afford the sort of massive bombardment that had become the norm on the Eastern Front. Instead they used willing local agents to pinpoint Soviet positions for sharp initial shellings to demoralise the green Russian troops and to cover the advance of their own infantry. In the centre, *XLIV Corps* and Turkish *III Corps* were generally successful, pushing through often disorganised Russian defenders to gain several key terrain features in the first few days. Near the Black Sea coast, Turkish *Third Army* also achieved most of its initial objectives, infiltrating the Soviet lines with the help of sympathetic locals and overwhelming several critical defensive positions. Turkish *Second Army* on the far right, however, was less imaginative in its tactics and made little progress at first. Similarly, the attacks of the weaker *Fourth* and *Fifth Armies* were tentative and slow against light British resistance on the Syrian and Iraqi fronts.

These early actions set the pattern for the next several weeks. De Angelis, with his Germans and Turkish *III Corps* pushed steadily ahead for the Tiflis valley, despite the frustrations imposed by difficult terrain, bad weather and inadequate air support. Turkish *Second Army*, however, managed only limited gains. Its attacks were poorly conducted and it received almost no assistance from the scarce *Luftwaffe* assets or its own air force. Furthermore, the Soviet defenders in the newly-organised 71st and 72nd Armies knew the ground almost as well as the Turks and offered stubborn, effective resistance. Nonetheless, by the end of September, Turkish *VIII Corps* was firmly ensconced south of Lake Sevan and occupied a 35-mile deep corridor along the railroad toward Tabriz.

The surprise success was the *Third Army*'s attack on Batumi. Conceived as a diversionary move against a vulnerable objective, Orbay had only hoped to pin down Soviet reserves and draw attention away from the principal attacks further south. Turkish tactics were reminiscent of the First World War, but their thrust overwhelmed the Russian 47th Mountain Division. Recently re-raised in the Caucasus after being destroyed in the 1941 campaign, the division included many ethnic Turks who happily

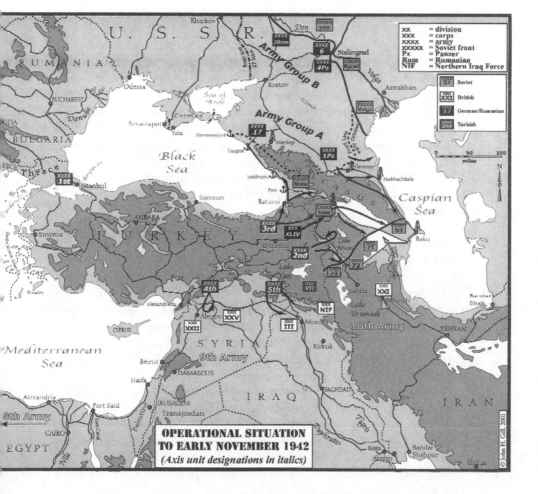

OPERATIONAL SITUATION
TO EARLY NOVEMBER 1942
(Axis unit designations in italics)

surrendered to their kinsmen at the first opportunity. As a result, *8th Division* of Turkish *X Corps* entered the outskirts of the city on 5 September to considerable jubilation in Ankara.

Unfortunately for the Turks, *8th Division* immediately ran into more determined opponents. A Soviet naval infantry brigade, supplemented by ships' crews and other hastily-assembled personnel, made each building a fortress while the Transcaucasus Front rushed in reinforcements and a new commander for 12th Army. The Turkish *8th Division* was quickly consumed and the *6th* and *16th Divisions* soon found themselves drawn into the maelstrom of Batumi, the 'Stalingrad on the Black Sea' as subsequent historians of 'the Great Patriotic War' have dubbed it. By the end of September, both sides were exhausted and the fighting temporarily degenerated into sniping and ugly skirmishes in the basements and alleyways of the ruined city. Efforts by Turkish *XI Corps* to cut off the city to the east and self-sacrificing assaults by some of the army's finest infantry battalions, however, eventually turned the tide and the city fell to the Turks in early October. Though costly for the Turks, the struggle for Batumi had also absorbed significant Soviet resources in manpower and munitions. As General Orbay bolstered *XI Corps* with units drawn from *IV Corps* and pushed north for Poti, therefore, he did so against an enemy that was rapidly approaching disintegration.

The loss of Batumi imperiled the entire Russian defence line to the north and only the exhaustion of the Turkish *Third Army* spared the Soviets an immediate catastrophe. With four of the North Caucasus Front's armies in danger of being cut off and the Black Sea Fleet threatened with extinction, Stalin, however, faced a crisis. The dire situation was compounded by *Army Group A*'s successes. Although *First Panzer Army* was stalled near Groznyy, the end of September saw *Seventeenth Army* finally overcome desperate Soviet opposition to capture Tuapse, trapping in the process more than 10,000 Russian Army and Navy personnel who had been unable to escape from the battle lines at Novorossiysk.

While the Turks and Germans hammered at Russian defences in the mountains, the Allies struggled to craft a coherent strategic response to this new threat. From the Kremlin's perspective, Stalingrad was the first priority, but as the crisis in the south developed, Stalin adjured his top military advisors 'don't forget the Caucasus front.'[24] The Soviet leader had no intention of abandoning the increasingly imperiled land link between the Black Sea and the Caspian. Beyond the loss of crucial oil resources and the destruction of the Black Sea Fleet, such a retreat would have dealt a grievous psychological blow to the nation and the army, while encouraging the USSR's many dissident populations. Moreover, it was by no means clear that the forces currently engaged could even be evacuated. Instead of retreating, Stalin therefore dispatched as many reinforcements from the Stavka Reserve as the requirements of the Stalingrad struggle and limited transportation capacity would permit. Units from central Asia and the

Soviet occupation forces in Iran were also added, boosting combat power but stretching logistic support, especially for the formations facing the *First Panzer Army*. Of particular importance was the arrival of the 53rd Army, assigned the task of preparing emplacements for a final defence of Baku as its sister army, the 58th, was to hold Makhachkala to the north.

Most sinister of the reinforcements were the numerous detachments of the notorious internal security troops (NKVD) and Lavrenti Beria himself, the chief of the secret police. With ruthless efficiency, Beria expunged any hint of anti-Soviet sentiment in the rear areas and, by his very presence, served as a menacing reminder to commanders of the consequences should they be perceived to fail in their duties. His intervention, however, was only partially successful. Where Soviet control remained, discontent was indeed contained, but the ethnic Turkic peoples became an important source of Axis intelligence and supplied large numbers of eager if untrained recruits for Ankara's army. Moreover, Beria's insistence on inserting himself into the Red Army's command structures and tactical decisions only served to exacerbate the confusions and contradictions of an increasingly inchoate situation.

New approaches to the Western Allies indicated the degree of Moscow's alarm. In 1941 Stalin had rejected any suggestion of British or American combat troops appearing on Russian soil. The critical situation of the Transcaucasus Front, however, forced the suspicious Soviet leader to reconsider. London, which had been planning such a move for more than a year under the code name Velvet, was prepared to comply and Washington agreed to assist, even though the diversion of resources might endanger the American determination to invade Western Europe at the earliest feasible time. Despite the Japanese threat to India and a renewed offensive by Rommel timed to coincide with the opening of Dessau, every possible Allied plane and soldier was, therefore, funneled to Syria, Iraq and Iran as summer turned to autumn in the crisis year of 1942.

Herculean efforts by planners and logisticians, however, had only produced limited results when Churchill and Roosevelt decided to commit Allied forces inside the USSR. Though granted imposing titles, the British Ninth and Tenth Armies were hodgepodge mixtures of untried, partially-formed units and battered veteran outfits recovering from the calamitous summer battles in the Western Desert. The British thus made extensive use of deception to inflate the strength of the forces arrayed on the Turkish frontier. Brigades were depicted as divisions and newly-created formations were credited with full combat capability. When the 10th Indian Division shipped from Cyprus to Syria, for example, it left behind its 25th Brigade to defend the island as the '25th Indian Division'. Similarly, the green Polish corps training and organising in central Iraq was touted as a powerful, battle-ready force of all arms. Owing to these deficiencies and the primitive transportation infrastructure in the region, the force Churchill sent to Baku in late September was initially limited to XXI Indian Corps with three infantry divisions (5th British, 5th and 8th Indian) with no appreciable armour component.

Churchill's decision and Stalin's acquiescence were prompted by the collapse of the Russian defences around Tiflis. Weeks of punishing combat on the frontier had exhausted the men of Lt General F.N. Remezov's 45th Army. They held on doggedly, however, until the first days of October when the two German divisions, leaving behind a thin screen to keep up appearances, slipped away to their right to attack a weak sector of the Russian line. The 45th Army crumpled, and the German *Jäger*, sensing victory, pressed ahead against evaporating resistance. Fortunately for the Allies, *XLIV Corps* had almost no motor transport and the Russian 53rd Army had moved into position north of Baku several days before the German breakthrough. Furthermore, the Turks on the southern flank of the penetration, poorly supplied and weakened by detachments, could hardly dent the Russian defences. As a result, when the *97th* and *101st Jäger Divisions* crashed into 53rd Army, the Germans were at the end of a weak logistical chain through rugged mountains, poised for victory but near the end of their tether.

Though de Angelis was stretching his logistics near to the breaking point, his men and their Turkish allies had already achieved a significant victory. By smashing in the back door of the Soviet defences in the Caucasus, *XLIV Corps* and the Turkish *Third Army* had forced the Stavka to evacuate the remnants of the Transcaucasus Front's 12th Army and four of the North Caucasus Front's eight armies. Thousands of prisoners and tons of stores fell into Axis hands as the Soviet troops fled east along a narrow corridor under constant harassment by German artillery and the few available *Luftwaffe* aircraft. The Black Sea Fleet ceased to exist, its sailors transferred to the Red Army or the scanty Caspian Sea flotilla. Bitterly-fought rearguard actions and the rugged terrain held up the pursuers and days would pass before *Seventeenth Army* cleared the final defenders out of Sokhumi and Poti, but the loss of Tiflis and the Black Sea coast represented a dreadful blow to Soviet morale. The defeat in the south also paved the way for *First Panzer Army* to renew its drive on Groznyy, which fell on 14 October, and Makhachkala, which the *13th Panzer Division* entered one week later after slicing through the incomplete field works hastily constructed by the 58th Army. The cover of the next issue of the *Wehrmacht*'s magazine, *Signal*, featured haughty and determined infantrymen standing watch on the shores of the Caspian Sea. In grim despair, Stalin demanded the British launch an immediate counter-attack.

A counter-attack was indeed in preparation, but Russo-British friction, supply shortfalls and transportation difficulties imposed what Stalin considered an unconscionable delay. In the meantime, the untried troops of the 53rd Army endured a vicious struggle with *XLIV Corps* outside Baku as the German veterans strove to crush the defenders and win the city with its oil. Finally, in the last week of October, with the 53rd Army near its breaking point, XXI Indian Corps struck the German right flank with a powerful surprise attack. Led by the experienced Jats and Punjabis of the 9th Indian Brigade, the 5th Indian Division drove through rugged terrain to threaten the lone road and railroad that represented the German line of communications back to Turkey. Simultaneously, the British hit the German positions in front of Baku, but coordination problems with the local Soviet commanders deprived their attack of its full effect. Several days of see-saw fighting ensued before low ammunition stocks brought the British offensive to a halt. The Germans held, and the British withdrew to better defensive positions, the failure of the counter-attack inflaming Anglo-Soviet acrimony. The German advance had been halted, but Allied offensive power was for the moment expended.

In the south, the Allied situation was somewhat brighter. An *ad hoc* command called Northern Iraq Force (6th Indian Division and some local levies) tied in with the Russians west of Lake Urumiah and threatened the left flank of the Turkish *Fifth Army*. At the same time, III Corps dealt a heavy blow to the Turks north-west of Mosul, with the 31st Indian Armoured Division making its combat debut by overrunning elements of the Turkish *64th Reserve Division* while the Arab Legion Mechanised Brigade harassed the weakly-held Turkish flank. On the Ninth Army's front, XXII Corps lost some ground to renewed attacks by Turkish *Fourth Army*. Lt General W.G. Holmes, the Ninth Army commander, however, refused to commit his reserves, preferring to preserve XXV Corps (8th Armoured Division and 10th Indian Division) for a thrust he was planning to split the two Turkish armies. Perhaps most important was that the RAF, by dint of good flying and extraordinary maintenance support, was able to clear the Turkish Air Force from the Syrian skies, exposing the ground troops and their logistics to incessant air attacks. These southern successes, however, were far from decisive and did not suffice to influence the fighting in the north.

Pluto and Grenadier

As October ended, the Allied battle lines in the Caucasus were in a shambles. Though *XLIV Corps* was stalled in front of Baku, dangling at the end of a tenuous line of supply, lead elements of *Army Group A* had approached the city from the north along the Caspian coast, and *First Panzer Army* was transferring responsibility for the Baku front to *Seventeenth Army* in order to prepare to carry its attacks north from Makhachkala. Desperate to forestall the next Axis assault and regain some ground before winter put an end to major operations, the XXI Corps staff was pleasantly surprised when their Russian liaison officer suggested a renewed attack to throw back *XLIV Corps* and the Turks. The joint Russo-British operation was christened Pluto and, although the British did not know it at the time, the Red Army intended it to be a small prelude to Uranus, a great offensive to encircle the Germans at Stalingrad. Lt General E.P. Quinan, commanding Tenth Army, recommended that Ninth Army undertake a simultaneous attack to distract the Axis and draw off Turkish reserves.

In the event, the Ninth Army's operation, codenamed Grenadier, suffered repeated delays and did not open until Pluto was well underway. Nonetheless, when it finally began on 1 November, Grenadier was initially successful. While the reinforced III Corps (2nd British Division, 31st Indian Armoured Division) occupied Turkish *Fifth Army*, XXV Corps cracked the seam between the two Turkish armies and raced north, breaking one Turkish division and capturing another almost intact. Demoralised by British air superiority, Turkish *Fifth Army* fell back hastily, forcing *Fourth Army* to abandon its gains as well. Resistance solidified as the advancing British and Indian columns came up against the mountains of Turkey proper, but the success of Grenadier precluded any effective reinforcement of the Turkish forces in Russia and absorbed fuel and munitions that had been earmarked for the *Second* and *Third Armies*. Combined with the British Eighth Army's victory at El Alamein, Grenadier thus staved off the Axis threat to the Suez Canal for the immediate future.

By the time Grenadier opened, however, Pluto was already losing steam. To the south, a pincer attack by the 72nd and 73rd Armies did inflict heavy losses on the Turkish *XII Corps*, but came to a halt in the face of a desperate rearguard action fought by the *4th Cavalry Division*. Near Baku, *XLIV Corps* was the principal target of Pluto. Weakened by weeks of unremitting combat, and low on food and ammunition after RAF bombers had repeatedly interdicted the frail Turkish rail system, de Angelis had been expecting an attack and had skillfully positioned the *97th* and *101st Divisions* along with two attached Turkish divisions to counter the anticipated Allied advance.

The wisdom of his dispositions was soon made evident. Although the effort cost heavily in casualties and severely depleted the limited Axis ammunition reserves, the Germans and Turks repulsed the Allied attacks with considerable loss. After three days of bitter fighting, de Angelis still held most of his ground, seeming to vindicate Hitler's insistence on standing fast. Over the next several days, his corps was reinforced by four Turkish regiments arriving from the central reserve in Ankara and ammunition stocks were replenished by redistributing supplies from *Seventeenth Army*. The British and Indian XXI Corps, on the other hand, though able to retain some of its gains, was temporarily spent as an offensive force. Its mission thus ended in failure despite great exertions and high casualties when the weather finally brought major operations to an end in mid-November.

Desperate options

Taking stock in the second week of November 1942, the Allied leaders faced a grim situation of desperate choices. The view from the Kremlin was deeply gloomy. The disaster in the Caucasus had wounded the Red Army badly, shaking its psychological foundations as well as consuming thousands of men and large quantities of material. Though Baku remained in Allied hands, the oil situation was growing critical and German forces were realigning themselves to threaten the lower reaches of the Volga. If the *Luftwaffe* could make enough aircraft available, Soviet shipping across the Caspian Sea could face prohibitive losses, endangering the slender link to their remaining sources of oil as well as to the huge range of supplies arriving from the West via Iran.

Furthermore, the involvement of Turkey in the Axis cause and the apparent 'liberation' of millions of Turkic peoples in the Caucasus raised the terrifying spectre of ethnic unrest for the Soviet regime in the vast stretches of Central Asia. If Berlin could handle them adroitly, the populations of the Caucasus could develop into an enormous asset for the Axis powers and a dangerous rear area foe for Moscow.

While Beria clamped a tighter hold on Central Asia, the Stavka grappled with more immediate operational questions. A Soviet counter-attack was imperative, but the physical and psychological damage of the Caucasus defeat, especially the reduction in oil supplies, meant that offensive operations would be limited, if possible at all. Prior to the catastrophe in the south, two great counter-offensives had been in planning for November: one called Uranus to cut off the German thrust toward Stalingrad and another, Mars, designed to eradicate a massive German salient west of Moscow. Clearly, one of these at least would now have to be cancelled and whichever one was undertaken would be both more doubtful and more dangerous. What Stalin and his generals had previously approached with confidence now became a desperate last throw of the dice.

The politicians and generals in Washington and London were equally worried. There were several important and encouraging developments: Operation Torch was proceeding well, the British Eighth Army was pursuing Rommel out of Egypt and Operation Grenadier had at least removed any Turkish threat to the Suez Canal until the spring of 1943. The debit side of the ledger, however, was dark indeed. In the first place, Turkey's accession to the Axis meant that there was no longer a neutral obstacle to a German thrust toward the Suez Canal from the north. Even worse, the Axis triumph in the Caucasus placed potentially powerful German forces in a position to sever the Iran corridor to Russia and, come the spring, to seize Baku in preparation for a strike south toward the vital Persian Gulf oil fields. Looming ominously over these threats, of course, was the terrifying possibility that Russia might come to some accommodation with Hitler and drop out of the war entirely.

These imminent threats to vital Allied interests imposed daunting operational and logistical requirements. The Ninth and Tenth Armies with their supporting air components would have to be reinforced to preclude any further Axis progress towards Baku, the Persian Gulf or Suez. This would divert at least one American armoured division, a large number of scarce fighter and bomber squadrons and significant logistical assets away from the anticipated struggle in Tunisia and southern Europe.[25] The constriction of the Iran corridor to Russia also meant that Britain and the US would have to resume the vulnerable Murmansk convoys at the earliest feasible date in order to demonstrate all possible support for their Soviet ally. The urgent need to relieve pressure on the USSR also led to renewed strains on the alliance as both the Americans and Russians increased their calls for a Second Front in western Europe at an early date in 1943.

The Germans also faced crucial strategic decisions as November approached its midpoint in 1942. The most important issue was the future employment of *Army Group A*. It was clear to everyone in Hitler's headquarters that the drive to conquer Stalingrad would continue. Yet, at a time when every available unit was needed to reinforce Tunisia, maintain the Reich's defences in Western Europe and repress the growing insurgency in Yugoslavia, a significant number of German formations would have to be maintained to bolster the Turks in the Transcaucasus, keep pressure on the Allies and prepare for an offensive to Baku and points south in the spring. Several divisions at least would be required to pursue the retreating Russians to the lower Volga and several might be sent to Stalingrad once they had refitted, but would they be enough to tip the scales in the *Wehrmacht*'s favour? *Luftwaffe* assets were even more scarce than ground troops. Stretched to its limits to prosecute the fighting at Stalingrad and in North Africa while supporting land operations and defending the Reich against the Anglo-American bombers, the German air arm could barely maintain a token presence in Turkey. Would those few squadrons be adequate to counter the growing Allied air strength? None of these questions had easy answers, but Hitler, the dull rumble of battle from Stalingrad notwithstanding, took satisfaction in his success in the Caucasus and looked forward to 1943 with great anticipation.

The reality

This scenario examines the serious German efforts to enlist Turkey in the Axis cause from 1940 through 1942 and refers to the actual inducements and threats presented to Ankara during that time. Germany's strategic situation in the spring and summer of 1942, the state of Turkey's military preparedness, Allied plans and the basic Allied forces available are also factual. Proceeding from this factual foundation, we can use the scenario as a historical laboratory to consider two questions. What would have had to change to allow such a significant alteration of Turkey's actual behaviour? And if the Turks had joined Hitler, what would have been necessary to ensure success?

For the first question, the key factor for Turkey's participation in the war was its leadership. Inönü, Saracoglu, Menemencioglu and Cakmak, though divided in other ways, were all united in their desire to keep Turkey out of the war. They certainly feared the Soviet Union, but they were equally wary of becoming another of Hitler's puppets. For them, the best outcome was one in which Berlin and Moscow held one another in check and thus created international space in which Turkey could pursue its own interests unencumbered. At the same time, Turkey's leaders held German military power in high regard and exhibited an especially deep alarm at the prospect of air attack on their cities. They thus resisted London's approaches and carefully steered a course between both sides to avoid what they were sure could only be ruinous involvement in the conflict raging all around them.

To make this scenario work, therefore, differences among the Turkish leaders were exaggerated to permit a coup and the rise of a fictional pro-German clique. In fact, although these men might have had leanings one way or another, they remained Turks first and foremost, keeping their own national interests firmly in view at all times. It was also necessary for our purposes here to ignore President Inönü's tight control of the country. As Saracoglu and other discovered, they all served at the president's pleasure and found themselves dismissed if their views or activities strayed too far from his intentions.

The second question this scenario illuminates concerns the requirements for military success against the USSR, assuming that Germany had coaxed Turkey into joining the Axis. The answer is deceptively simple: more German ground and air forces. It is unlikely that the Turks, given the state of their army and air force, could have prevailed alone in an attack into the Transcaucasus. The Soviets did send six divisions and four brigades north from the Turkish frontier in August as *Army Group A* drove south from Rostov, but they always kept a close watch on Turkey and did not denude the border.

In addition there were Red Army troops available in Iran and in the Stavka Reserve which could have been used (albeit at a cost in transportation and logistic assets) had Turkey shown signs of tying its fate to Germany's. Depletion of the Stavka Reserve might have had an effect on the abortive Operation Mars, the counterpart offensive to Uranus in central Russia during November 1942, but it is highly unlikely Stalin would have allowed any diminution of the forces committed to the key struggle at Stalingrad.

We must not underestimate the severe pressure Operation Blue exerted on the Soviets, but a real prospect of victory in the Transcaucasus could only have come with the insertion of German troops. Burdened, however, with Rommel's expeditionary corps, counter-insurgency requirements in the Balkans, and the need to guard against Allied adventures in Western Europe (made most vivid to Hitler by the Dieppe raid in August 1942) on top of the truly staggering commitment in the East, there were simply not enough German forces at hand to conduct Operation Blue properly, never mind provide an additional expeditionary command in Turkey, without giving up some other cherished commitment. Any diversion to Turkey could only have come at the expense of *Army Groups A* and *B*.

This piece has focused on ground troops, but the provision of adequate air support would have proven much more problematic. Even *Army Group A* found itself nearly stripped of *Luftwaffe* assets by late summer as the fight for Stalingrad intensified. The Turks probably could have held off the limited British and Commonwealth assets in the Middle East and Iran/Iraq as portrayed here, but, barring astoundingly good Axis luck or abysmally poor Russian performance, significant achievements in the Transcaucasus were unlikely without a substantial German presence beyond the lone corps in this scenario.

Bibliography

Blau, George, *The German Campaign in Russia: Planning and Operations* (US Army War College, Carlisle, 1983).

Border Troops in the Great Patriotic War (Nawka, Moscow, 1968).

Brett-James, Antony, *Ball of Fire* (Gale & Polden, Aldershot, 1957).

Conner, Albert Z., and Poirer, Robert G., *Red Army Order of Battle in the Great Patriotic War* (Presidio, Novato, 1985).

Boog, Horst; Rahn, Werner; Stumpf, Reinhard; and Wegner, Bernd, *Das deutsche Reich und der zweite Weltkrieg* (Deutsche Verlags-Anstalt, Stuttgart, 1990).

Deringil, Selim, *Turkish Foreign Policy During the Second World War* (Cambridge University Press, Cambridge, 1989).

Erickson, John, *The Road to Stalingrad* (Westview, Boulder, 1984).

Grechko, Andrei A., *Battle for the Caucasus* (Progress, Moscow, 1971).

Gwyer, J.M.A., and Butler, J.R.M., *Grand Strategy* (HMSO, London, 1964).

Hinsley, F.H., *British Intelligence in the Second World War* (HMSO, London, 1981).

Howard, Michael, *Strategic Deception* (HMSO, London, 1990).

Joslen, H.F., *Orders of Battle of the Second World War* (HMSO, London, 1960).

Kershaw, Ian, *Hitler 1936–1945: Nemesis* (Penguin, London, 2000).

Kolinsky, Martin, *Britain's War in the Middle East* (Macmillan, London, 1999).

Krecker, Lothar, *Deutschland und die Türkei im zweiten Weltkrieg* (Klostermann, Frankfurt, 1964).

Lucas, James, *Hitler's Mountain Troops* (Arms & Armour, London, 1992).

Motter, T.H. Vail, *United States Army in World War II, The War in the Middle East, The Persian Corridor and Aid to Russia* (Department of the Army, Washington DC, 1952).

Moyzisch, L.C., *Operation Cicero* (Coward-McCann, New York, 1950).

Oender, Zehra, *Die türkische Aussenpolitik im Zweiten Weltkrieg* (Oldenbourg, Munich, 1977).

Papen, Franz von, *Memoirs* (André Deutsch, London, 1953).

Playfair, I.S.O., *The Mediterranean and the Middle East* (HMSO, London, 1960).

Sandhu, Gurcharn Singh, *The Indian Armour* (Vision, New Delhi, 1987).

Schramm, Percy E., ed., *Kriegstagebuch des Oberkommando der Wehrmacht* (Bernard & Graefe, Munich, 1982).

Schultz, Friedrich, *Reverses on the Southern Wing* (US Army War College, Carlisle, 1983).

Shtemenko, S.M., *The Soviet General Staff at War 1941–1945* (Progress, Moscow, 1985).

Tarnstrom, Ronald, *Balkan Battles* (Trogen, Lindsborg, 1998).

Tieke, Wilhelm, *The Caucasus and the Oil* (Fedorowicz, Winnipeg, 1995).

US Army, European Command Historical Division, 'Decisions Affecting the Campaign in Russia (1941/1942)', MS #C-067b.

Weber, Frank G., *The Evasive Neutral* (University of Missouri Press, Columbia, 1979).

Weinberg, Gerhard, *A World at Arms* (Cambridge University Press, Cambridge, 1994).

Ziemke, Earl F. and Bauer, Magna E., *Moscow to Stalingrad: Decision in the East* (US Army Center of Military History, Washington, DC, 1987).

Notes

1. Statistics drawn from Ziemke & Bauer *Moscow to Stalingrad*, pp. 283–95.

2. Actual quote cited in Kershaw, *Hitler 1936–1945*, p. 506.

3. Actual quotes taken from 'Decisions Affecting the Campaign in Russia (1941/1942)', US Army, European Command Historical Division, MS #C-067b; and Ziemke & Bauer, p. 296. Both are from Halder, but the second actually dates to November 1941, before the great defeats of the winter.

4. Actual quotes from May and March 1942, cited in Kershaw, pp. 513–14.

5. Hitler on 5 August 1942 quoted in Boog, *et al.*, *Der Globale Krieg*, vol. VI of *Das deutsche Reich und der zweite Weltkrieg*, p. 117.

6. Actual Jodl assessment quoted in Krecker, *Deutschland und die Türkei im zweiten Weltkrieg*, p. 225. The Bulgarian Army was seen as keeping Turkey in check.

7. An actual incident from early 1941 recorded by the *Sicherheitsdienst* officer in the Ankara embassy, in Moyzisch, *Operation Cicero*, pp. 7–9.

8. On Papen's recommendation, Hitler did write a letter to Inönü in February 1941 and the Germans hosted General Erden on a tour of the Eastern Front in November of that year.

9. Quotes paraphrased from Weber, *The Evasive Neutral*, p. 146 citing exchanges between the German Foreign Ministry and von Papen in May 1942.

10. Fall Gertrud was actually the German contingency plan for military occupation of Turkey, Schramm, *Kriegstagebuch des Oberkommando der Wehrmacht*, vol. III, pp. 1349–50.

11. Actual quote cited in Oender, *Die türkische Aussenpolitik im Zweiten Weltkrieg*, p. 150.

12. Hitler quote from 23 November 1940 in Deringil, *Turkish Foreign Policy During the Second World War*, p. 112.

13. Von Papen quote from 13 May 1941 in *ibid.*, p. 117.

14. The quote refers to Inönü's attitude toward the briefing he received from Erden after the latter's tour of the Eastern Front in 1941. Cited in *ibid.*, p. 131.

15. Papen, *Memoirs*, p. 479.

16. Actual quotes from Turkish officers in Deringil, pp. 38–9. Thanks to Mr. David Ryan for invaluable assistance with order of battle data, and to Mr. Rudi Garcia for concept review. Thanks also to Ms. Kate Flaherty, Still Pictures Branch, National Archives, for prompt and courteous help with the photos.

17. The second quote is actually from a historian, the first is from a British air attaché's report in 1937. Both in *ibid.*, pp. 33–5.

18. Actual quote in Schultz, *Reverses on the Southern Wing*, p. 145. The German corps was actually organised as indicated under General de Angelis.

19. Quotes are actual. Hitler quote in Lucas, *Hitler's Mountain Troops*, p. 133. Actual assessment of the British Chiefs of Staff, March 1940 in Deringil., p. 94.

20. Quotes from Hinsley, *British Intelligence in the Second World War*, vol. III, pp. 83–103.

21. Though little known, the Allied units mentioned here and later actually served in the Middle East, Iraq and Iran during the second half of 1942, though often at reduced strength. Of the British forces, only XXII Corps and 'Northern Iraq Force' are invented. The Soviet 71st, 72nd and 73rd Armies are invented, but represent likely command arrangements in the face of an invasion. The Transcaucasus Front and 12th Army were real, but had been disestablished by October 1942; they are retained here for command and control purposes. The Soviet 53rd Army was in Central Asia.

22. Quotes from actual reports in *Border Troops in the Great Patriotic War*, pp. 450ff.
23. First quote is actual, cited in Schramm, vol. II, p. 617. Second quote is fictional.
24. Actual Stalin quote on 12 September 1942 cited in Erickson, *The Road to Stalingrad*, p. 189.
25. The planning for an American armoured division and for a major US air presence in the Middle East or Persia/Iraq are actual.

7
KNOWN ENEMIES
AND FORCED ALLIES
Sicily and Kursk, 1943

John D. Burtt

'It is better to have known enemies than a forced ally.'
Napoleon.

Introduction

The huge meeting room was silent as the assembled generals watched *Khozyin* ('the Boss') warily as he paced the floor, cigarette smoke exploding from his lips accentuating his dangerous anger. The news they had delivered was bad and Josef Vissarianovich Stalin was not known to 'enjoy' bad messages. Their summer attacks against the Fascists had been hideously expensive in terms of men and tanks; and worse, the offensives had gained little.

'What of our Allies?' Stalin demanded suddenly, with biting sarcasm.

'The same,' Zhukov replied. 'No appreciable movement.'

'They are waiting for us to destroy the Fascists and ourselves,' Stalin snapped, throwing the reports on the table. 'No longer,' he sighed, accepting the unthinkable. The abhorrence he felt at discussing an armistice with the Fascists was only slightly less nauseating than the disgust he felt at the Western Allies for forcing it on him.

The situation

In late 1942, Allied and Soviet offensives shattered the fragile stalemate that existed between the European belligerents. In North Africa, the British Eighth Army attacked Generalfeldmarschall Erwin Rommel's *Deutsches Afrika Korps (DAK)* at El Alamein. After two weeks of intense combat, the supply-starved and outnumbered Axis forces were forced into retreat. To make matters worse, Allied troops landed to the west in Algeria and Morocco on 8 November 1942, threatening to trap Rommel between converging forces. Then on the Eastern Front in mid-November, Soviet spearheads broke through the flank forces on either side of the German

Sixth Army as it struggled in the morass of Stalingrad. Within days the Army was cut off and surrounded.

Hitler reacted as he always had in other crises, demanding his forces hold at all costs. Rommel was able to get his particular hold order rescinded quickly, but the delay trapped three good Italian divisions. Hitler ordered German troops to Tunisia to hold a bridgehead open between the converging Allied forces.

As his troops retreated, Rommel flew to Germany to meet with his Führer; he intended to demand adequate supplies or a complete withdrawal from Africa. However, his timing was poor. Caught in the middle of the *Sixth Army*'s developing crisis, Hitler had little time for Rommel and less patience. He categorically refused to consider a withdrawal from Africa and demanded Rommel return to his troops and stop the Eighth Army. The field marshal left the meeting a very discouraged man.

The New Year brought a drastically changed situation, particularly in the east. Field Marshal Erich von Manstein's Winter Storm operation to relieve the *Sixth Army* had failed. A second Soviet offensive had broken open the front. Hitler had to reconsider his earlier decision. The men he had impulsively ordered to Tunisia would have made a significant difference on the Eastern Front.

The Italians now posed the largest problem. Their *Eighth Army* in Russia had been virtually destroyed in December by the Soviet offensive.[1] The defeat at El Alamein and the subsequent retreat added to the continual tale of combat disasters suffered by his Axis partner. Pulling out of Tunisia now would undoubtedly cause Mussolini's and Italy's utter collapse. Such an event would leave his southern flank wide open to the Western Allies. A compromise was needed to buy time.

In Tunisia, Rommel's *DAK* finally came to rest in the Mareth Line, a set of pre-war French fortifications built, ironically, to defend Tunisia against the Italians. Montgomery's Eighth Army stopped in Tripoli, to reopen the destroyed port and regroup for their next assault. The United States, Free French and British forces of First Army, under British Lieutenant General Sir Kenneth Anderson, were pushing into Tunisia from Algeria. The German reinforcements had been organised in January into the *Fifth Panzer Army* under General-Oberst Hans-Jürgen von Arnim. His forces included the *10th Panzer Division*. New orders came for both German commanders from Hitler – do what they could to delay the Allies, then begin pulling their veteran troops out.

With the British to the east settled in to regroup, von Arnim and Rommel saw the opportunity to use their interior lines to strike the Allied troops in the western part of Tunisia with their combined forces, driving them back from the Eastern Dorsale. Then they could combine to strike the British if necessary.

On 14 February 1943, von Arnim attacked out of the Faid Pass with his *10th* and *21st Panzer Divisions*, overrunning a battalion of US armour and two battalions from the 34th Infantry Division and opening a huge gap in the Allied defences. The Americans lost over 80 per cent of their tanks and had 1,400 men captured. Next *10th Panzer* pushed north toward the flank of the Allied line defending the Fondouk Pass while *21st Panzer* pushed for the city of Sbeitla. Elements of the US 1st Armored Division were shoved roughly aside with heavy losses; a hasty counter-attack did nothing but provide the German gunners with targets, losing 50 of 54 tanks. Two elements added to the demoralisation of the defenders. Accompanying the Germans was a company of Tiger heavy tanks whose 88mm guns tore through everything the Americans had. Worse, Allied air cover, when it appeared at all, attacked everyone indiscriminately. The Americans fell back, ceding the town, and its huge stockpile of supplies, to the attackers.

By the end of the second day, the Allies were pulling back all along the line. To the west, the Germans moved toward Sbiba, threatening Thala and the vital port of Bône.

To make matters worse, Rommel's *DAK* had advanced from the south and captured Feriana and the airfield at Thelepte from its US 1st Infantry Division defenders, capturing over 60,000 gallons of fuel. A *DAK* taskforce hit the Free French behind the Western Dorsale and Rommel's desert veterans flanked and captured the Kasserine Pass after a fierce fight, sending the Allied defenders retreating toward Algeria. The US 1st Armored Division had lost over 2,500 men and 112 tanks in the fighting, over half of its combat power. Anderson and US II Corps commander Major General Lloyd R. Fredendall responded to the crises by sending reinforcements haphazardly into the line, intermingling units and creating massive command problems.

The Germans pressed troops north and west, but they backed off when they hit determined resistance. British troops and armour from V Corps moved south to restore the Allied line, but they were savaged by sudden attacks. In one German attack, a captured Valentine tank led the way into a British strongpoint south of Thala, helping the attackers destroy 30 tanks and 28 artillery pieces and capture 600 men before withdrawing.

With the western forces in disarray, the Axis pulled back through the passes and turned their attention toward the British, but Montgomery had not budged from his line at Medenine. Deciding not to attack that fortified position, Rommel chose instead to leave a small mobile delaying force at the Mareth Line, knowing it could be flanked, and to build better defences at Wadi Akarit to the north.

Hitler succeeded in getting his delay.

Strategic choices

By the middle of March 1943, the battlefronts had again stabilised. Both Allied fronts in Tunisia were quiet. In the east, von Manstein had managed to concentrate his armoured forces and strike back at the over-extended Soviet spearheads. His counter-attack in the Ukraine destroyed three Soviet armies and recaptured the city of Kharkov, but mud, casualties and exhaustion stopped the German advance. The respite gave Hitler the chance to consider his options for the coming summer season.

The problems and concerns he faced were nearly global. In the East, despite the reprieve that von Manstein's success had gained him, he knew the battles would recommence as soon as the spring mud dried. To the north an increasingly hostile Sweden and a war-weary Finland threatened his position in Norway.[2] The United States had already offered to mediate between Finland and the Soviet Union, something Hitler had refused to allow. To the south, his Balkan allies were shaken by the disaster at Stalingrad and looking for a way out. Neutral Turkey was actively seeking to establish a Balkan pact under its leadership. Losing the Balkans would deprive Germany of significant resources – oil, bauxite, cadmium, and more.

And again, there was Italy. Now ejected from their African colonies, and facing the prospect of war on their own soil, the Italians under Mussolini remained questionable. With his attention focused on the Western Allies and the threat they posed, the Italian leader was pushing for Germany to make the Mediterranean theatre a higher priority for troops and equipment. Defending his country would take more than he had. Of the 94 divisions Italy had recruited, fully a third had been destroyed in Africa and on the Eastern Front – over 130,000 men were lost when the *Eighth Army* was overrun alone. Another 30 were stuck in the Balkans fighting partisans.

But Mussolini knew that any change in Hitler's priorities would require resolution of the two-front-war problem. He began suggesting either a negotiated peace with Stalin or the development of an East Wall – a fortified defensive zone against the Soviets. Hitler publicly rejected any possibility of negotiations with Stalin, although privately he had authorised a peace feeler the previous December. Stalin, with his armies on the attack, had rejected the feeler.

Hitler could not ignore Mussolini completely, regardless of his personal opinions about the Italian's capabilities. To do so would lead to an Italian surrender and worse problems. In one respect Hitler realised that Mussolini was right – the war in the east had gone badly and an outright military victory, something Hitler had thought inevitable in 1941, was unachievable. He would have to accept wearing his enemies down, or winning a significant enough victory to negotiate from a stronger position.

With those thoughts in mind, Hitler ordered some repositioning of troops, strengthening Greece with two divisions and the Balkans by four. In addition he formed a new command under Rommel in northern Italy, to be built around the veteran *1st Panzer Division*. These troops would be used to defend Italy or, as he feared, disarm the Italians in the event they collapsed.

Then he turned his attention to his most pressing problem – the east. He decided that some sort of limited offensive was needed with the goal of consolidating his defensive position, throwing the Soviets off balance, eliminating their immediate reserves, and demonstrating to his allies that Germany was still dominant. The most obvious target for such a limited attack was the bulge around the Ukrainian town of Kursk. Eliminating that bulge would destroy all the Soviet troops within the bulge as well as any reserves the Soviets sent to rescue encircled forces, and would shorten his front line by nearly 150 miles. Thus on 13 March Operations Order 5 was sent out. It predicted that the Soviets would soon attack and all defensive measures were to be upgraded. *Army Group Centre* was to prepare to attack the Kursk salient from the north while *Army Group South* would prepare to strike from that direction. His subsequent Operations Order 6 gave the specifics of what he called Operation Zitadelle, and two other operations, (Habicht and Panther) aimed at gaining more room in the industrial Donets Basin. The earliest date for the attack was set as 3 May 1943.

In the west, Britain and the United States were recovering from the setbacks in Tunisia. Lieutenant General George Patton arrived to take command of the US II Corps and rebuild it after its disastrous baptism of fire. Montgomery's Eighth Army reopened Tripoli, resupplied itself and prepared for further operations. The setback had been severe but neither ally was overly concerned. They continued to look ahead.

Strategy for the war differed dramatically between Britain and the US. The British saw the Mediterranean theatre as the sole region where they could reasonably meet (and beat) the Germans in 1943. In addition, they felt there was a strong possibility that Italy could be knocked out of the war. The United States, however, saw the Mediterranean as an unnecessary sideshow. The American leaders wanted a cross-Channel attack as soon as possible, so they could drive straight into Germany, end the European portion of the war, and turn their attention to the Pacific and Japan. They had agreed to the Torch landings in Morocco and Algeria solely in return for Britain's commitment to invade France in the autumn of 1943. But when the Allies convened the Casablanca conference in January of that year, both sides knew that a cross-Channel assault would not be possible that year. With that hanging over the proceedings, they acrimoniously hacked out their next step, finally agreeing to follow up their 'victory' in Tunisia with the invasion of Sicily. Unfortunately, because of the US reluctance toward all things Mediterranean, Sicily was seen as the end product of the allied advance, rather than one part of a more coherent plan.

Once the decision was finally made, planning started for the Sicilian operation. Initial decisions established that General Dwight D. Eisenhower would be the Commander-in-Chief, with British General Sir Harold Alexander as his deputy and overall ground commander. After that, the decision-making broke down completely, aided by the fact that there were five separate planning sites involved: Washington, London, Cairo, Rabat, and Algiers.

By April 1943, three months later, there was still no agreed plan of action. The best they had come up with was having a British Eastern Task

Force, under Montgomery, land at widely spaced sites from Gela to Syracuse. The British landing was to be concurrent with a US Western Task Force under Patton landing near Palermo. However, when apprised of the plan, Montgomery exploded and flatly rejected it. He felt the planners were underestimating the Axis resistance and demanded, in a wholly insubordinate fashion, that the landings be more concentrated. His nominal superior, Alexander, finally agreed after nearly undercutting any authority he had left by suggesting the decision rested with Churchill. Part of Alexander's concerns rested with the distrust he had of US combat capability, stemming from their abysmal performance during the Axis attacks in February. This lack of trust was particularly galling to the Americans because they felt, with considerable justification, that many of their problems in Tunisia were created by faulty dispositions ordered by British General Anderson.

The new plan had the British Eighth Army, with three divisions, land near Syracuse while the newly named US Seventh Army, also with three divisions landed at Gela. The plan angered the US commanders, especially Patton, who saw their part in the operation reduced from capturing a key Sicilian port to protecting the British left flank. Patton was further angered when his request to replace the green 36th Infantry Division, tapped for the invasion, with the veteran 1st Infantry Division was turned down by Eisenhower who wanted to give more American troops combat experience.

While the Allies finished their battles in Tunisia and Hitler moved his resources around, the Soviets also took the respite provided by the *rasputitsa* (the Russian name for the muddy/roadless weeks of the spring thaw) to consider their next moves. Despite the loss of Kharkov and the sad end to their winter offensive, they had been very successful in pushing the Germans back. Stalin felt he had the manpower and material to keep the initiative by attacking as soon as the ground firmed up.

His generals thought otherwise and recommended caution. They knew, based on two years of fighting the Fascists, that the Germans would be attacking when the roads cleared – both to shore up their faltering alliances and to exact some revenge for the loss of *Sixth Army*. A study of their maps showed them the same thing the maps showed the Germans – the Kursk salient was an obvious target for a Fascist attack. This was confirmed by their spies – and by the Western Allies' Ultra intercepts (although, as always, the source was disguised when such information was passed to the Soviets). Stalin's generals, led by his chief troubleshooter, Marshal Georgi Zhukov, suggested they allow the Germans to attack, wear down the assault troops and armour with a defensive battle, then launch counter-offensives against a weakened foe. For the moment Stalin took their advice.

In early April he ordered the Kursk salient – and all other front lines – to prepare extensive defences in anticipation of the German attack. To insure the Germans would, in fact, be stopped – something the Soviets had yet to do – Stalin established the Steppe Military District with six full armies, three tank corps and one of his new tank armies,[3] a total of 580,000 men, 9,000 guns and 1,600 tanks. This deep reserve would be used to blunt any significant German success and provide the troops for the ensuing counter-attacks. Once the Germans had been stopped, the Soviets would unleash their attacks first into the Orel salient north of Kursk (Operation Kutusov), then against Kharkov to the south (Operation Rumiantsev). The overall goal would be to drive the Germans back to the Dnepr River or beyond.

The buildups

Even as the decisions were being made and implemented, other events were having their impact, especially in the west. In late March the Allies struck again in Tunisia, this time from both directions. The American II Corps, four divisions that had been rejuvenated under Patton's forceful command, moved against Gafsa and put pressure on the defenders at El Guettar. Three days after the US moved, Montgomery's Eighth Army assaulted the Mareth Line. In both cases the well-fortified defenders made the Allies pay for each yard. But the odds were against the Axis and the dual crises made von Arnim move troops away from Tunis toward the threatened zones.

The Allied attacks stalled the transfer of troops out of Tunisia. The transfer had been slow anyway – much slower than the transfer into the country. Allied strength on the sea and in the air made the move slow, but internal problems made things worse. Rommel had expected his veteran *DAK* troops to be withdrawn first, but Reichsmarschall Hermann Göring interfered, demanding his 'elite' *'Hermann Göring' Panzer Division* be given priority. The argument had finally been resolved with elements of the *'Hermann Göring' Division* and the *21st Panzer* sharing the withdrawal along with an equal number of Italian troops. In all only nine battalions of German troops were able to get out of Tunisia before the Allies attacked.

Once the US and British attacks got underway, it was only a matter of time before the Axis forces were overwhelmed. The basic problem was supply. Von Arnim had told his superiors at *Comando Supremo* in Rome and in Berlin that he would need 140,000 tons of supplies per month to hold on to Tunisia. But in March less than 30,000 tons was delivered. In the face of Allied air and naval superiority, the Italian Navy and Axis air forces simply could not keep the troops supplied with the food, fuel and ammunition they needed to defend the bridgehead.[4]

In mid-May the inevitable happened – Axis forces in Tunisia surrendered, sending more shockwaves through the Axis alliance, especially Italy. Mussolini's former supporters became more active in seeking to oust him. Multiple conspiracies began to take form. In Berlin, Hitler had to divert his attention from Zitadelle back to Italy. He immediately offered five new divisions to Mussolini for Italian defence. The Italian leader turned down the whole request, stating three divisions and 300 tanks would suffice. The response made Hitler suspicious of a possible Italian doublecross. He ordered that Rommel's command in Northern Italy be expanded to thirteen divisions and established Operation Alaric – a plan to hold the western Alpine passes open and disarm the Italians.

Hitler's troop movements into the area were still ongoing. There was little at present to stand in the way of an immediate Allied assault on Europe proper. This was especially true if the Italians collapsed. Most of his generals expected the Allies to follow up their African victory with an attack on Sicily, with a concurrent invasion of the Italian mainland at Calabria to isolate the island. There was a single German division on the island, *Division 'Sicily'*, and it was rebuilding. In addition the *'Hermann Göring' Panzer Division* was regrouping in Italy itself. A tour of Sicily by the Commander-in-Chief, South, General Albert Kesselring, left serious doubts as to the Italians' ability to defend their own soil. They had four mobile and six coastal divisions on Sicily, but Kesselring described the defensive preparations as *Reisenauri* ('one hell of a mess'), with the fieldworks 'so much gingerbread' and the coastal divisions 'hopeless.'

This came at a time when preparations for Zitadelle were being assessed and changed. Hitler had already postponed the attack once to allow new weapons systems to reach the attacking forces. Panther and Tiger tanks, and Elefant self propelled anti-tank guns gave the Germans a superior technology over the Soviets, but production was slow. The delay was making his generals nervous. In early May, General Walter Model whose *Ninth Army* was to spearhead the attack from the north, shared aerial photographs showing extensive defensive preparations in his zone of attack. Field Marshal von Manstein, in charge of the southern assault, was seeing the same thing. He felt he could succeed if the attack took place now, but the battle would be a toss-up in June. The conference ended with Hitler expressing concern but providing no real decision other than to continue preparations and expect more delays.

As the Germans reconsidered, the Soviets and Allies continued their plans.

In the East, the Soviet buildup around Kursk was being done on a massive scale. Over 1.3 million men and 3,500 tanks had been assembled in the Central and Voronezh Fronts to contest the coming assault. But the numbers were not the whole story. Each front had developed up to six defensive lines, filled with battalion defensive positions and anti-tank strongpoints. On the Voronezh Front alone, the Soviets had dug nearly 2,600 miles of trenches, 300 miles of anti-tank obstacles, and laid over 600,000 mines. As an example, the 6th Guards Army, expecting an attack by von Manstein's armour, had placed 69,000 mines and 327 pillboxes in its main line of defence, with 20,000 mines and 200 pillboxes in its second. Backing these armies were the front reserves that included the 1st and 2nd Tank Armies, with the Steppe Front as the ultimate reserve. Also in support were three full air armies with 2,600 aircraft.

On the German side the Zitadelle buildup continued. General Model's

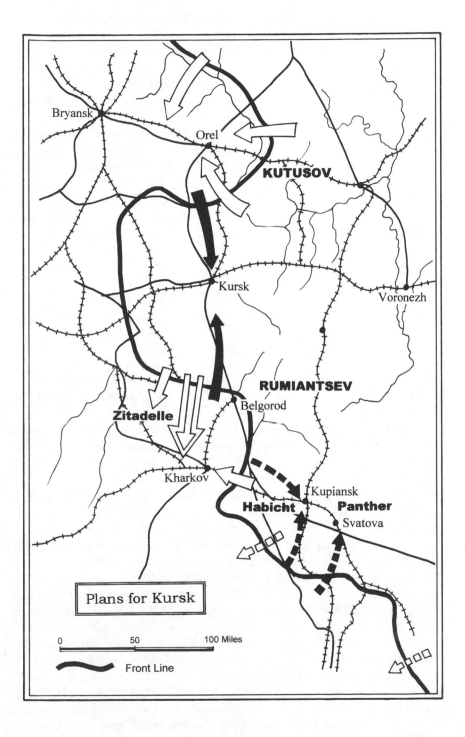

Plans for Kursk

0   50   100 Miles

Front Line

Ninth Army, scheduled to lead the northern assault, had built up to a force of some 330,000 troops, 600 tanks and 425 assault guns. In the south, von Manstein's main attack force, General Hermann Hoth's *Fourth Panzer Army*, had assembled 225,000 men and over 1,000 tanks and assault guns. Despite the massive buildup, there was rampant pessimism among the commanders about their chances due to the myriad delays and the very evident Soviet preparations.

In the west, preparations for Sicily, called Operation Husky, continued as well. Ultra intercepts had indicated the Axis were expecting an attack on Sicily, so efforts were being made to confuse the issue with bombing and reconnaissance flights over Greece, Sardinia and Corsica. The British suggested a more novel approach; in an operation they called Mincemeat, they planned to float a body ashore in Spain with letters from Alexander indicating Greece was the next target. Eisenhower turned down the suggestion as impractical.

Then, in early June, a major storm erupted between Germany's opponents. Stalin had been demanding the Allies open a significant Second Front to take some of the pressure off his nation. Informed officially of Allied plans to invade Sicily and postpone a cross-Channel attack until 1944, he exploded. He told Churchill and Roosevelt that their delay was creating grave difficulties for his people, making them feel alone against the Fascists. He pointed to the horrendous casualties suffered by the Red Army and called Allied losses 'insignificant'. Operation Husky, in his opinion, was wholly inadequate. He needed an attack that would divert a significant number of the 200-plus German divisions facing him. The comment struck a sore point with Churchill who had been stunned when the Husky planners had informed him they could not guarantee success if more than two German divisions were encountered. Despite reassurances from both Roosevelt and Churchill, Stalin remained implacable, accusing the West of deliberately allowing his nation to destroy itself while defeating Fascism.

In June, the Western Allies took steps to neutralise a threat to their Husky plans. The targets were the small islands of Pantelleria and Lampedusa that stood between Malta and the Tunisian shoreline. Both islands had Axis airfields and listening posts that threatened the security of the Husky transport fleets. Pantelleria was considered the primary threat and a difficult obstacle because 15 battalions of coastal guns in pillboxes and 12,000 entrenched troops defended it. On 7–11 June over 5,400 tons of bombs were dropped on the island, blasting emplacements but causing only about 130 casualties. However, as the British brigade assigned to assault the island approached, the garrison surrendered, ostensibly because of the lack of water. Lampedusa surrendered the next day.

The fall of the two fortresses showed the Axis that Sicily would be the next target – and indicated to the Germans how well the Italians would defend their own soil. Once again, Hitler had to switch his attention to the Mediterranean from the east.

On Sicily, the only German division on the island had been redesignated the *15th Panzergrenadier Division*, built around three rather than the normal two Panzergrenadier regiments. But it was also integrating another Panzer battalion into its organisation, which would make it in effect a very strong Panzer division (and it would shortly be renamed as *15th Panzer Division*). Its troops were virtually all veterans, as were their leaders. In Italy, the *'Hermann Göring' Panzer Division* was nearly finished regrouping after its Tunisian withdrawal, regaining its infantry strength to complement its strong Panzer regiment. It received orders to transfer to Sicily. Two other divisions were rebuilding in Italy – the *29th Panzergrenadiers* and *26th Panzer*. Further north, Rommel had collected the *1st Panzer Division*, but only one of the promised eight other divisions, to hold in readiness for Operation Alaric.

Apart from the military aspects, the political climate in Italy would have been humorous had the impact not been so significant. German intelligence began picking up bits and pieces of a wide variety of conspiracies against Mussolini, all highly vocal but totally disorganised. However, the German Ambassador to Italy, Hans von Mackensen, reported one coup was serious but also told Berlin that one of Italy's more extreme Fascists, Roberto Farinacci, had offered to lead a counter-coup against plotters in Mussolini's own Fascist Grand Council.[5] The Germans began to take the political problem seriously.

On 18 June, a week after Pantelleria fell *Oberkommando der Wehrmacht* (*OKW*), the German Armed Forces High Command, recommended to their Führer that Zitadelle be cancelled in order to keep strategic reserves free to respond to any threat. Again Hitler chose not to make a decision, still torn between needing the reserves and needing a victory over the Soviets.

But less than a week after *OKW* made its recommendation, the choice was taken away from the German leader. Two separate spy sources reported to Stalin that Zitadelle was no longer planned. 'Werther' reported that '*OKW* does not wish to provoke a large scale Russian offensive in the central sector under any circumstances.'[6] The Soviets had put their fronts on alert for the German assault three times in May and once in June, just prior to the spy reports. Some of the commissars were pushing for Stalin to attack first. But the Soviet leader had demurred thus far. He knew the risk of attacking where his strength was concentrated – he would be driving right into the fresh, unbloodied troops the German had amassed – but he also knew that if he were going to attack anywhere, it would have to be where he had planned. To move his attack troops elsewhere would take reserves from the potential German attack zone and make him vulnerable if the Germans again changed their minds. With the spy reports now in hand, Stalin decided to wait no longer – against Zhukov's advice, he ordered the Red Army to attack.

The battle in the East

On 24 June 1943 the Soviets opened their offensive with two diversionary attacks. From the Southern Front, reinforced reconnaissance battalions crossed the Mius River and clashed with German outposts. That night, following a heavy barrage, the 5th Shock and 28th Armies attacked along a twelve-mile sector of the German *Sixth Army*'s defensive line toward Stalino. The same day, the Southwestern Front sent its reconnaissance battalions across the northern Donets River, followed by the 1st and 8th Guards Armies, with the 23rd Tank Corps for exploitation.

Both attacks made slow progress against strong German defences, developing small bridgeheads across the rivers but failing to penetrate much past the first defensive lines. But the attacks succeeded in their main purpose. Von Manstein dispatched most of his *III Panzer Corps*, the *6th* and *19th Panzer Divisions*, plus the *168th Infantry Division*, south to deal with the threats to their southern flank.

Then it was the Soviets' turn to be surprised. Their plans had called for a ten-day delay between the diversionary attacks and the start of Operation Rumiantsev, their main attack toward Kharkov, to allow the Nazi reserves to commit to those areas. However, as they waited, intelligence came in that made them alter their plans even further. Partisans around Bryansk reported that the Germans were building a new defensive line near the city, and that they were pulling stockpiled supplies out of their forward supply dumps near Orel. It appeared that they were preparing to withdraw from the Orel salient that was the target of Operation Kutusov, the follow-on attack to Rumiantsev. In fact, *Army Group Centre* had no orders from Hitler for any such withdrawal; its commander, Generalfeldmarschall Günther von Kluge, had ordered the preparations of what he called the Hagen Line started as he and *Ninth Army*'s General Model organised their arguments in favour of a withdrawal. Such a withdrawal would shorten the German line significantly, making more reserves available. To Stalin, however, such a withdrawal meant that the *Second Panzer Army* and *Ninth Army* would escape his trap. This was unacceptable to him and he ordered Kutusov implemented immediately.

The original plan for Kutusov called for concentric attacks from the north, east and south into the Orel salient. On the north face, the Western Front's 11th Guards Army, along with two tank corps, massed over 700 tanks and almost 4,300 guns for their breakthrough. In addition the Soviets had planned to exploit this hole with their new 4th Tank Army, but the schedule change caught this unit still in transit. To the east the Bryansk Front's 3rd, 63rd and 61st Armies prepared a straight-ahead assault, with the 3rd Tank Army and its 730 tanks moving up to exploit. Finally on the southern face, the Central Front had three more armies ready to attack with the 2nd Tank Army ready to follow them. All told, the Soviets were to unleash 750,000 men in 67 divisions and 2,300 tanks on the German forces in the Orel salient.

Three infantry corps of the *Second Panzer Army*, totalling some 14 divisions, defended the line with the *5th Panzer Division* in immediate support. Behind them stood Model's *Ninth Army* with its two full-strength Panzer corps. Von Kluge also had an additional five Panzer divisions in deep reserve. Aerial reconnaissance picked up Soviet troop movements to the east, allowing the troops some advance warning of the impending attack, but on the north face, the German defenders had no such warning.

Kutusov started on 28 June with the normal Soviet practice of sending their reconnaissance battalions into the German defences to probe for weaknesses and redefine lines of advance. In addition to this activity, Stalin unleashed his *relsovaya voina* ('war on the rail lines') – thousand of partisans armed with explosives attacked the rail lines leading in and out of the salient. Over 10,000 demolition charges went off, disrupting German movement and, Stalin hoped, pinning two German armies in the salient to be destroyed by his converging forces.

Early on 29 June the 11th Guards Army assaulted their portion of the line. Massing almost all their tanks and guns on a ten-mile stretch of the German defences, the deluge devastated and overwhelmed two infantry regiments and the 40 tanks that held that portion of the line. Despite counter-attacks by the *5th Panzer Division*, the assault penetrated almost six miles, just short of the German second line.

To the east the Bryansk Front's assault was far less successful. The German defenders, reinforced by corps anti-tank reserves, stalled the initial push by the 3rd and 63rd Armies, destroying over half their armour. The Soviet infantry barely gained two miles against these heavy losses. The commitment of the 1st Guards Tank Corps the following day also stalled quickly in the dense German defences, and was stopped completely as the *2nd* and *8th Panzer Divisions* arrived to seal the penetration.

The second day of the attack saw the 11th Guards continue their success, committing the 1st and 5th Tank Corps to breach the second German line and gain another three miles. By 1 July three Panzer divisions, the *12th*, *18th*, and *20th*, had arrived to blunt the advance. However, the success of the Western Front's advance worked against it as its flanks were left open by the stalled drive coming from the east. The massed Panzers smashed the 5th Tank Corps and threatened to cut off the entire breakthrough. The Soviets countered by throwing the 50th Army into the breach, but it was not the mobile force they needed. 4th Tank Army was still in transit.

On 2 July the Central Front opened its drive from inside the Kursk salient, with the 13th, 48th and 70th Armies attacking. They met stiff resistance, even on their limited front, and barely made it through the first German line in a replay of problems further north. The 2nd Tank Army, waiting for the breakthrough, was stalled in the open; *Luftwaffe* airstrikes tool a heavy toll on the waiting tanks. It took two full days for the Central Front's infantry to hammer a hole large enough for the 2nd Tank Army to drive through. When it finally did, it ran into highly accurate anti-tank fire, mainly from the dug in *656th Anti-tank Detachment*, made up of Elefant self-propelled anti-tank guns. These weapons – an 88mm gun in a turretless tank – proved deadly in long-range combat. The 2nd Tank Army's 16th Tank Corps lost 75 per cent of its strength – 150 tanks – in a single engagement while only killing three Elefants. As they reeled back from the losses, the Germans followed up with a counter-attack by the remainder of the *XLVII Panzer Corps*.

For the next five days, the Soviets hammered at the Germans, but the fresh and mobile Panzer divisions stalled virtually every threat, striking at the flanks and forcing the Soviets to defend their small gains. During this period, German intelligence was stunned when aerial reconnaissance photographs showed two large tank formations closing in on the Orel battlefield. In addition, despite defeating the Mius and Izyum offensives, they began seeing massed movement south of Kursk near Belgorod, indicating another Soviet attack pending. It was becoming obvious that the Soviets had been able to mass far more combat power than the Germans had ever suspected.

On 3 July the main Soviet attack began as Operation Rumiantsev opened. There was nothing fancy about these plans, authored by Georgi Zhukov himself. He massed almost five complete armies (5th Guards, 6th Guards, 53rd, 69th and part of the 7th Guards) at the point of the main attack, backed by two tank armies, the 1st and 5th Guards. Two days after this attack opened up, two more armies would attack on their right; three days after that, two more armies on the left. Overall, three Soviet Fronts – Voronezh, Steppe and Southwestern – concentrated 990,000 men, 12,000 guns and 2,400 tanks at the point of decision.

Opposing them was Hoth's *Fourth Panzer Army* and *Army Detachment 'Kempf'*. Well rested infantry manned the front lines, with the *7th Panzer Division* in immediate support. There were multiple defensive lines established – Kharkov had seven protecting it from the north and three lines to the east. Belgorod, closest to the front, was protected by defensive lines and fortified heavily. Backing the infantry up was the mobile power that had been assembled for Zitadelle – the *XLVIII* and *II SS Panzer Corps*. *Army Group South* was missing only the two Panzer divisions sent successfully to destroy the breakthrough on the Mius River. Additionally, the *3rd SS Panzergrenadier Division 'Totenkopf'* had been temporarily detached from the *II SS Panzer Corps* to operate against the Izyum bridgehead. Altogether, though, the Germans fielded 350,000 troops and some 900 tanks.

When Zhukov attacked, the disparity in strength at the point of attack was decisive. The guns opened fire at 05.00, the infantry struck at 08.00 and by noon, the first German line had a six-mile hole torn in it. Both exploiting tank armies plunged into the hole and by the end of the day had driven some 15 miles into the German defences. Zhukov's infantry lagged the advance by some nine miles as they dealt with the German defences.

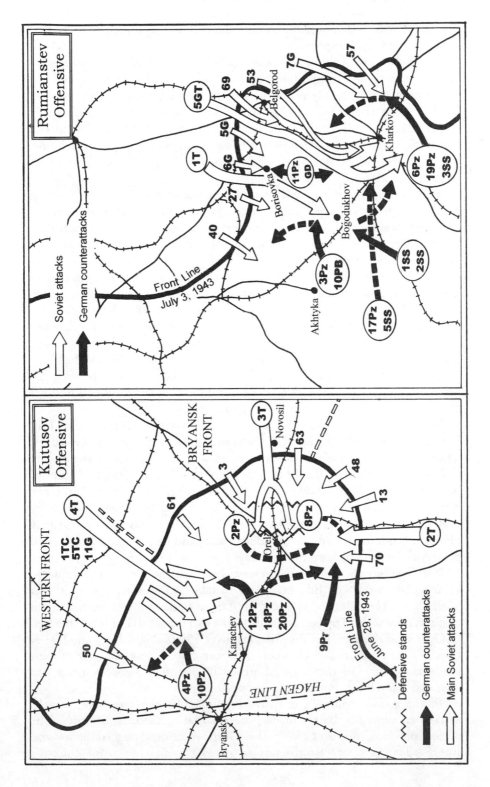

This gap would widen over the coming days and create an opportunity that von Manstein could exploit.

When the massive blow fell near Kharkov, Hitler had been considering *Army Group Centre*'s suggestion to withdraw from the Orel salient. His initial impulse was to say no, as he had done many times before, but the Tunisian disaster still hung in his mind. With the Kharkov front suddenly ripped open, the reserves he could have used to hold Orel were unavailable. On 4 July he gave permission to von Kluge to withdraw to the Hagen line. Six days later, when the Allies invaded Sicily, the permission became an imperative order.

To the north, von Kluge and his army commanders still had the problem of the continual Soviet pressure and the approaching armour. Fortunately for them, Stalin and his generals made it easy. They committed each tank army separately as it arrived, allowing the Germans to use their interior lines to counter each threat.

The 3rd Tank Army arrived first from the east and, rather than exploit the shallow breach made by the 3rd and 63rd Armies, its commander, General P.S. Rybalko, decided to force a separate breach. The attack, on 6 July, was generally successful, with the momentum of the shock force carrying it over seven miles through German defences, but casualties in men and equipment were heavy. Diverging directives from Stalin and his front commander further split up Rybalko's diminished combat power. The orders left the tank army vulnerable to counter-attacks by the *2nd* and *8th Panzer Divisions* that stopped each piece separately.

By the time the 4th Tank Army arrived and went into action on 13 July, it was apparent to the Soviets that the Germans were evacuating the salient. They tried to step up the pressure to eliminate as much of the enemy strength as they could. But Stalin's primary mobile force, the 2nd and 3rd Tank Armies, had been devastated – from a strength of 450 and 730 tanks respectively, each army now fielded fewer than 60 tanks. Pursuit by infantry was too slow to be effective. Thus 4th Tank Army was sent in virtually alone. It ran into an ambush of hidden tanks and assault guns and lost 50 per cent of its strength on the first day.

With the Soviets' last mobile reserve blunted, the Germans completed their withdrawal by 20 July, managing to take 53,000 tons of supplies out with them. They destroyed every military installation and burned grain crops as they went. The Soviets could point to a huge tract of land liberated in Operation Kutusov, but they had lost over 550,000 casualties and 80 per cent of their armour. The Germans had been hurt, losing almost half their tanks and guns, but the targeted armies of the offensive were intact and effective behind a strong defensive position.

To the south, Zhukov's offensive continued as the two wing attacks started on time, but barely made progress against German defences. The added pressure, however, kept the German armies pushed apart and interfered with their effectiveness in dealing with the crisis. Zhukov's infantry became embroiled for days around the towns of Graivoron and Borisovka, trying to encircle and destroy the elements of five German infantry divisions. Counter-attacks by the *11th Panzer* and *'Grossdeutschland' Divisions* held the escape routes open and got most of the troops out, hampered severely by heavy artillery fire from the encroaching Soviets.

The rescue efforts around Borisovka delayed the German response to the invading tank armies, but insured that the 1st Tank Army was operating with minimal infantry support. On 10 July two Panzergrenadier divisions, the *1st SS 'Liebstandarte Adolf Hitler'* and *2nd SS 'Das Reich'* launched a counter-attack at the exposed Soviet spearhead near Bogodukhov. The next day the *3rd Panzer Division* and *10th Panzer Brigade*, with some 200 new Panther tanks, struck the embattled Soviets from the opposite flank. The new tanks showed they were superior to the enemy tanks they faced – when they worked. Far too many fell victim to mechanical failure. However, the two flank attacks shattered the 1st Tank Army and severely damaged the tank corps preceding the 40th Army's advance that attacked *3rd Panzer* with a flank attack of its own.

While the 1st Tank Army was battling for survival, Zhukov set up his set-piece assault on Kharkov. He planned to have the 53rd Army and part of the 5th Guards Tank Army attack the city from the northwest, while the Southwestern Front's 57th Army attacked it from the southeast. A direct frontal attack by the 7th Guards Army, and an encircling move by the remainder of the 5th Guards Tank Army would force the Germans to evacuate the city or be trapped inside.

But the loss of the 1st Tank Army left the German mobile forces free to concentrate on the threat to Kharkov. The *III Panzer Corp*s, recently arrived from the Mius battle, would move directly up the Donets from Izyum and attack the 57th Army in the flank with *'Totenkopf'* in support. *'Liebstandarte'* and *'Das Reich'* would attack the encircling tanks, and *Army Group South*'s main reserves, the *17th Panzer Division* and *5th SS Panzer 'Wiking'* would attack the Soviet threat in the northwest.

The two sides collided on 15 July. The next two days of swirling tank battles saw both sides lose heavily. But the concentrations that the Germans could throw at the exposed Soviet spearheads proved too much. A divided 5th Guards Tank Army took a toll on the attacking Germans, but was completely shattered with 95 per cent of its armour destroyed. Without an armoured shield, the Soviet infantry units were forced to halt their own attacks and defend. Both the 57th and 7th Guards fell back after resisting the German assaults for several days, opening up the rest of Zhukov's forces to flank attacks from the southeast. By 21 July the Soviet attack was spent. There was general movement back toward the river lines, but there were multiple towns and villages that Soviet troops held, creating a patchwork of isolated islands of resistance in the sea of German armour. The Germans had little infantry strength to deal effectively with these isolated positions and their armoured was battered and exhausted.

The Soviets held on to some bridgeheads over the Donets, but the significant victory they were seeking fell terribly short. Two more carefully built up tank armies had been ruined and over 2,000 tanks had been destroyed in three weeks of intense fighting. Another 480,000 men had fallen, nearly half during the pull back and mop ups. The Germans had suffered as well, losing 60 per cent of their armour, but they had taken the tremendous body shot the Soviets had prepared and stayed intact.

For now the east quieted down as both sides licked their wounds.

The battle in the West

When the news that the Germans were cancelling their Kursk offensive to build a strategic reserve came out of Moscow, the Allies were stunned. Nervous intelligence officers tapped every source they had looking for signs that the Germans were moving more troops into Sicily. They identified Rommel's new command in Northern Italy, but little else. Ultra gave no indications of major movements – but it had also given no warning of Zitadelle's cancellation.[7] When the Soviets struck in the east and pinned the Germans down, Allied fears subsided and Husky continued.

On 9 July 1943, Axis aerial reconnaissance found the huge Allied invasion armada – 2,600 ships carrying 180,000 men – moving toward Sicily; Husky was beginning.

On Sicily, the Axis forces were better prepared for the invasion, thanks to the two-month respite following the fall of Tunisia, but nowhere near prepared enough. In nominal command of the 230,000 Italians and 40,000 Germans was 66-year-old Generale d'Armata Alfredo Guzzoni. Recalled out of retirement, the energetic Italian had only been on the island for six weeks – enough time to know his defences were inadequate. His mobile and coastal divisions were poorly trained, poorly equipped, poorly supplied, and poorly led. Only his *'Livorno' Assault and Landing Division* was close to strength. His troops were divided into two corps. The *XVI Corps* had the task of defending eastern Sicily with the *'Napoli' Division* and two coastal divisions. The *XII Corps* defended the western half of the island with the *'Aosta'* and *'Assietta' Divisions* and three coastal divisions. In addition to these corps, there were three separate naval fortress areas at Messina-Reggio, Trapani, and Augusta-Syracuse that were better armed and prepared for defence.

In reserve, Guzzoni held the *'Livorno' Division* and the two German divisions under his 'command'. He wanted to keep all three concentrated for one massive counter-attack once the main Allied landing was identified. However, Kesselring disagreed with the dispositions, wanting the German divisions split to cover both sides of the island. Guzzoni gave in. The *'Hermann Göring' Panzer Division* newly arrived in Sicily and at full strength, was stationed to guard the west. In the centre Kesselring placed the *15th Panzer*, supplemented by a company of Tiger tanks. With the exception of a regimental group posted near Catania, *15th Panzer* was concentrated. Its men and officers had been on the island for months and knew the area well. Hitler named Major General Fridolin von Senger und Etterlin, an experienced Panzer commander as well as a diplomat, to head up Germany's forces on Sicily, ostensibly under Guzzoni.

Fortunately, von Senger and Guzzoni held similar tactical views on how to defend the island, despite the difference in dispositions – each intended to counter-attack with the weight of his reserves. Von Senger, and his immediate superior, Kesselring, especially wanted an immediate attack against the chaotic beachheads.

On the night of 9 July the first phase of Husky went into action as the British 1st Airborne's 1st Airlanding Brigade was transported over the island in 169 gliders. The mission of these 2,000 paratroops was to land outside Syracuse near the Ponte Grande Bridge and hold it until relieved by the 5th Infantry Division the following day. Unfortunately, the glider convoy broke apart due to anti-aircraft fire, high winds and smoke that obscured the target area. Sixty-nine gliders landed at sea, killing over 250 troops. The rest of the gliders were scattered over the island – only twelve landed anywhere near their target. With incredible courage, a single platoon captured the bridge and by daylight had collected some 90 troops to hold the vital span.

The second air phase of the operation went as poorly as the first. Paratroops of the 505th Regimental Combat Team from the US 82nd Airborne Division were supposed to be dropped northeast of Gela around midnight to block any enemy movement toward the US landing beaches. Many of the 266 C-47 aircraft lost their way flying to Sicily and encountered the same conditions that had fractured the glider convoy. The 3,000 paratroops were scattered over a thousand square miles of the island. As a result, this elite fighting force was reduced from a potent weapon to a scattered nuisance.

The landings commenced at 03.00, 10 July 1943. The British landed the 50th Northumbrian and 5th Divisions of Lieutenant General Miles Dempsey's XIII Corps between Avola and Cassible southwest of Syracuse, with support from 3rd Commando and the 1st Special Raiding Squadron. Further south around Pachino, Lieutenant General Sir Oliver Leese's XXX Corps put the 1st Canadian and 51st Highland Divisions ashore with the 231st Brigade in direct support. There was very little organised resistance to the landings; most of the problems came from the high seas that pushed landing craft as much as 6,000 yards off course. But, by mid-morning, the British had troops ashore and were beginning to push out toward their first objectives.

To the west the US Seventh Army was also landing at the same time. The independent 3rd Infantry Division landed on both sides of Licata, taking the small port handily with the help of the 3rd Ranger Battalion. East of them, the 36th Division, part of Lieutenant General Omar Bradley's II Corps, landed at Gela where it met stiff resistance. The first attack into the port was repulsed, but the second, aided by engineers and Rangers, was successful. Finally, Bradley's other division, the 45th Infantry Division, landed unopposed near Scoglitti.

Resistance began picking up as the landing forces moved off their beachheads. In the first major setback elements of the 5th Division, moving to relieve the 1st Airborne troops holding the Ponte Grande Bridge, arrived too late. After holding out for hours, the paratroops, reduced to fifteen men, surrendered when their ammunition ran out. By mid-afternoon when the relieving troops finally arrived, their initial advance was repulsed, then the charges reset by the enemy brought the bridge down in front of them. Movement toward Syracuse was halted while the engineers gathered equipment to re-bridge the river.

Axis counter-attack plans began with the movement of the *15th Panzer* toward the US beaches. The 45th Division, supported by the M4 Sherman tanks of the 753rd Tank Battalion, captured Comiso airfield and was advancing against the field at Biscari. They overran the Italian defenders, but ran head on into the Germans. The Shermans were no match for the Tigers that accompanied the attack and the infantry had to fall back, suffering heavy casualties as they retreated.

Early on 11 July the counter-attack hit the beachhead in full force. The green 36th Division, a Texas National Guard unit, held its own for a while, but without enough anti-tank support began caving in before the Panzers. While *15th Panzer* pushed forward, another Italian-German force struck Gela itself, forcing the US defenders out. A counter-attack by engineers and Rangers retook the town briefly, but it fell again to another concerted Axis effort. The Ranger battalion was virtually destroyed in the fighting. The survivors joined the 36th Division at the beachhead, where naval gunfire aided the defence.

But the potential disaster at Gela became secondary to the disaster that befell the British that day. General Montgomery came ashore early that morning and, while he was moving forward, a lone Bf 109 strafed his entourage, killing his chief of staff and seriously wounding the Eighth Army commander himself. News of Monty's wound spread quickly and the loss of their beloved leader devastated the troops, bringing the entire army to a virtual halt.

Offshore, Patton responded to the crises on the beaches by landing the last regiment of the 36th Division and an initial task force from 2nd Armored Division to counter the Panzers. The reinforcements stabilised the situation, but the US Seventh Army found itself with two separated beachheads, both under sporadic attack, and no port, which limited supply. The Germans beat back several counter-attacks, inflicting losses on the American tankers as they kept their pressure up.

That night Patton also committed another reserve – the 82nd Airborne's 504th Parachute Regiment. Unfortunately, bad luck dogged this airborne attempt as much as the first two. As the transports approached Sicily, the

Allied fleet, still nervous from a day of Axis air attacks, opened fire with a withering anti-aircraft barrage. Twenty-three aircraft were shot down and many others damaged in the horrific mistake. The paratroops lost 10 per cent of their number before the drop, including their assistant division commander, and were scattered over a wide area.

While the Seventh Army struggled to fight off Axis counter-attacks, the British struggled with their personal loss. Alexander, as stunned as the army by Montgomery's loss, seemed unable to cope with the situation. On 12 July, more than a day after Monty's injury, Alexander came out of his funk to announce that XXX Corps commander Leese would take over command. Leese was an obvious choice; he was Monty's protégé and a good corps commander. But he was far more volatile with his subordinates than Monty and prone to obscene outbursts. With the change in command finally made, Leese attempted to get Eighth Army rolling again.

Guzzoni, Kesselring, and von Senger were aware that the attacks at Gela had probably done as much damage as they could. Allied naval support and increasing air attacks were providing enough of a shield to keep the Panzers from pushing the landings into the sea. They could replace infantry losses by combing the German rear area units but they had also lost a lot of tanks, including virtually all their Tigers, and these losses were almost impossible to replace. And with both German divisions attacking the Americans, very little stood in the way of the British except the Italians, who, apart from the 'Livorno' Division, were surrendering in large numbers. Von Senger sent orders to his division commanders to pull back from the beaches, out of naval gunfire range, and commence mobile delaying tactics.

Kesselring debated sending more troops to the island, given the poor performance by the Italian coastal divisions. He was still concerned that the Allies would land on the Italian mainland and cut off Sicily. While the situation clarified, he dispatched his elite paratroops to the airfields near Augusta to bolster the defenders.

On 15 July Leese finally got Eighth Army moving again, sending the 5th and 50th Divisions straight at Syracuse. But the delay had cost the British heavily. Rather than a few assorted troops in their path, and the bulk of the enemy engaged with Seventh Army, they found an enemy substantially strengthened with high quality troops. The 5th was bloodily repulsed in its attack, but the 50th managed to force and hold a bridgehead across the Anapo River. Though fighting was bitter, both Syracuse and Augusta fell four days later.

As XIII Corps operated on the coast XXX Corps moved inland. The 51st Division attacked Palazzola on the main highway and was making progress against the Italians, when the *15th Panzer* struck from the flank. The Highlanders were thrown back several miles before regrouping to stop their pursuers. As soon as resistance stiffened, the Panzers pulled back. Later that night, the Germans struck at a brigade from the 50th Division before pulling back into fortifications around Palazzola.

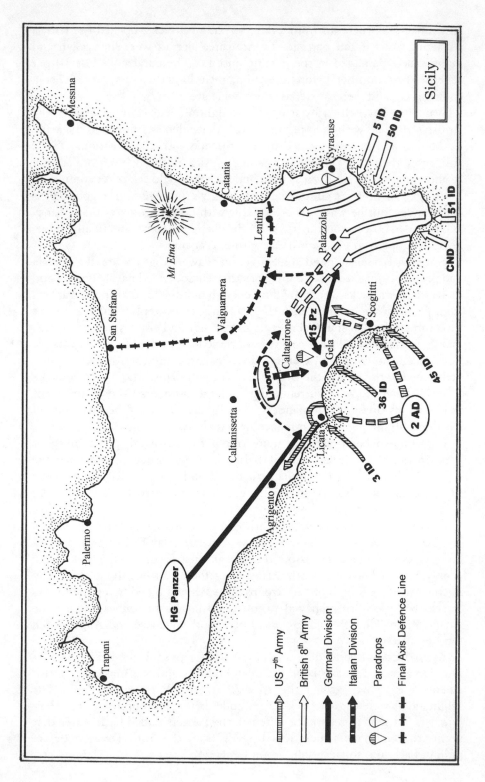

Sicily

Messina

Catania

Mt Etna

Lentini

Palazzola

Syracuse

5 ID

50 ID

51 ID

CND

San Stefano

Valguamera

Caltagirone

Gela

Scoglitti

115 Pz

Livorno

45 ID

Caltanissetta

36 ID

2 AD

Licata

3 ID

Agrigento

HG Panzer

Palermo

Trapani

US 7th Army

British 8th Army

German Division

Italian Division

Paradrops

Final Axis Defence Line

In the American sector, the German retreat allowed Seventh Army to retake Gela from its tenacious *Livorno* defenders. Inland, a taskforce from 2nd Armored pushed ahead, slowed by a series of well-defended positions that compelled the Americans to try slow flanking manoeuvres. Their opponents, the *Hermann Göring* Panzergrenadiers, battle-hardened and tested in Tunisia, pulled out of each position just prior to the attacks and withdrew to fresh defences. By 20 July, however, the Americans had advanced enough to secure the beachhead and Patton went onto the defensive to regroup, resupply, and add badly needed replacements to his bloodied regiments.

With a storm hampering operations, Patton and Leese met with Alexander to discuss further plans. The meeting became as stormy as the weather. Leese began by attacking Patton for US 'failures'. The British commander was livid at the attacks by *15th Panzer* which had severely hurt his troops and stalled their drive. In his view, the United States combat troops were not protecting his flanks as the invasion plan envisioned. He presented these views in an angry, foul outburst that shocked everyone in the room. Alexander, who silently agreed with his subordinate, did nothing to tone down the remarks. Patton, who had earlier received a stinging rebuke from Eisenhower for the airborne disasters, finally exploded, citing Leese's unimaginative tactics as the real reason the British were not moving. Alexander eventually stepped in to quell the recriminations. Although the shouting subsided, the participants remained volatile and angry.

As the meeting proceeded, the commanders ran headlong into a problem that had been ignored throughout the Husky planning sessions. There had been little thought as to operations after the landings had been established. Taking the city of Messina quickly to trap Axis forces on the island and prevent reinforcements was the obvious goal, but there had never been a master plan or strategic blueprint on how to accomplish that goal. There had never been any coordination between armies, either through their own efforts or through 15th Army Group. Now, with the bitterness of the earlier words still ringing, the Allies had to come up with plans.

With the forces on the east coast stymied and facing a series of easily defended river lines, the original British plan of taking Messina from that direction was impractical. Leese demanded the Americans face west and hold their present line, while Eighth Army moved northeast to cut the island in two. Patton vehemently protested the relegation of Seventh Army to being bystanders. But Alexander went along with Leese's overall plan. He ordered Patton to finish regrouping and not become heavily engaged.

While the Allies argued and the Sicilian defenders dug in, events were coming to a head in Italy itself. The fall of Syracuse and Augusta triggered the anti-Mussolini plotters into making their move. But Roberto Farinacci informed the Germans that the head of the Fascist Grand Council, Dino Grandi, was planning to oust Mussolini at a Council meeting on 24 July. Kesselring met with the Italian leader to warn him of the plot, but

Mussolini dismissed the idea, stating Grandi was fully on his side. Stymied from that direction, the Germans took direct action – Gestapo agents grabbed Grandi at his home and spirited him away. Bereft of its leader, the coup subsided.

On 22 July, while the Germans were finishing their withdrawal from the Orel salient and the armoured clashes around Kharkov were dying down, the Eighth Army attacked. XIII Corps tried to breach the line of defences on the Lentini River and failed after three days of hard fighting. The Highlanders struck again at Palazzola, but were battled to a standstill by *15th Panzer*. However, after several days, the Germans withdrew from the battered town voluntarily to avoid being cut off. Further west the Canadians attacked Vizzini along the main highway and had a difficult time against the dug-in Italians, who were supported by a *Kampfgruppe* from the *15th Panzer*. After nine days of fighting, the Canadians finally dislodged the Axis with help from the Highland Division.

While the British were slogging ahead, the Americans were regrouping and reinforcing their beachhead. The battered 36th Division was pulled out and replaced by the 9th Infantry Division. The Texas division's baptism of fire had been a hard one; apart from the troop casualties, five senior staff officers were relieved along with six battalion commanders. With two battalion commanders captured during the fighting, the 36th Division would enter its next fight with new leaders.

Patton refused to sit quietly, regardless of his orders from 15th Army Group. As soon as 2nd Armored and the 45th 'Thunderbird' Division had built up, he sent them on a 'reconnaissance in force' against the town of Caltagirone. Capture of this town would begin to open the way across the island. After several days the Thunderbirds fought their way into the town, only to be pushed out again by *Hermann Göring* troops. A battalion of the 2nd Armored arrived to stop the German pursuit and begin the push back toward the town.

At the end of July, with his attacks across the Lentini stymied and Vizzini in his hands, Leese demanded Patton pull away from Caltagirone and give Eighth Army possession of the vital highway for his drive across the island. Patton, whose troops were battling back into the city, refused.

Leese immediately went to Alexander, demanding that Patton be relieved for insubordination and disobeying direct orders not to 'become engaged'. Alexander flew to Sicily to meet with Patton personally. The American made an impassioned argument that the British were not in a position to take the town and he was. To pull back, Patton stated, would be a gift to the Germans.

Alexander was noncommittal to the Seventh Army commander, but flew directly from his meeting to Eisenhower's headquarters where he dumped the problem on his superior's lap. Eisenhower, exasperated by the internecine arguments and the slow process of the campaign, compromised. He ordered Patton to take the town, then turn it over to the British. In a closed-door session, he also told Alexander to take control of 15th Army Group or be relieved himself.

On 2 August 1943, Caltagirone fell to the 45th Division, when the *Hermann Göring* Panzers and Panzergrenadiers fell back. II Corps commander Bradley, still livid about the orders from above, grudgingly ordered his troops to pull out. Moving XXX Corps and its support into the town delayed any British action for several days as Leese's command was woefully short of transport. While XXX Corps was moving into position for its next push, Leese also brought the 78th Division into Syracuse to bolster battered XIII Corps along the coast.

While the transfer was being made, Patton ordered Bradley to shift his attack toward Caltanissetta further west, then unleashed a surprise. He amphibiously leapfrogged a regiment of the 3rd Infantry around the Axis western defences to land at Porto Empedocle, where the attack quickly captured the small port and the larger undefended town of Agrigento. The move unhinged the Axis defences and the Italians pulled back into the hills, opening up the coast road to the west.

Von Senger ordered all German troops on the western half of the island to move into a large arc around volcanic Mount Etna. Guzzoni, shocked and angry at the German withdrawal, ordered his troops to resist. Over the next several days, it became clear, however, that the Italians were no match alone for the fast-moving Americans.

By 7 August, with the British drive just getting underway and the Americans closing in on Palermo, Patton sent a strongly worded suggestion that the British look at leapfrogging units around Axis strongpoints. He even suggested landing the US 1st Infantry Division at Marina di Catanzara on the Italian mainland to isolate the island and break open the front.

Three days later, however, two Ultra intercept bombshells took the Allied focus away from Sicily and onto the ominously quiet Eastern Front.

Endgame

The first bombshell was an order to Rommel to send the *1st Panzer Division* south to join the *26th Panzer* and *29th Panzergrenadier Divisions* under the *XIV Panzer Corps* headquarters en route from the east. He was also told to expect the *II SS Panzer Corps*, then activate himself as commander, *Army Group Italy*, under Kesselring. Knowing that substantial reinforcements were heading for Italy was bad enough but the second Ultra intercept was worse. The orders went to all German army group, army and corps commanders, telling them to prepare for a series of defensive shifts in connection with the expected armistice with the Soviet Union.

Stalin, after having his concentrated combat strength shattered at Orel and Kharkov, had indeed entered into armistice negotiations with Germany. He was angry and disappointed at the results of his massive offensives – the losses left him little capability to attack and thus robbed him of the initiative. He grew increasingly bitter that the Western Allies seemed unable to break through two German divisions while he fought off a hundred times as many. This left him feeling that the West was forcing him to destroy himself along with the Germans. Ultimately he knew any armistice with Germany would be violated at some point, but he was determined that this time it would be to his advantage. Until then, he thought, let the Capitalists and the Fascists bleed each other for awhile. He ordered his Commissar for Foreign Affairs, Vyacheslav Molotov, to open secret negotiations with his hated enemy.

For Hitler, the armistice was a compromise as well. Although his forces had stopped the Soviet attacks and inflicted massive casualties, his own armies had been hurt, too. Short on men and equipment, and exhausted from the intense combat of the last few weeks, they were in no condition to follow up their defensive victory with an offensive of their own. Stalemate could only lead to more battles and, with the West knocking at Europe's side door in Sicily, he would end up confronting the same no-win options he faced in early 1943. Armistice was acceptable for now.

Churchill and Roosevelt were stunned by Ultra's implied turn of events. Churchill likened it to the same gut wrench he felt when the 1939 pact between the Soviet Union and Germany was announced.[8] Both men immediately sent their ambassadors to meet with Stalin. The Soviet leader had little to say to either man other than to confirm his decision to settle with the Germans. When pushed for an explanation, he exploded, stating that his nation had lost a million sons in the past month and demanding to know what sacrifices the West was making. With that he dismissed his visitors.

In mid-August, while the German-Soviet talks were nearing completion, the Allied political and military leaders met again in Casablanca. As the first order of business they reviewed their military situation. On Sicily, there was slow progress against the stiff enemy line that curved around Mount Etna. US forces were clearing out the western half of the island, while the British probed for a weak spot. Quality Axis troops were starting to appear in the lines against them, despite Allied air interdiction. The straits between Messina and Reggio had become ringed with dense anti-aircraft defences that both protected the troops crossing and allowed more supplies to flow. Allied movement forward was becoming even more difficult than it had been before. In addition to the worsening military situation, Mussolini's political fortunes were stable for the time being. Italian troops from the Balkans were being brought home, replaced by a slow trickle of German divisions from the east. With Grandi's disappearance, the Italian leader's opposition had been subdued. The possibility of Italy falling out of the war now seemed unlikely without a solid Allied victory in Sicily.

The differing US and British strategic viewpoints again emerged in the talks. Churchill wanted to continue the Mediterranean campaign, threatening German Europe along a wide front. The United States was caught in a quandary. Its air campaign against the Reich was just beginning to pay dividends, but without an Eastern Front, the bombers would face heavily reinforced *Luftwaffe* interceptor squadrons. As much as the US wanted a cross-Channel attack, Roosevelt had to admit the American and British armies were not ready to take on the Germans alone. With little progress in Europe and few strategic options, public opinion in America would demand the President turn his full attention toward the Japanese.

Reluctantly, both men concluded that a Germany unhampered by a Soviet enemy would be able to augment its forces in the Mediterranean and make an Allied position on Sicily untenable, especially from a logistics point of view. Orders went out to 15th Army Group to withdraw the Seventh and Eighth Armies from Sicily. Although the two leaders left each other with renewed vocal assurances of continued support against Hitler, they both knew that, to all intents and purposes, the war in Europe was over.

The reality

In reality, Hitler did little reassessing in early 1943. His decision to defend Tunisia failed, trapping 250,000 Germans and Italians. In the east, despite his own misgivings – and those of his leading generals, he chose to initiate Operation Zitadelle in July, throwing his Panzer reserves into the attack. It failed and the weakened German forces were unable to counter the subsequent Soviet attacks. As historians note, the Soviet offensives did not end until Berlin fell. The messages about the cancellation of Zitadelle were in fact received by Stalin, but he waited several days and German troop movements showed him the operation was still on. In the west, the deception Operation Mincemeat was not turned down by Eisenhower and succeeded in spreading the scarce German resources into Greece, Sardinia and the Balkans. And despite the muddled planning and mistakes, the Allies succeeded in capturing Sicily – after Montgomery just missed being wounded by a strafing aircraft on D-Day. The campaign there sealed the end of Mussolini's regime, and Italy capitulated less than a month after the island fell.

Bibliography

Deakin, F.W., *The Brutal Friendship: Mussolini, Hitler and the Fall of Italian Fascism* (Harper & Row, New York, 1962).

D'Este, Carlo, *Bitter Victory: The Battle for Sicily 1943* (HarperCollins, New York 1988).

Erickson, John, *The Road to Berlin: Stalin's War with Germany* (Yale University Press, New Haven, CT, 1999).

Glantz, David M., *Soviet Military Intelligence in War* (Frank Cass, Portland, OR, 1990).

Glantz, David M., and House, Jonathan M., *The Battle of Kursk* (University Press of Kansas, Lawrence, KS, 1999).

Mitcham, Samuel W., and von Staffenberg, Friedrich, *The Battle of Sicily*, (Orion Books, New York, 1991).

Sadkovich, James, *The Italian Navy in World War II* (Greenwood Press, Westport, CT, 1994).

Notes

1. The Italians were not the only German ally to lose armies on the Eastern Front. The Romanian Third and Fourth Armies were destroyed in the fighting around Stalingrad as well.

2. Unlike Italy, Romania and Bulgaria, Finland was not Germany's 'ally'. The small country was a 'co-belligerent' and had joined the war to redress the results of the Winter War of 1939 with the Soviet Union. Finland called its participation the 'War of Continuation'.

3. The 1943 Soviet tank army was an organisation consisting of two tank corps and one mechanised corps, plus supporting units. It totaled 37–45,000 men and 6–700 tanks. It was the equivalent of a German Panzer corps and capable of sustained independent deep operations.

4. The Italians lost 319,000 tons of shipping from February through May 1943. Over 60 per cent of the losses occurred in port from allied air attacks. Ultra intercepts also tracked and targeted tankers making sure that the mobility of the Axis forces was limited. See Sadkovich, *The Italian Navy in World War II*.

5. Roberto Farinacci had once been the Secretary of Italy's Fascist Party, when, in 1924, he had led a purge of the government. He clashed openly with Mussolini, who considered him too violent and extreme. Mussolini had him removed from office and, although still a party member, Farinacci had not held any other high position. See Deakin, *The Brutal Friendship*.

6. 'Werther' was thought to be Major General Hans Oster, the second in command of the German military intelligence and counter-intelligence organisation, the *Abwehr*, under Admiral Wilhelm Canaris. The other spy reporting the cancellation was 'Lucy', Rudolf Rössler, an anti-Nazi German working out of Switzerland with senior *Wermacht* sources. See Glantz, *Soviet Military Intelligence in War*.

7. This was, of course, because Hitler had not officially cancelled the offensive.

* 8. Churchill discusses his thoughts in some detail in his memoirs, *The Broken Crusade* (HMSO, London, 1948).

8
THE LUFTWAFFE TRIUMPHANT
The Defeat of the Allied Bomber Offensive, 1944–45

David C. Isby

'There is a might-have-been which is more true than truth.'
William Faulkner, *Absalom, Absalom.*

Over a five-month period, from October 1943 to March 1944, the *Luftwaffe* succeeded in defeating both the US and British bomber offensives against Germany. Both of these offensives, at different times, had effectively to stop the deep penetration attacks that both considered vital for their strategic impact. Their own heavy losses and the lack of evidence of the impact the bombers were having on the German war machine forced Allied airmen to re-consider how to continue their bomber operations.

For their part, the Germans were faced with another set of decisions that had to be made to ensure that these successes were not fleeting. The German check to the Allied bomber offensives was obviously not decisive. How both sides reacted to these German victories in late 1943 and early 1944 amounted to a turning point in the war in Europe, even though the impact of the decisions made by each side was not seen to be decisive for many months thereafter.

Background to defeat

The British bomber offensive of 1940–41 was largely ineffective militarily, killing more British aircrew than German citizens at its targets but, by late 1942, the bomber offensive was being waged in deadly earnest. By the end of that year the US Army Air Force's Eighth Air Force was entering combat over occupied Europe and the RAF had made its first massed thousand-bomber raids and started to inflict significant damage on German cities.

The *Luftwaffe* reacted strongly, pulling back fighters from other fronts and massing flak guns. The German war economy, now being belatedly mobilised, geared up to meet the bomber offensives. Production priorities were set to build ammunition for flak guns, cutting into the quantity available for the Army for ground combat.

In January 1943, at the Casablanca Conference, Roosevelt, Churchill and their staffs established the bomber offensive as a major element of Anglo-American strategy against Germany, putting a seal on decisions made pre-war and included in the Anglo-American ABC-1 report of 1941. In July 1943 the potential power of the bomber offensive was shown by the destruction of Hamburg. Albert Speer, now directing the German war economy, feared that if Hamburg were to be repeated throughout Germany over the summer of 1943, a different city burning each week, Germany would crack. The threat was not only from British night area bombardment. The Eighth Air Force precision daylight bombing attack on the synthetic oil plant at Huls showed that, done right, this type of attack could be devastating to high-value targets.

But it did not happen. No other cities burned like Hamburg nor were any oil plants damaged like Huls for the rest of 1943. Instead, the *Luftwaffe*'s efforts – improvised rather than well planned – delivered Germany from the bomber threat in 1943.

In the summer and autumn of 1943, the *Luftwaffe* fought the US daylight bomber offensive – which relied on unescorted bomber formations striking key industrial targets – to a standstill. The Germans had to improvise an integrated air defence system far more extensive than the one which defeated them in the Battle of Britain. A US maximum effort against the 'soft underbelly' of the German war economy, the oil refineries at Ploesti, Romania, cost 54 B-24 Liberators and its low-level attempt at decisive accuracy proved to be unrepeatable. The Eighth Air Force lost 60 B-17 Flying Fortresses on the 17 August Regensburg–Schweinfurt raid. Finally, in October, 148 heavy bombers were lost on four missions, 60 of them on the 14 October return to Schweinfurt. With anything from an eighth to a third of the force being lost in each major attack, the USAAF was forced to suspend the bomber offensive against Germany after the second Schweinfurt raid.

With the USAAF halted, it was the turn of the RAF night offensive against the cities of Germany to carry the burden of the Allied Casablanca strategy. RAF Bomber Command was confident of success, with improved navigational aids and radar, more Lancaster bombers, and new tactics, including the use of the Pathfinder Force to mark targets. Bomber Command set out to land its decisive blow. It failed. In the 'Battle of Berlin', the RAF was unable to inflict decisive damage on Berlin or any of the key cities it targeted, while suffering unsustainable losses. The climax came with the March 1944 Nuremberg raid, when 96 bombers went down. The RAF also had to curtail its operations against Germany.

The 1944 bomber offensive

However thankful the Germans may have been for these successes, no one – from the leadership in Berlin down to the fighter pilots – was under any illusion that this was more than a respite. Spring weather in 1944 would surely bring about decisive battles that would determine the success or failure of the bomber offensive.

As with many decisive battles, the decisions made after the German victories were pre-figured or constrained by other ones. In fact, many of the critical decisions that shape the outcome of a conflict are inevitably taken years before, some in long-ago days of peace. The victor is found, in the bright light of hindsight, to have paved the way to success – and the loser to defeat – by a series of decisions that may not have seemed important when they were made.

For the *Luftwaffe* to be able, in 1944, to convert the Allied setbacks of previous months into a lasting and significant defeat required the Germans to have made right decisions in the preceding years. These were fundamental decisions on the doctrine of a modern defensive air wars: what means shall be employed and how shall they be employed? To make these decisions more than theoretical, they had to be enabled by another set of decisions, on the mobilisation of the German war economy, its priorities, and the direction of the war. Some doctrinal decisions required fundamental changes to the nature of the National Socialist regime.

To make the *Luftwaffe* victories of 1943–44 decisive also required the Allies to make wrong decisions as well as for the Germans to make the right ones. Again, key decisions were made years before anyone would know these would become decisive. Doctrinal questions were key. These had been made, in many cases, pre-war, in the years when both the RAF and USAAF were advocating and evolving strategic bombing capabilities and their political leaders were looking for a way to win a major war without repeating the battles of 1916.

Compounding the problem of evolving a dearly-purchased doctrinal view to meet a changing threat was the fact that the nature of the bomber offensive was such that there were neither guides in previous experience nor immediate readings of victory and defeat. The RAF and USAAF had indeed thought about strategic bombing campaigns pre-war, but had never come close to carrying them out. In an air campaign, there were no vital terrain features to win or lose, no towns or hills to give their name to battles and signal victory or defeat. Rather, victory and defeat were determined not by whose flag was planted on the battlefield but, in the manner of modern war, by statistics. The numbers of aircraft lost, the rate of loss (often the key indicator) and their trends and apparent repeatability, the number of available replacements and the tons of bombs dropped were all closely watched. What was harder to determine was the effect of all these indicators. Air forces, trained to think in turn of readiness rates and flight hours and receptive to modern technology, can delude themselves faster than any other service if they put their minds to it.

For a modern military force, the supply and quality of information is as important as that of ammunition. Yet, even if the information is available, deciding which elements of it are important and which will be used to guide operations, may twist its impact. In the final analysis it was hard to change a losing strategy if it was not apparent to its practitioners that they were indeed losing.

The key German decisions

There was nothing any decisions in 1943–44 could do to redress Germany's fundamental strategic dilemma of having to wage a two-front war with weak or distant allies against enemies who, if lacking in proficiency, had greater resources and access to technology. But such decisions could sustain the German strengths at the operational level of war that had brought them close to victory in 1939–41 and, conceivably, could negate the strategic advantages of Germany's enemies.

The key German decisions that made the changes to the *Luftwaffe* more than mere speculation – on how to mobilise their economy fully – were made before the bomber offensive started to have militarily significant effects.[1] The Germans were, early on, faced with the question of what would be the nature of the Second World War. Would it be a short, victorious war waged with as little internal political cost as possible or was it to be a massive struggle of countries, ideologies, and, in Nazi eyes, races? From these fundamental decisions – or the refusal to make them – came the basic framework that determined how many weapons and of what type would be available to defend Germany.

The key decisions of 1940–41: fully to mobilise the economy of not just Germany, but that of all occupied and Axis Europe as an integrated economic superpower to wage a long, technologically demanding, war were hard ones. They were not easily reconciled with the demands of National Socialist ideology – though advocated by some leading ideologues such as Reinhard 'Hangman' Heydrich – nor with German popular opinion. The motivation for this change was that the Germans knew the US was planning to gear up the world's largest economy for war as early as mid-1941. Indeed, the information had been both in reports from the German embassy in Washington and in US newspapers.[2] The change was that Hitler and the leadership decided to take this threat seriously.

The *Luftwaffe* also had to undergo a change away both from Göring's National Socialist romantic vision of air combat – which did not even represent what was taking place in 1918 – and, more important, its role in overall German operations from that which had proven successful in 1939–42. This meant that the response to the growing Allied air offensive had to be envisioned as improving the defences of the Reich. This was a vital change and against the deep-seated views of Hitler, whose belief in offensive operations led him to stress attacks against Britain, first by aircraft and later by the 'vengeance weapons', guided missiles. Hitler's instinct was to defend Germany by attacking Britain.[3]

Changing this was another of the key decisions that made possible German victory against the bombers. For this to be done required Hitler and the national leadership to make decisions through a rational and relatively objective process. This was difficult, for the National Socialist ideology stressed 'thinking with the blood', and what was seen as the iron law of races and struggle trumped other considerations, but was eventually accomplished. This meant that Göring was eased aside and replaced by General Adolf Galland, the fighter ace and General of the Fighter Force, as head of the *Luftwaffe*. The *Luftwaffe* would have to be transformed. The *Luftwaffe* had to be made capable of winning a defensive air campaign.

Making this all possible was a cold-eyed triage of capabilities and forces. The bomber force was de-emphasised. Bomber production was cut back. A proposal to use emerging jet combat aircraft designs primarily as 'Blitz bombers' was disregarded. Operational bomber units, many still weak from their defeat in Operation *Steinbock*, the retaliatory 'Baby Blitz' ordered against Britain, were combed for skilled aircrew, especially for night fighter units. The V-weapons programme was also cut back. A defeat of the Allied bomber offensive would remove much of the German demand for retaliation that motivated the programme.

Many of the results of these decisions would not be seen until 1943–44 but they made possible the mass production of the implements of war that could turn the temporary defeat of the bombers into something more long-lasting and costly: Messerschmitt 262 jet-propelled day and night fighters, Focke-Wulf 190D piston-engined fighters (the most effective of Germany's pre-jet fighters), high-powered engines and the aviation fuels to run them, advanced radars, and much more.

The hardest decision was that the *Luftwaffe* prevailed over Speer in arguing for quality in place of some quantity in aircraft production. Speer's original goal was to boost the number of military aircraft produced by Germany wherever he could. He thought it was less important that they were older designs than that numbers be kept up. This approach, which could have led to Germany ending the war with large numbers of obsolescent, fuel-less fighters waiting at dispersal sites, was changed by one of the 'key decisions' to move to a technologically sophisticated integrated war-fighting approach.

The *Luftwaffe* realised that it could not sustain a force with a large number of inferior fighters. This led to a decision to increase Fw 190 production in place of that of the Bf 109, which was to be replaced by the interim Me 209 and Me 309 piston-engined designs until Messerschmitt production capability transitioned purely to the Me 262 in 1945. In the words of Johannes Steinhoff, one of the *Luftwaffe*'s young fighter leaders on whom the burden of combat operations was placed, 'The war in the air is a technological war which cannot be won by a technologically inferior fighting force, however high its morale or dauntless its resolution.'[4]

The most significant decision was in the development of jet fighters. The Germans early on recognised the potential of the jet fighter as a bomber destroyer – by day and night – and closed down a range of other research and development projects to achieve an early production capability. They decided to push the production Me 262 as an interim fighter type despite the limitations of its Junkers Jumo engines in both design and materials. The Germans also realised that the Me 262 would have to be developed not just as a fighter but as part of an integrated weapons system with a revolutionary new weapon, the 55mm R4M air-to-air rocket.

Other decisions were required to ensure that these weapons and systems would be used effectively in combat. Improved leadership and staff work were central to the transformation of the *Luftwaffe*. It became an integrated air defence system with a consequent build-up of fighters, radar, flak and a well designed and well thought out battle management system linked with secure landline communications. This required bringing forward a new generation of leaders – the generals who gained success during the *Blitzkrieg* did not transition easily to a defensive war – who had been thrust forward by success in the cockpit. Supplementing these leaders were staff officers trained in the best German practice, a combination of pre-war General Staff officers who had been sent to the *Luftwaffe* and the more promising *Luftwaffe* veterans who had been sent through staff training.

Galland was to become commander-in-chief of the air defence of the Reich. He was empowered to make hard decisions and give orders that would be obeyed not only by the different military services, but by the myriad of state, party, and local institutions that were trying to counter the effects of the bombers. Such a strong degree of unity of command – in effect, combining operational, administrative, and research and development responsibilities – and confidence in the commander by the national command authorities was hitherto unknown in the Third Reich, but events were to show that nothing less was required for survival, let alone victory.

The Allied reaction

It was not enough that the Germans made the 'right' decisions. The Allies had to make the 'wrong' ones. Where the Germans replaced their leaders, the Allies retained theirs. The leaders of the 1943 bomber offensive, Air Marshal Arthur Harris and Lieutenant General Ira Eaker kept their positions. These leaders had made decisions for the bomber offensive that had been, in retrospect, the result of tunnel vision on the goal of victory through strategic bombing. Thus, the key decision the Allies made was to carry on much as they had before their defeat by the Germans, but to do it harder and with more aircraft.

The Allied strategic air forces were certainly not the first military forces to be led into defeat by how their pre-existing doctrine failed in the face of the harsh audit of the battlefield. Any institution finds it difficult to learn. It has been argued that organisations in general and military organisations in possession of a strong sense of doctrine in particular, are insensitive to change in their environment.[5]

While the Germans made broad and fundamental changes in aircraft, organisation and technology from that which they had used in 1943, despite their success against the bomber offensive, the Allies decided not to make similar changes. They had seen success – at Hamburg and Huls – and believed that what was required to reach it again was to repeat the process longer and with more resources.

The RAF and USAAF alike remained committed to strategic bombing theory as they had tried to implement it in 1943.[6] The British remained committed to striking not at any one specific industry, but at Germany's will and capability to resist through striking at the urban population, and its administrative and transportation centres. The USAAF was reluctant to modify its pre-war reliance on a doctrine based on mass formations of unescorted heavy bombers destroying critical targets through precision daylight bombing.[7]

Even though the bomber had failed to get through in 1943, its proponents thought that repeating the procedure would succeed. The USAAF believed that, as its B-17 and B-24 bombers were better suited to daylight than night operations, that they would avoid the problems that Bomber Command had encountered with navigation and poor accuracy in the opening years of the war. The American Way of War tends to look to victory through superior doctrine and resources, and the leaders of the Army Air Force were determined to run their own air arm and its operations independently. However, the failures of 1943 had put the military and political masters of the air arms on notice. They would not write further blank cheques for resources without results.

The decision to go on as before despite indicators that it is not working is certainly not an unknown response in air warfare. Harris viewed the US targeting of German industries with scarce-disguised contempt and refused to be swayed from his offensive against German cities even to interfere with the dispersal of the ball-bearing industry from Schweinfurt. The US Eighth Air Force had continued with its bombing of German U-boat pens in French ports long after it was considered to be ineffective largely because of the training it provided for the bomb groups.[8]

Military organisations often fail to adjust their strategies or standard operating procedures to meet specific circumstances, especially when these are in flux. Rather, they tend to look for numerical indicators that support the belief that the circumstances actually represent the preferred case, the one they had prepared to deal with. As a result, rather than responding to the actual situation, many military organisations make decisions and implement policies that reflect the preferred approaches and worldview of those making the decisions regardless of the harsh realities faced by those at the sharp end of the equation.[9]

The 'cult of the offensive' has been identified as the view that military organisations have fixed preferences in strategy and will always prefer offensive ones.[10] This theory holds that evaluation of the effectiveness of operations in aid of this strategy is not carried out if the results are even potentially contradictory to the organisation's preference for offensive action.[11] Where the Germans had stopped looking at the wrong numbers to determine whether they were 'winning' or 'losing', the Allies had embraced them. Those evaluating the bomber offensives became concerned with how much effort was put into them – sorties flown and tonnage dropped – but appeared uninterested in the overall results.[12] They could determine bombing accuracy quite well, but RAF Bomber Command, for example, placed a great deal of value on the number of acres of German cities it burnt out rather than the more difficult question of how this affected the German war effort.

One of the key questions was how much credence to give to the claims of unescorted bomber formation gunners. The decision-makers were well aware that every German fighter that went down would be claimed by every gunner firing at it, but were they to believe actual losses were one-tenth of those claimed? Two-thirds? Some other number? Here, the tendency was to believe the figures that meant good news, that in a battle of attrition between bomber gunners and the fighters, the fighters were losing. But whether this meant they were winning or losing overall was a judgement that eluded the decision-makers.

The most significant decision that led to the defeats of 1944 was the increased hostility towards the use of long-range fighter escorts as part of the bomber offensive. The idea of re-engining the North American P-51 Mustang with the Packard-built Merlin engine was put aside as it was deemed there was no requirement for such a fighter. The USAAF's doctrine, worked out before the war, did not include a 'strategic fighter' such as a long-range P-51. The USAAF had looked at large two-engine designs such as the Bell YFM-1A Airacuda, Lockheed XP-58 and the Northrop XP-61 that had been envisioned in its original air war plan AWPD-1. This led to a decision not to increase the number of escort fighters above that in 1943. Doctrine rather than adaptation carried the day.

Because doctrines, rather than research and development issues were driving decision-making, there was no increased emphasis on the P-38 or modifications to the P-47 to allow it to carry twin drop tanks to extend the range of fighter escort. Drop tanks had been considered pre-war and were seen as redundant.[13] The heavy losses of 1943 were not seen as calling for fighter escorts beyond those already provided. Some indicted even those escorts then available – P-47s and Spitfires – as reducing the effectiveness of the bombers' defensive armament. The bomber was going to get through to its target in daylight.

The RAF had long distrusted the concept of fighter escorts.[14] It was also reluctant to commit its most advanced Mosquito night fighters to escort duties over Germany for fear of compromising their advanced radar systems once shot down and because operating without their ground controlled intercept capability would leave them vulnerable to German night fighters.

Even though the German bomber operations against Britain had been largely defeated by early 1944, the bulk of the night fighter force remained defending against its resumption.

Compounding the problem was the long lead-time inherent in fabricating modern weapons, organising and training the fighting forces that used them, and in the research and development required both to keep existing weapons viable and to provide their eventual replacements and counters to enemy innovations. The decision to invest in the strategic bomber offensive long pre-dated the Casablanca Conference. It was reflected in a wide range of US and British decisions made throughout 1940–42. This meant that even if the bomber offensive were to be defeated decisively in 1944, the Allies would be unable to make a clean break from their investment in strategic bombing and reinvest it elsewhere. Ford's massive Willow Run plant would still be turning out bombers, not landing craft, even though landing craft were, by 1944, proving to be the great Achilles heel of being able to translate economic capability into military force. Had the decision to curtail the bomber offensive been made earlier, some of the resources could have been made available to address the Allies' great strategic need, that for landing craft, especially LSTs (landing ships, tank) and a more responsive and flexible strategy might have been possible. The allies had made the investment in strategic bombing long before the defeats of late 1943. For them to have invested the resources that went into the bomber offensive into more LSTs and better rifle platoon leaders would have required decisions to be made long before then.

'Big Week' leads to the Big Blow

The first opportunity the Germans had to demonstrate the improved capabilities for their integrated air defence system was in mid-February. Then, taking advantage of the week of good weather common in mid-winter in northern Europe, the USAAF decided to announce its return to the offensive mission with a series of attacks on the German aircraft industry. The goal was both to push back the rising tide of German aircraft production and to force the *Luftwaffe* fighter force to impale itself on the defensive fire of the bomber formations.

Over the course of two weeks of maximum-effort air battles that pushed both sides to the brink of exhaustion, considerable damage was done to several German factories but, without deep penetration fighter escort, the bomber rate of loss was even higher than that experienced in 1943. While German losses to the short-range escorts and the bomber guns were not inconsequential, without long-range strategic fighters that could take the war to the enemy fighter force, then the bomber-destroying system that worked so well in 1943 would not only remain intact, it would improve.

After the costly attacks of 'Big Week', the USAAF shifted its objective again, to join with the RAF in the closing stages of the 'Battle of Berlin', as Harris had urged them to do since October. The planning for a series of long-range daylight attacks on Berlin was underway even as 'Big Week' ended. The Germans, aware that the RAF's continued offensive against Berlin would likely lead to pressure on the USAAF to join in, were planning to meet it at the same time.

The *Luftwaffe* leadership did not perceive the defeat of the bomber offensive as simply the end product of an industrial process. They did not think that allocating greatly increased resources to the defence of the Reich would inevitably and of itself produce a large number of shot-down bombers. They realised that the operational skill that had made possible so many of their victories in the early years of the conflict had often been absent from the campaign against the bomber offensive. The command and technology changes made prior to 1943 enabled the *Luftwaffe* to implement initiatives in 1944 that they had been unable to use in earlier air battles.

The principles of mass and annihilation had been enshrined in the German way of war since the days of General Alfred von Schlieffen and his study of the Battle of Cannae in the nineteenth century but, in 1943, the *Luftwaffe* was unable to apply these to defeating the bomber offensive. Though they could impose a general high level of attrition on the overall attacking forces, the Germans were concerned that this was a cost that the Allies, with their superior manpower and industrial bases, could sustain if they had the will. The Germans had been able to inflict heavy losses, to be sure, but the goal of a Cannae-style air battle, leading to a decisive concentration against part of the enemy force and its destruction, was not within their grasp. If part of the enemy force was destroyed, rebuilding it would not simply be a matter of adding new replacements to an existing, if diminished, trained cadre. The German plan aimed at removing bomber groups from the enemy order of battle as thoroughly as ground battles could remove enemy divisions, what a later age would call targeting the enemy's force reconstitution capabilities.

In February 1944, however, the Germans started planning for what was termed 'The Big Blow'.[15] This would be an attempt to mass all of German interceptor strength against part of a daylight bomber raid. Galland selected for his target the first US daylight bombing raid on Berlin that he believed was coming. Fighters were brought in from throughout the Reich. Fighter groups were concentrated into larger formations capable of putting massed interceptor formations together. Over 1,000 sorties – perhaps as many as 3,000 – could be launched at an incoming US long-range attack.

The first 'Big Blow' fell on the first US daylight mission to Berlin on 6 March 1944. The battle turned into the largest of the war so far. The US bombers fought their way through to the target and back but several bomb group formations were either totally destroyed or reduced to a handful of bombers. Total losses far exceeded those which had halted the daylight air offensive in October 1943. Galland had found a way to maximise a key indicator: the number of German fighter sorties in defence of the Reich required for a bomber kill. In the 1943 battles, the number had been about

10. Now, with the qualitative improvements in the fighter force and the massing of formations starting to show, the number started to go down. The improvements in the air defence system meant that fewer sorties were wasted through failing to intercept the bombers.

The USAAF repeated its contribution to the Battle of Berlin twice more within the following week. Losses were high on both sides, but, at the end, without long-range strategic fighters to take the initiative against it, the *Luftwaffe* remained master of the sky over Berlin much as the RAF had remained over London in 1940. The USAAF, without strategic escort fighters able to prevent the Germans from concentrating fighter forces to make them more effective and forced to allow the enemy's twin-engine fighters to pick off stragglers at their leisure, had conceded the operational initiative to the *Luftwaffe* fighter force.

The pre-invasion bombing decision

With the heavy USAAF losses over Berlin and the RAF losses reaching their height over Nuremberg in March 1944, the strategic bombing offensive was largely shifted to targets in support of the upcoming invasion. This required moving the USAAF attacks away from German industrial targets – over the protests of the American airmen – and RAF attacks away from German cities – over the protests of the British airmen – and using them to hit transportation and tactical targets in France. While the German de emphasis of the V-weapons programme limited the need to devote sorties beyond those absorbed by some decoy 'No-Ball' V-1 ramp sites, the pre-invasion air offensive now assumed greater strategic importance. It was becoming increasingly obvious that attacks on German industry would not limit the flow of munitions and fuel that would be required by the German Army in the upcoming battle.

These defeats in effect undid the Casablanca decision to emphasise the bombing offensive. What they could not easily undo were the allied decisions, made largely in 1941–42, to invest heavily in the air war and in heavy bombers. Roosevelt, Churchill, the Combined Chiefs of Staff, and Eisenhower and his staff at SHAEF had never been of one mind about the wisdom of making the bomber offensive a cornerstone of strategy. The airmen running the bomber offensives had been, and so had been given the opportunity to proceed in their own way. Now that this had resulted in heavy losses for small gain, with the political costs that entailed, the Allied leadership re-fashioned their strategy. However, with the two bomber offensives' earlier defeats now compounded, the switch to a pre-invasion bombing campaign provided a respite for the Allies to rebuild. They could also make plans for the resumption of the bomber offensive once the invasion was established ashore.

With the German fighter force now largely pulled back to defend the Reich itself and beyond the reach of the Allied fighter force, it was thought that the pre-invasion bombing offensive would force the *Luftwaffe* to return to bases within the range of Allied fighter cover. Because the *Luftwaffe* had continued to become stronger since 1943 but had largely concentrated in Germany, air superiority would have to be secured after the invasion started rather than through the defeat of the *Luftwaffe* fighter force in the months before the invasion.

However, the increasing tempo of air operations over France and the likelihood of an invasion in the summer of 1944 led to a new division inside the German high command. Should the newly reinforced fighter force be held in reserve to continue the defence against the bombers once the strategic bombing offensive resumed or should it be committed to contest air superiority over the invasion?

It was not only the fighters that the defeat of the strategic bombers had allowed to join in the fighting in Normandy. The Germans pulled large numbers of 88mm flak guns out of Germany and were able to move them towards the invasion. The defeat of the bomber offensive had even made the coast defences of Normandy stronger, for they allowed steel and concrete that would otherwise have been required to create hardened and underground facilities for German industry to be available for the Atlantic Wall.[16]

Galland argued strongly to keep the fighters as a strategic reserve, that once they had defeated the strategic bombers they should not be committed simply to provide cover over the forces in the field. But he was overruled. It would have been impossible for the *Luftwaffe* to continue to claim a large percentage of the Reich's resources and not join in what promised to be a decisive battle over France. But once they were committed, they were well within the effective range of the superior numbers of high-quality RAF and USAAF day fighters.

The invasion

The *Luftwaffe*, undefeated by the bomber offensive, was ready to meet the 1944 D-Day landings in full strength, though most of its fighters and fighter-bombers had to deploy forward in the weeks after the invasion started. The resulting air battles over Normandy were the largest of the war. With both sides contesting control of the air and trying to concentrate air-ground assets at decisive points, the fighting resembled a much larger and more sophisticated version of the air combat over the Kursk offensive in 1943. The Germans were able to contest air superiority over Normandy throughout June and July. German fighter-bombers were able to inflict considerable damage on the crowded beachhead.

But, in the end, the superior numbers of the Allied fighter force told. 'Big Week' had tried to bring the *Luftwaffe* fighter force to battle by attacking a target it could not abandon and defeating it by the fire of unescorted bombers. Over Normandy, the Allies found a target the *Luftwaffe* could not abandon – the German Army – but this time the mass of short-range but otherwise very effective Allied fighters were there to carry out the destruction effectively. The *Luftwaffe* fighter force was away from the integrated air defence system that it had successfully built to defend the Reich. Without the radar warning and the fighter controllers, as the Battle of Normandy wore on, the German fighters were increasingly forced to defend their bases in France. Even though the German decisions about their economy had narrowed a technology gap that otherwise would have been even more disastrous and overwhelming, the German fighter force was forced into a decisive battle over Normandy and, as Galland had feared, largely destroyed.

Over Normandy, the Allied strategic bomber forces were frequently committed to support of the ground forces. Despite the spectacular concentration of firepower that could be delivered by large-scale carpet bombing in front of ground attacks, difficulties with coordination of forces often led to disappointing results or, worse, fratricide. The failure of the strategic bomber offensive did not free up the Allied bomber forces to redress the balance of the ground war. The Allied heavy bombers proved to be poorly suited for that.[17]

The use of the strategic bomber force against interdiction targets in France proved to be more effective. While, in the absence of strategic bombing against the transportation industry in Germany, the dispersed and increasingly integrated war economy was able to produce the goods and resources, it was getting this through to the fighting forces in Normandy that proved difficult. The Allied interdiction effort, even though reinforced with strategic bombers, could never cut off the German forces in Normandy. But they could prevent the Germans from ever massing enough reserves of fuel, ammunition, or replacements to take advantage of any of the repeated Allied tactical setbacks to go over to the offensive and throw the invasion into the sea.

Despite the failure of the bomber offensive to defeat either Germany's cities, industry, or air force before D-Day, the Allies were still able to make the invasion of Europe a success. The allies succeeded despite the fact that the bomber offensive had consumed vast amounts of resources in the US and especially in Britain, in terms of money, industrial production, research and development and allocations of quality manpower. As it was, the main problem with the Allied forces in Normandy was not in a lack of materiel and resources but in the ability to turn them into a sustained operational success other than through a series of battles of attrition. While the de-emphasis on the bomber offensive provided some higher quality manpower for the allied ground combat forces, what limited the benefit was the ability to train this manpower up to its full potential Having the bombers available for tactical support because they were not engaged in striking Germany did not increase the fighting capability of allied ground forces. Rather, it made them demand the bombers as part of any offensive operations despite their poor performance.[18]

The German Army was able to withdraw from Normandy in good shape.

There was sufficient fuel coming from the strategic synthetic oil plants and the Soviets were still a long way from the Ploesti oil fields. With sufficient fuel, even the Allied interdiction campaign was unable to deprive Germany's mechanised units of their tactical mobility.

The return to strategic bombing

The German Army had been pushed back to the boundaries of the Reich by the autumn of 1944 but few thought the war would be over by Christmas. With the bomber offensive defeated, Germany was able to go into the decisive battles of 1944–45 with its air force having suffered heavy losses over France, but with the backbone of the Reich's integrated air defence system unbroken. More significantly the German war machine was free of the diversion of having to devote a large percentage of its total output to defence against the bombers. Industry and infrastructure alike were largely preserved from destruction and disruption. German morale, protected from the impact of bombing, remained high.[19]

The impact of this was first felt on the Eastern Front. The bomber offensive had been intended to provide a 'second front', as the only major Anglo-American offensive in western Europe before D-Day. Its inability to make an impact on the German war machine had been reflected in high casualties and slowed advances for the Soviets in 1943–44, though the bulk of the *Luftwaffe* was still concentrated for the defence of Germany.

The Allies were in a position to return to the bombing campaign after the breakout from Normandy. The refusal to develop and employ long-range escort fighters was now less critical with the availability of forward bases and the German loss of their forward radars reduced the warning time available to the integrated air defence system. The potential seemed to be there for the Allies to reverse their earlier setbacks and resume the bomber campaign the airmen envisioned.

What prevented that – and turned the resumption of the bomber offensive into an even costlier setback than those that had occurred earlier – also had its roots in the rationalisation of the German war economy. This had allowed the rebuilding of the air defence of the Reich with Me 262 jet day and night fighters.

The Me 262 had entered full rate production in May 1944. It was the best example of what the rationalisation of the German war economy was able to produce in the absence of effective bombing. Increased investments in research and development had extended the service life of the Junkers Jumo engines to 25 hours. This was hardly an engineering triumph, but it made the new fighter feasible to mass-produce.[20] The new fighter still had many teething troubles, but with the R4M rocket developed with it, the Me 262 proved to be an order of magnitude more effective as a bomber destroyer than even the best piston-engined fighters were. That there were now fighters over Germany meant much less to the fast-moving Me 262, which, if skillfully flown, could fly past escort fighters to get to the bombers.

The Me 262s were soon inflicting crippling losses on the daylight bomber raids, but the main German goal was to build up an effective force of these before the daylight bombers could carry out their campaign against the oil and transportation industries on which Germany's war economy depended. Galland again decided to emphasise the principles of mass and concentration for an improved version of the 'Big Blow' before the bomber offensive started inflicting substantial damage.

The jet-powered version of the 'Big Blow' followed the successful pattern of the first, concentrating on an Eighth Air Force raid on oil refineries at Leipzig, generating several thousand sorties and destroying several hundred American bombers. However, only the superior performance of the Me 262 made this *Luftwaffe* victory possible, for the piston-engined German fighters were finding it increasingly difficult to hold the Allied fighters, now based on the continent, at bay. But with the Me 262/R4M weapons system, the Germans had, in fact, the counter to B-17/B-24 class bombers flown in tight formation. It combined speed and lethality in a way none of the piston-engined fighters, single or twin engined, had done. At night, the Me 262B night-fighter was highly lethal, regularly shooting down the Mosquito pathfinders that Bomber Command depended on for its increased accuracy.

The final effort

With Germany resisting into 1946 – the additional resources made possible by the defeat of the bombers kept the Russians on the Vistula and kept Romania and its oil in the war – the Allies were forced to re-invent the strategic bombing campaign yet again. The US strategic bombing forces in Europe were largely rebuilt with modified Boeing B-29s, diverted away from the Pacific War. Meanwhile, the first of the massive six-engine piston B-36s and the four-engine jet B-45s were coming into service.

Some of the new US bombers also went to veteran RAF Bomber Command units. This was significant because the British war economy was no longer able to keep up after years of near-total mobilisation, Bomber Command became less of a factor in the 1946 campaign, despite the introduction of Avro Lincoln and Vickers Windsor heavy bombers. Britain had invested so much of its resources in the previous bomber offensives there was little more to give , and the RAF was increasingly reliant on what the US could transfer.

It would now be a high-altitude war, with bombers operating at 30,000 feet or more, above the reach of the flak. To deal with the German jets, there were the large numbers of piston-engined fighters that, if individually non-competitive with the Germans, were still effective in operating against their bases.[21] But US industry was also able to produce large numbers of P-80 and P-84 jet fighters, which joined RAF Meteors and Vampires. Though these lacked range, their use of forward bases was supplemented by increased work on British-developed mid-air refuelling techniques.

To meet this, the German war economy – still fully functioning – was able to field the first of the 'secret weapons' made possible by the rational re-ordering of research and development priorities. Me 263 rocket fighters provided high-altitude point interception capability and the first *Wasserfall* surface-to-air missiles supplemented increasing numbers of 105mm and 128mm flak guns for high-altitude defence.

Though the Germans were still able to challenge the bomber offensive as the Allied armies pressed at the borders of Germany in the spring and summer of 1946, there was one element of the Allied investment in technology that they were unable to counter. The first atomic bomb was dropped on Berlin, followed a few days later by one on Dresden. It took a further ten bombs – all the US had – over the spring and summer of 1946 finally to bring about victory through airpower. The Soviet Army was able to push over the Vistula. Romania switched sides. The Western Allies were able to push bridgeheads over the Rhine.

This finally brought about the collapse of the German war economy though it required an additional five months of often-bitter broken-back conflict before German unconditional surrender was forthcoming.

Conclusion

The *Luftwaffe*'s triumph against the combined bomber offensive proved to be Germany's disaster. All Germany won from the heroic struggles of its defenders was primacy on the atomic targeting list above Japan. There was nothing the *Luftwaffe* could do to stop the inexorable development of atomic weapons. What their victory over the bombers provided was an extension of the war that enabled the revolutionary impact of these weapons to have the final, decisive impact on the war in Europe.

The German military of the Second World War was good at securing operational success – winning a major battle or campaign – but could not convert this to a lasting solution to Germany's fundamentally insoluble strategic problem of fighting a multi-front war against enemies with much greater resources. Only where the opponents lacked the time or space to deal with German operational success or the flaws in their war-fighting capability prevented their resources from being effectively used – as in 1940 – were the Germans able to gain a strategic success. But even this – like the *Luftwaffe*'s success in 1944 – proved transitory.

The reality

The 'might have been' here shows the significance of the Allied bomber offensive against Germany. Its counterfactual absence suggests that its impact cannot be easily 'dis-aggregated'. The effects of the most effective phase of the bomber offensive – 72 per cent of the total tonnage was dropped after D-Day – were integral with other effects on the German capability and will to resist. Post-war conventional wisdom, that the bomber offensive could not reduce German industrial production nor crack civilian morale and that its impact was limited to keeping German fighters and flak at home rather than in Normandy, is largely contradicted by more recent writing.

I have been guided by Max Weber's 1905 suggestion that counterfactuals should change as little as possible. The second-order impacts of changing the values, goals, and contexts in which decisions were made are impossible to predict. It is often difficult – or irrelevant – to treat them properly, especially in the type of causation that evolves along the 'for want of a nail' path of impact escalation.[22] Friedrich Engels' image was that history was a 'parallelogram of forces' and that to move one corner would affect parts of the figure far away and in unintended ways.[23]

The Allies proved on a number occasions in both world wars to be as committed to doctrinal solutions as did those that led to the defeat of the bomber offensive in this scenario. The cult of the offensive and the self-delusion by numbers were all too real. However, the US strategic bombing offensive in Europe actually proved to be very good at learning.

The German changes to their fighter force and industrial programme that could lead to victory in 1944 are generally those identified, with the benefit of hindsight, by Adolf Galland in post-war interrogations, as among those omissions that cost Germany the war. The 'Big Blow' was a Galland project in 1944 that was never implemented.

Bibliography

Avant, Deborah D., *Political Institutions and Military Change. Lessons from Peripheral Wars* (Cornell University Press, Ithaca, 1994).

Boog, Horst, ed., *The Conduct of the Air War in the Second World War* (Berg, New York, 1992).

Clodfelter, Mark, *The Limits of Airpower* (The Free Press, New York, 1989).

Davis, Richard G., *Carl A. Spaatz and the Air War in Europe* (GPO, Washington, 1993).

Evans, Richard J., *In Defense of History* (Norton, New York, 1999).

Galland, Adolf, *et al.*, *The Luftwaffe Fighter Force. The View from the Cockpit* (Greenhill Books, London, 1998).

Gooderson, Ian, 'Heavy and Medium Bombers: How Successful Were They in the Tactical Close Support Role During World War II?', *Journal of Strategic Studies*, v. 15, n. 3, September 1992.

Isby, David C., *Fighter Combat In The Jet Age*, (HarperCollins, London, 1997).

Konvitz, Josef W., 'Bombs, Cities and Submarines: Allied Bombing of the French Ports 1942–43', *International History Review*, v. 14 n. 1, February 1992.

McFarland, Stephen, *America's Pursuit of Precision Bombing, 1910–45* (Smithsonian Institution Press, Washington, 1995).

Miller, Stephen, ed., *Military Strategy and the Origins of the First World War* (Princeton University Press, Princeton, 1985).

Murray, Williamson, *Strategy for Defeat* (Air University Press, Maxwell AFB, 1983).

Overy, Richard J., *The Air War 1939–45* (Europa, London, and Stein & Day, New York, 1980).

Paret, Peter, ed., *Makers of Modern Strategy: From Machiavelli to the Nuclear Age* (Princeton University Press, Princeton, 1985).

Posen, Barry R., *The Sources of Military Doctrine* (Cornell University Press, Ithaca, 1984).

Price, Alfred, *The Last Year of the Luftwaffe, May 1944 to May 1945* (Arms & Armour, London, 1991).

Price, Alfred, *Luftwaffe. The Birth, Life and Death of an Air Force* (Macdonald, London, and Ballantine, New York, 1970).

Rosen, Stephen Peter, *Winning the Next War: Innovation and the Modern Military* (Cornell University Press, Ithaca, 1991).

Speer, Albert, *Inside the Third Reich* (Weidenfeld and Nicolson, London, 1970).

Stephens, Alan, ed., *The War in the Air, 1914–1994* (Air University Press, Maxwell AFB, 2000).

Van Evera, Stephen, 'Why States Believe Foolish Ideas: Non-Self Evaluation In Government and Society', Paper presented at the American Political Science Association annual meeting, 1988.

Weber, Max, 'Objective Possibility and Adequate Causation in Historical Explanation', in *The Methodology of the Social Sciences* (Free Press of Glencoe, Glencoe, Ill., 1949 (1905)).

Werrell, Kenneth, *Who Fears? The 301st in War and Peace* (Taylor, Dallas, 1991).

Zisk, Kimberley Martin, *Engaging the Enemy: Organization Theory and Soviet Military Innovation 1955–91* (Princeton University Press, Princeton, 1991).

Notes

1. On the timeframe, see Speer, *Inside the Third Reich*, p. 239.
2. Murray, *Strategy for Defeat*, pp. 103, 134.
3. Price, *Luftwaffe*, p. 94
4. Quoted in Galland, *The Luftwaffe Fighter Force*, p. 215.
5. See generally: Avant, *Political Institutions and Military Change*; Rosen, *Winning the Next War*; and Zisk, *Engaging the Enemy*.
6. On strategic airpower theory in general, see: Overy, *The Air War 1939–45*, pp. 5–25; and MacIsaac, David, 'Voices From the Central Blue', in Paret, *Makers of Modern Strategy*.
7. See generally: McFarland, *America's Pursuit of Precision Bombing*, especially pp. 182–6.
8. Konvitz, 'Bombs, Cities and Submarines: Allied Bombing of the French Ports 1942–43', pp. 40–3
9. The USAAF was less likely – or able – to fall into this type of problem than its successor, the USAF, which has been the subject of several case studies on this type of bureaucratic behaviour. See generally: Clodfelter, *The Limits of Airpower*.
10. Posen, *The Sources of Military Doctrine*, p. 50.
11. See generally: Van Evera, 'The Cult of the Offensive and the Origins of the First World War', in Miller, *Military Strategy and the Origins of the First World War*; also Van Evera, 'Why States Believe Foolish Ideas'.
12. On the tendency to look at tonnage rather than results, see the Spaatz quotation in Werrell, *Who Fears?*, p. 83.
13. Davis, *Carl A. Spaatz and the Air War in Europe*, p. 61.
14. Overy, p. 15. Murray, 'The Influence of Pre-War Anglo-American Doctrine on the Air Campaigns of the Second World War', in Boog, *The Conduct of the Air War in the Second World War*, pp. 238–40.
15. On the 'Big Blow', see Galland, *op. cit.*, pp. 176–80.
16. On the competition between German industrial hardening and the Atlantic Wall, see Overy, 'World War II: the Bombing of Germany', in Stephens, *The War in the Air, 1914–1994*, pp. 123–5.
17. Gooderson, 'Heavy and Medium Bombers: How Successful Were They in the Tactical Close Support Role During World War II?'
18. Gooderson, p. 367

19. On the impact of bombing on German morale, see Overy, p. 208, and Murray, *Strategy for Defeat*, p. 300. While some sources hold that the bombing stimulated German morale, the weight of the evidence is that it took a considerable toll.

20. Price, *The Last Year of the Luftwaffe, May 1944 to May 1945*, p. 176.

21. Isby, *Fighter Combat In The Jet Age*, see chapter 1 generally.

22. Weber, 'Objective Possibility and Adequate Causation in Historical Explanation', in *The Methodology of the Social Sciences*, pp. 164–88.

23. Quoted in Evans, *In Defense of History*, p. 118.

9
HITLER'S BOMB
Target: London and Moscow

Forrest R. Lindsey

'As for my participation in making the bomb, there was no choice. The original discovery that made it possible was made in Germany, and we had believed that the German scientists were ahead of us in the development of a nuclear weapon. I shudder to think what would have happened if Germany had been first to acquire the weapon.'
Eugene Wigner, physicist.

The beginning of the end

Professor Heisenberg was startled and more than a little bit uneasy when he was summoned in the middle of the night. It was unprecedented for anyone to summon him to anything, since as the top theoretical physicist in the country and a Nobel Prize winner, he was used to some degree of deference. Nonetheless, when the black-uniformed SS officers came for him at his home, he dressed quickly and quietly got in the car. In Hitler's Germany, you did what you were told when the SS came for you.

He was led to a large darkened building up a wide stairway to the last office in a hall. When the door opened he was seated in a dimly lit and sparsely furnished office whose main features were a very large desk and a portrait of the Führer centred behind it on the wall. His escorts left him there alone and for several minutes all he could hear was his own breathing. For a second, he closed his eyes and thought of what he might have done to be brought to this room. His meeting with Niels Bohr the previous month[1] – was that seen as something treasonous? Were some of his conversations with his fellow scientists overheard? He opened his eyes and stared across that giant desk into the unblinking gaze behind the flat, round-rimmed glasses of Heinrich Himmler.

'Good evening Herr Professor', the Reichsführer said without expecting an answer. 'I understand that you have made some exceptional contributions to our Fatherland in the field of atomic fission.' Heisenberg was surprised that this was what the Reichsführer wanted to talk to him about, yet this was hardly a secret. 'We need a weapon that will decisively crush our enemies and you and your department have the best chance of giving Germany this weapon', Himmler continued. A flash from Himmler's glasses dismissed the reflexive shrug from Professor Heisenberg that was meant to say that he did not think that an atomic bomb was possible yet. 'The SS under my direction is taking over the leadership of this project as of this moment. You will be given everything and anything that you will need. You will have the highest priority for funds, materials, and workers.'

Himmler paused for a second to make his final point as clearly as possible, 'You will continue the leadership of your department as a member of my SS with full authority to lead as you choose. You will have any scientists, engineers and technicians that you choose — including any that may be prisoners of the Reich.' He paused again to let that last item fully sink in — he was allowing Heisenberg to recruit Jewish prisoners from the concentration camps. 'You must succeed at any cost. The British and the Americans are working to have the same weapons so we must have them first. When you succeed, you will have done great service to your Fatherland and your Führer and you will be amply rewarded. If you fail, the price will be beyond your imagining. Goodnight, Herr Professor.'

After the SS car had dropped him off, Heisenberg spent a long time sitting helplessly on the steps in front of his home. He felt like a man who has been standing in the water at the beach when a large ocean wave strikes him and carries him along, tumbling and choking, powerless.

It was very clear to him that he had no one to appeal to, no power above the Reichsführer to avoid his future. He had quietly advocated a passive resistance to bomb development among his scientific community and he had even hinted that he would not help the Nazis get one during his meeting with Bohr in Copenhagen, but that was over now. He knew only too well that the man in that darkened room meant exactly what he said and that he had all of the power he needed to make Heisenberg do what he wanted. After a long while, Heisenberg opened his door and went inside.

Heisenberg's Special Weapons team — the 'Uranium Club' — grew geometrically as more physicists and engineers and workers were brought in to the new facilities dedicated to the nuclear weapon project. Thanks to Albert Speer, materials and supplies poured in and the funding was literally limitless. Branches were established throughout Germany and occupied Europe to assure that the facilities and capabilities were under one leader, one focus. Naturally, the security at each of these facilities was immeasurably tightened as the responsibilities transitioned to the SS. The cyclotron near Paris, the heavy water plant in Norway, the uranium mines in Czechoslovakia and much more all became part of Himmler's direct sphere and therefore Heisenberg's as well.

The work on a functioning reactor, various methods of isotope separation and research on the many mathematical models for chain reactions in fissionable material were conducted simultaneously. The unspeakable became much more possible every day the research went on and, under the SS, that was every day of the week.

Bits of information, hints, clues trickled out of Germany to the Allies despite the best efforts of the SS and the *Gestapo* and the *Abwehr*. The Allies devoted an ever greater portion of their intelligence collection effort to the discovery of where the Germans were in atomic design[2] and the various commando entities and resistance movements increased reconnaissance and planning. Yet from all external signs, the German effort was unusually quiet. Unknown to the Allied codebreakers at Bletchley Park, Himmler had prevailed on his communications sections to adopt a whole new code system over and above the existing Enigma method to deal with the heightened communications security requirements for the atomic project. All communications concerning the Special Weapons Project would be kept on this network and sent on landlines whenever possible. One could not be too careful.

By September 1943 the Special Weapons Project had made significant breakthroughs; the first functioning atomic pile had been used to conduct controlled fission experiments and the role of slow neutrons was proven for the initiation of chain reactions within fissionable material. The concept of enriching uranium to form a new, more fissionable element was successfully demonstrated and the breeder reactor was born in Germany. For the first time, a working atomic weapon would be a certainty and with the experience of the last two years of warfare it was clear that the war would last long enough for it to be built – and used.

Hitler was kept advised of the progress of the atomic team nearly weekly. References crept into his speeches that hinted at a new 'super-weapon that no power on Earth can resist'. As the Allies came closer to the Reich, as the bombing by the British and Americans intensified, Hitler became more and more involved in the development process and for the first time, targeting this new monster bomb became the primary issue.

The combined efforts of several of Heisenberg's U-235 and uranium enrichment plants had produced several kilograms of fissionable material by January 1944 and the Führer was notified that within two to four months, two weapons would be available for testing. As was typical of Hitler, he directed that the tests be carried out on actual targets. Within the highest echelons of command, Hitler's senior staff were briefed on the expected capabilities of these first atomic weapons and their recommendations were that they should be used against Red Army concentrations opposite *Army Group Centre* in Byelorussia and against the expected Allied landings in France. Hitler would have none of that. These new weapons would be used against his enemies' cities to break their wills and to exact revenge for the destruction of Germany's cities. With Hitler's final word on the subject, planning for the employment of the first two weapons began.

The first element of the plans was to determine the specific targets. Next, the bomber crews would have to be trained in the special characteristics of atomic weapon preparation, arming, and employment. Bombers were modified for the nearly 4,500kg weight and increased bulk of these bombs, and preparations made to allow the crews the capability for in-flight arming and if necessary, disarming of the bombs.

The crews and the planners learned that atomic weapons work best if detonated at medium altitude above a target: the primary destructive capability of the atomic explosion is a massive spherical shock wave that expands until it touches the surface of the Earth. There it reflects back against itself to form a compounded wave that travels rapidly away from the centre of the burst, smashing everything in its path. The scientists also mentioned the enormous heat and ionising radiation that would come from the explosion of the weapon but it was not known just how much of a factor these destructive effects would have on a target.

Since the last major Allied conference in Tehran in December 1943, the Allied focus had been the destruction from the air of German industry and the German will to fight as the Allied ground forces advanced in the East and slowly up the length of Italy. The Allies would open a second front on continental Europe as soon as possible to relieve some of the pressure on the Red Army. In the Pacific, the Japanese faced an inexorable tide of naval advances since their defeats at Midway, then Guadalcanal, then the Gilberts and the Marshalls and now the Allies were on the doorstep of their key bases in Saipan and Formosa and the Philippines.

In March 1944 alone over 2,000 tons of high explosive and incendiary bombs rained on Berlin and it was clear that the American and British air forces were only beginning to reach their stride. It was also clear that the German air defences were incapable of stopping them.

In carefully protected communications with Roosevelt, Churchill sought to discuss the analysis of Hitler's progress towards an atomic bomb. While the Germans were communicating about everything but nuclear matters, the silence itself was telling. Most of the identified laboratories and facilities had been targeted for bombing or commando attacks but it was clear that feverish activity was still present. Churchill was sure that it was only a matter of time and not much time at that. Roosevelt described as fully as he felt he could, the status of the Manhattan project and his estimate that working weapons would be available some time late in 1944. Neither man was sure that they could beat the Germans to the punch and with the invasion of Europe approaching quickly the possibility of a German atomic attack strongly affected planning. All of England was one big military staging area for the largest amphibious attack in history and everything depended on surprise, good weather, air superiority, and luck.

Hell's Arrival

'But what I want is annihilation – annihilation effect.'[3]
Adolf Hitler.

Even as the Allied leaders were preparing for their next phase of offensives, events had already moved inexorably to a new and terrible future: specially prepared and heavily escorted Heinkel 177 bombers took off from French and Polish airfields into the dark night sky. Late in the morning of 15 April 1944, just before the first glimmer of dawn in Moscow and at 03.22 in London, intense, blinding light and searing heat erupted, followed within one or two heartbeats by irresistible waves of moving earth and walls of titanic pressure. For the two cities and millions of sleeping people it was the end of the world.

Hitler's revenge had arrived.

The first few hours after the attacks, after the last echoes of the loudest man-made blasts ever heard on Earth faded, it was eerily still around the world as the news began to travel. In the two bombings the leadership and nerve centres of two of the major Allied powers had been instantly silenced. For the British and to a degree the American leadership in England, communications with the capital were completely gone and confusion reigned. Fires throughout central London, from the East End to Westminster, burned out of control and the entire centre of the city, from the Tower of London to Whitehall was grey and burning rubble without signs of life. The surprise attack had been particularly cruel for the victims who had been near windows or just above ground: the atomic flash ignited any exposed flammable material out to a radius of three miles from the weapon's hypocentre. Human beings are flammable material at those temperatures.

Photo-reconnaissance Spitfires were sent to get the first pictures of the damage to London and then back to get the film developed. Army units were trucked in from bases all over Britain to try to rescue survivors and these first soldiers to enter the outskirts found themselves encountering clumps of terribly burned people and saw for themselves the first signs of a new terror, radiation sickness. In a world war in which every possible atrocity had been tried, the Nazis had introduced the most monstrous of them all.

In Moscow, tens of thousands of survivors were slowly finding their way away from the ruins of the city. The German bomb had exploded above the exact centre of the Kremlin, crushing the ancient walls into rubble and evaporating centuries of history. Those who had been travelling on Moscow's Metro were mostly lucky enough to survive but were now facing the sealing of the entrances at the city centre and were in the dark, stumbling in the search for an open way to the surface. For those who made it to the surface, fires and poisoning awaited them and no leaders were left to tell them what had hit Moscow and what dangers they faced now. In a single, cataclysmic stroke, the Soviet political leadership, the central hub of rail transportation, and the top level government communications systems were completely gone.

Hitler was the happiest anyone remembered seeing him. The new atomic weapons had done even better than he had been assured that they would. His enemies had been dealt crushing blows, unrecoverable blows! Photos taken at first light over London and Moscow were already on the table in front of him and his staff. They were confirmation of the devastation the super-bombs had caused. Little remained in the way of recognisable landmarks, except for the layout of the rivers, and it was obvious that the aiming points he had specified were achieved. The Kremlin and Buckingham Palace did not exist any more and in their places were huge, shallow debris-filled craters. Now, he was sure, the Allies would have to end their war against him. With these weapons the world would be his again.

In London and Moscow, the silence began to give way to the cries of the victims and then the sounds of rescue personnel digging through the rubble. Tens of thousands had died in a single moment and many more tens of thousands would die of their injuries yet. Throughout Britain, the Soviet Union, and then all of the Allied and the occupied countries, a wave of horror and disbelief passed through every corner. Then as the full scope of the atrocity began to become clearer, bitter resolve replaced fear.

In Britain, Winston Churchill and the majority of the political and military leadership and command and control facilities survived. The Royal Family did not. They were in Buckingham Palace directly under the fireball and their country grieved for them as they tried to account for their own loved ones in London. The American forces in Britain assisted the British authorities in every way they could, providing troops, facilities, equipment, food, and power generators for the recovery efforts. For a while, the war came to a stop. The bombing of Germany continued but at a somewhat reduced pace while leadership and coordination were re-established.

In the Soviet Union, the situation was even worse: Stalin had ordered that Moscow's citizens stay in the city, even to the point that the NKVD had been shooting people who tried to leave. Many more people were in Moscow than wanted to be when the bomb exploded and the tall concrete apartment buildings built quickly for housing the maximum numbers of people had crumbled onto them when the shock waves had hit. The casualties were enormous and there were no significant supplies of food, clean water, or medicines to help them. Even with the catastrophes that had occurred throughout this war for the Soviet people, this was a monstrous blow. Stalin and much of the Politburo had disappeared since the explosion, as had the NKVD headquarters in Dzerzhinsky Square. For the many political organs of the Soviet government there was no leadership, no direction, no help. The help that did come, feeble as it was, came from individuals and small groups and, soon after, from the Red Army. Where the all-present Communist Party had been, a vacuum had replaced it and the Soviet nation reeled. Moscow was also the hub of the state rail system and its destruction crippled deliveries of weapons and ammunition and supplies to the front. The Soviet people needed a hero and they got one: Marshal Georgi Konstantinovich Zhukov gathered his military leaders and the surviving members of the Party leadership and began the rebuilding of the essential mechanisms of control lost in the atomic bombing of Moscow.

Heisenberg had feared success almost as much as he had feared the consequences of failure. He and the other members of the 'Uranium Club' knew how horrific an atomic weapon would be and did not want Hitler to have one. But at his back at all times was the cool insistence of Himmler and his *SS*. Everywhere Heisenberg went, every conversation, every moment was attended. They were supportive, coolly friendly and ran to get whatever he wanted them to get, yet they were really waiting in the wings, like some kind of killer animals, waiting for the chance to torture and kill whomever they were told to torture or kill. As the scientific barriers to the working atomic bomb were overcome one by one, Himmler was congratulatory and additional honours and awards flowed. Whenever there had been difficulties, Himmler would appear unannounced and inspect the work with startling attention to detail. Hitler himself had visited once and Heisenberg had felt a surprising spurt of pride, replaced quickly by shame as he once again realised that he and his physicists would be parties to the mass extinction of thousands. He and his family had lost many friends and relatives to the Allied bombing campaign and the attacks came close to getting him several times. Sometimes the anger at these near misses and personal losses spurred him on but most of the time the rapid pace of progress towards an unthinkable weapon filled him with desperate anguish.

Now that day had come. The propaganda mills were churning out radio announcements and newspaper articles and newsreels trumpeting a 'magnificent victory'. The pictures of the stark landscapes that had been ancient and beautiful cities were posted everywhere and from what he could see, the people on the streets of Germany were cheerful. They believed the announcements that the war was almost over and that the Reich had won. Heisenberg hoped that the next bomb from the next Allied bomber would get him. Looking at the pictures of the horrors he and his team had created, he wished that they had got him a lot earlier. He looked upward reflexively when the evening air raid sirens and the booming of distant flak batteries announced the arrival of British bombers again. Maybe now, he thought, it will be my time.

At Southwick, the British Emergency Government and the Supreme Allied Commander, General Eisenhower, met to discuss the immediate requirements caused by the German attacks. The most pressing concern was if and when there would be another atomic attack. The most critical potential targets were the industrial cities of England and the bases with massed troops assembled for the invasion of Europe. The first priority was be to reduce the vulnerable populations of the likes of Birmingham, Manchester, Southampton and Coventry and to disperse the large military camps and staging areas into smaller, less lucrative targets. The invasion initially planned for May/June as Operation Overlord had to be suspended indefinitely until this powerful German threat was overcome or eliminated. The struggling landing at Anzio in Italy was the only hopeful operation in progress for the western Allies but it was also vulnerable: no matter how carefully planned, an amphibious operation must necessarily concentrate its forces into relatively small areas of beach, supported by closely clustered vessels. This type of concentration of forces was perfectly suited for an effective atomic attack. For now at least, Europe would stay in Nazi hands. The big question on Allied planner's minds was, how many of those things do the Nazis have – and where will they strike again?

For the Soviets under Zhukov, there were the same questions with the added burden of many more casualties than they had any capability to help. To the east and south of Moscow, radioactive fallout had spread for tens of thousands of hectares downwind and sickness had spread. Refugees from all of the areas around Moscow had crowded the available trains, trucks, and roads as they sought some relief, somewhere. It was a wet and cold April with shelter hard to find and many families struggled to survive in the fields and forests of central Russia. Zhukov still had a war to fight and his forces were massed and coiled to hit the Germans in Byelorussia. He could either wait for the Germans to use another atomic bomb on the Red Army or he could order them into the attack. An attack had another advantage – his troops would be in close proximity with the Fascists and if they wanted to use the atomic bomb on them, they would kill Germans too. His forces were ready and fuelled by an unquenchable hatred for the German enemy. At his command, the Red Army drove straight into the Germans.

In Washington and throughout the US, the German atomic attacks filled Americans with astonishment and fear. Could the Nazis hit our cities yet? Congress met to discuss emergency measures for the evacuation of New York, Philadelphia, Washington and other major potential targets for the Germans and called on the military leadership to increase the air defences of East Coast cities. President Roosevelt, though visibly more ill, met with General George Marshall and General Hap Arnold to plan for the one thing that would stop Germany, an atomic counter-strike against Berlin. The director of the Manhattan Project, Brigadier General Leslie Groves, assured the planners that they would have at least one, maybe two, working weapons of roughly the same power and characteristics as the German weapons by late October or early November with more available shortly thereafter. The B-29s capable of carrying the atomic bomb could be sent to England immediately and the crews, which were already in training, would accompany them there. Communications with Churchill confirmed the British leader's desire to annihilate Berlin, with Hitler in it, as soon as possible. Roosevelt ordered the preparations to move the bombing team to England and then sent Churchill the message 'Operation Counter-stroke has begun.'

The Nazis did not have any more atomic bombs, yet. The scientists and technicians were working hard to assemble enough material for the next bombs, but the painstaking, infinitesimally slow process of separating the fissionable isotopes from the large mass of non-fissionable material took time. All of the available fissionable material had been expended on London and Moscow and Hitler would have to wait a while longer for more. The Allied air forces were attacking around the clock with special emphasis on any likely location for atomic manufacturing or weapons storage or scientific research, which slowed the process. Roads, rail junctions, and where they could be found, underground factories received a rain of high explosives around the clock. The Allied air forces' efforts took a more desperate cast as higher rates of loss of aircraft and crews were accepted to ensure that the critical nuclear-related targets were neutralised.[4]

Hitler was surprised that the Allies had not capitulated yet. He fully expected calls for an armistice from the West, and for the Soviet Bolsheviks to collapse. Neither happened. The British and Americans had increased the day and night bombing attacks and the Russians were pounding his armies in the east. Apparently, they need more lessons. He directed Himmler to hurry up and get more atomic bombs ready.

The German Army continued to hold off the Americans and British in Italy on the 'Gustav Line' through the wet Italian spring. Fortress Europe kept its defences honed under Field Marshal Rommel's leadership and starting in June, the first of the V-weapons, the V-1 flying bomb, was fired at British targets. The main direction for concern for the Nazis was the east, as the Soviets seized Sevastopol and to the north, drove the Germans out of Byelorussia and into eastern Poland. The Red Army was unstoppable and, as the German combat units on the front found out, not in the mood to take prisoners. The Soviet supply system had been quickly rebuilt and as powerful barrages of massed artillery and Katyusha rocket fire rained on German defensive positions, the Nazis learned how effectively that new system worked.

Goebbels and his Ministry of Propaganda had kept up the momentum of encouragement that the atomic attacks had given the German public and trumpeted the terror that would soon result if the Allies did not stop bombing the Reich. As time wore on through the summer and fall, it was clear to everyone in Germany that the Allies had stepped up attacks from the air and the Russians were getting closer and closer. No matter how artfully crafted, the propaganda could not disguise the danger of the situation and the continuing losses in the east and the south. Germany's allies were collapsing and more troops had to be sent into Hungary and the Balkans to solidify the defences there. The worst blow came with the Soviet seizure of the Romanian oil fields. With that loss, the German war machine lost its main source of fuel and, without a lot of fuel, the Nazis could not hope to win the war through offensive combat. Despite these significant losses, Hitler believed that his 'wonder weapons' would save the Reich. The V-2 ballistic rocket had begun attacks on Britain and jet-propelled fighters and bombers were entering service in large numbers. Any day now, the next of his series of atomic bombs would be ready and the world had better beware. As he had ordered, plans were being completed for a long-range strike against the United States. New York City would be the next to go.

Heisenberg worked at what appeared to the SS as a feverish pace. He spent nearly all of his time in the underground facilities, tens of metres below the surface where there was neither day nor night. Living in the tunnels full time he did not have time to go home and see his family, so he sent them to join his sister in Bavaria until he could take some time off. Subtly, undiscernibly, he ordered more of the difficult-to-obtain materials and directed his team to work on related, yet non-essential areas. He was carefully delaying the completion of the next series of atomic weapons by obstructing the critical processes and concentrating on the less critical.

Heisenberg saw the pictures of the heaps of dead civilians and the rubble his bombs had created and he saw and heard the suffering of the slave labourers in the tunnels. Every night was torture as his dreams filled with the horrors he had created. The SS around him were as brutal and remorseless as ever and no day went by without seeing someone, usually one of the starving workers from the concentration camps, clubbed or shot or death near him.

Yet, if that was supposed to have the effect of spurring him on, it did not work.

Heisenberg had discovered something infinitely worse than his own torture and death. It was living with causing the suffering and death of innocent humanity. If he gave Hitler the next series of bombs before the Allies could finish their own, millions more would die and the evil that was Hitler and the whole Third Reich would win. Interestingly, it was Hitler who gave him the best rationale for delay: orders came through Himmler to build the next atomic weapons lighter. The new V-2 rocket had a useful payload of only 1,000 kilograms and Hitler wanted the atomic weapon adapted for use on it. That kind of engineering took time.

Counter-stroke

'Never give in – never, never, never. In nothing great or small, large or petty, never give in, except to convictions of honour and good reason. Never yield to force; never yield to the apparently overwhelming might of the enemy.'
Winston Churchill.

By September 1944 the 393rd Bomber Squadron, 509th Composite Group, had completely arrived in Britain and began conducting training operations far out of the reach of German 'snoopers' – the high-flying reconnaissance aircraft. Despite the propaganda coming out of Germany, no sign of another Nazi atomic attack was apparent. Intensive bombing at any and all potential atomic plants or assets had some effect, and for the time being the Allies could concentrate on getting the invasion going again. The weather on the Channel coast was terrible but any window that could be taken for the landing was being considered. The Germans were apparently so confident that the Allies were dissuaded from attempting an invasion by the threat of an atomic bomb attack, that they were moving several top divisions to the Eastern Front to try to stem the latest Soviet offensive. To General Eisenhower, the door was open again, as soon as the Allies' own atomic weapons were ready.

By mid-October, the 393rd Bomber Squadron was operationally ready and the first American atomic weapons were aboard the cruiser USS *Augusta* on its way across the Atlantic. Through a miracle of concentrated effort, the Manhattan Project team had assembled two uranium devices that they believed had a high probability of working as well as, or better than, the German weapons. They had wanted to try one out first at their test range in New Mexico, but the orders from Washington were clear: get the bombs to England to be used against Germany at the earliest possible date. Even as the weapons were secured below decks on the *Augusta*, Los Alamos scientists were making the last connections, the last adjustments, despite bouts of seasickness.

On 7 November 1944 General Eisenhower directed the invasion force to sea as a break in the weather was predicted for the morning of 9 November. As the force approached its debarkation points at 04.10 on the 9th, Eisenhower directed that a single preformatted message with one code word be transmitted to his air chief: 'Oblivion'. At that word, three B-29s lifted off towards Germany, joining with the streams of a thousand or so B-17s and B-24s taking part in bombing attacks all over Germany that day. One of those B-29s carried one of the Manhattan weapons, code-named 'Little Boy', while the other two B-29s carried navigation and recording equipment and had the secondary mission of close defence of the bombing aircraft if any German fighters made it to them through the escorting fighters. Instead of the usual custom of carrying the picture of a scantily clad lady on the plane's nose with some ribald saying, the lead B-29 carrying the atomic bomb had just the name of the pilot's mother painted on.

As dawn on 9 November arrived, the German defenders were stunned to see thousands of ships off the coast of Normandy. Paratroopers and glider forces had landed in France ahead of the main force during the preceding night but the German communications were so disrupted by the rampaging aircraft and the increase in French resistance activity that they were not aware of the whole scope of that night's actions. Hitler was awakened as soon as the Allied invasion was completely revealed. He was incredulous – how could they do this? He called Field Marshal Erwin Rommel's headquarters for an on-scene report and ordered the reserve Panzer divisions thrown into action. General Rommel kept silent. His reserves had been committed to the Russian Front over his strenuous objections months before.

Heisenberg heard the news broadcasts about the Allied landings in France and was as surprised as everyone else in Germany was. Then he understood.

It really was all over now. He packed a single leather briefcase and approached his *SS* 'escort' officer. He said that he had essential business in Berlin with Himmler himself concerning the atomic bomb project. Though surprised, the officer agreed and put in a call to the Reichsführer personally that Heisenberg needed to see him and that it was urgent. Himmler was pleased that he would have Heisenberg there – he had a number of important items to discuss with him and this would be the best opportunity. The message seemed to carry some promising news and this would be a good time to tell Hitler if they had the new bombs ready. Himmler put aside his morning meetings to take his staff car to Berlin.

The Allies streamed ashore against heavy resistance the whole morning and the casualties were heavy. US and British fighter-bombers were crushing attempts by the Germans to reinforce their defences and the toehold of Allied forces grew to a true defensible lodgment, an irresistible grip on the Continent. The Allies were back!

In emergency meetings in the Führerbunker in Berlin, Hitler and his general staff developed plans for the counter-attack in Normandy. Hitler was furious at Rommel for not following his orders and he blamed him for the successful landing of the Allies but a little of the edge was taken off his anger when he received a message from Himmler that he wished to update him on the atomic project. 'Good', Hitler thought, 'it's about time! My next bomb goes on the Allies at their beachhead! This will finish the British and the Americans once and for all.'

Heisenberg stepped from the train station and looked at his watch. It was nearly noon. The *SS* officer with him said something and as he looked across the street, Himmler's car arrived. The *SS* officer saluted with a stiff arm upraised and Himmler got out of his car to greet Heisenberg, a slight smile on his face. As they crossed the street, air raid sirens began howling and anti-aircraft batteries began firing some distance away. The escort officer wanted to head the group towards a shelter but Himmler waved him to silence.

'What is your important news, Herr Professor?' Himmler asked.

'Herr Reichsführer, I believe the Allies have their own atomic bombs now', Heisenberg said.

This was not what Himmler had been expecting to hear at all. He wanted to hear about the status of their next series of weapons, not the Allies' weapons. He frowned. His sources had told him that the soonest the Americans could hope to have their own atomic weapons would be at least a year away. Plenty of time. What was Heisenberg talking about?

Himmler was about to ask Heisenberg that question when he saw Heisenberg staring upward. Himmler and the *SS* officers looked to see what he was looking at. A small speck – or was that more than one plane? Very high up there and bright silver in the rare November sunshine. He looked back at Heisenberg and saw the physicist was smiling an odd smile and that there were tears in his eyes, streaming down his face. He started to say something but an enormous flash of light erased everything.

The ground heaved around the Führerbunker and the interior filled with dust and bits of the walls. Hitler and all of his staff were knocked to the floor and file cabinets fell over as the floor heaved in one direction and the walls in another. The Führer's first thoughts were that some assassin had bombed the next room, trying to kill him. The whole bunker complex was completely dark and filled with the smell of dust. As his senses began to return, he saw some emergency lights had been turned on and that his entire bunker had been damaged by something and every room and all of the halls were filled with debris. Had the Americans made a direct hit on his bunker? An officer reported that the entrances were sealed, blocked by something. The smell of smoke began to be stronger and the bunker itself, normally cold and damp, was stiflingly hot and getting hotter. Suddenly Hitler understood. The Americans had caught up and they had repaid the favour for London and Moscow. He knew what was outside the bunker on the surface and he also knew that none of them would live much longer. There was no communication with anyone outside and there was no escape from this concrete tomb. His only choices were slowly to cook or to suffocate, or if there was enough air, die of radiation poisoning. Hitler took his pistol from his pocket and climbed over the rubble into an adjoining room to take a different option.

After the message from the lead B-29 was received indicating that the attack had been successful, the Supreme Allied Commander released a message to the German people. In it he said that the Allied forces had returned to the European continent and that the Allies had destroyed Berlin with a single atomic bomb, like the ones used on London and Moscow. He said that the Allies had not wanted to resort to using that horrific weapon but that the first use by the Nazis without warning called for like measures to end the war. He said that the long terror of Nazi domination of Europe was over and that whatever it took to erase Nazism from the face of the Earth would be accomplished. He called on the representatives of the German people to surrender and to end this terrible war. He said that, if they did not, the Allies had more of these horrific weapons and would use them if necessary. Eisenhower finished his message with the hope that the German people would take the steps they needed to take to end this dark era and restore freedom and honour and peace to the world.

On 25 November 1944 representatives from Field Marshal Rommel's headquarters met with representatives of the Allied High Command to discuss the surrender of all German forces in the west. Hitler was dead and the world had to be returned to sanity again.

Very shortly after, the German forces in the east surrendered to the Soviets and the war in Europe was over. Now it was time for recovery and rebuilding and decontamination.

Turning his attention to the Far East, a tired and ill President Roosevelt sent a message to the Emperor of Japan containing similar points and informing him that atomic weapons were available for use against Japan immediately. Would more bloodshed and loss be necessary? The world's first nuclear exchange was over and history would never be the same.

The reality

The Nazis never got the bomb, perhaps because Professor Heisenberg did not have the inspiration to make the necessary breakthroughs the Allied scientists did or because he dragged his feet and implied to Speer and the others that it was 'impossible' because he was against giving Hitler such a terrible weapon. No one will ever know for sure, but it is a safe bet that the Nazis would have used the atomic bomb if they had had it. I have made a reasonable guess that Hitler would have attacked London and Moscow and considering the vicious and criminal use of thousands of randomly 'guided' V-1s and V-2s against the civilians of London and Antwerp and Brussels, I cannot imagine Hitler missing a chance for even more evil. Interestingly enough, the Nazis must have thought they were closer to having the atomic bomb than most historians thought: a specially prepared Heinkel He-177 bomber was discovered in Czechoslovakia at the end of the war, modified to carry an outsized nuclear weapon underneath it.

The idea of Himmler taking over the atomic weapons project is based on the actual takeover by Himmler of the rocket development project at Peenemünde.[5] As with this story, Himmler and his SS boosted the funding and material priorities for the A-4 Project (V-2) and, as in this story, used slave labour liberally to build the missiles under inhuman conditions despite determined Allied bombing attacks aimed at halting the programme.

Approximately 22 months to build a bomb is theoretically possible if Heisenberg and his team had been given full priority and support. They had a lot of the most critical material, uranium, thanks to captured Belgian stocks from the Congo and the Czech mines. The advancement of the American atomic development effort from the actual first test shot at Alamogordo New Mexico in July 1945 to an attack on Berlin in November 1944 is also theoretically possible: several delays came from errors in the processing of U-235 from the more common U-238 isotope and a respectable amount was lost due to an error at the Oak Ridge calutron facilities. Had this material not been lost, the bombs might have been ready months earlier. The scientists under Oppenheimer's leadership also had a tendency to 'admire the problem' at times. The time used for elaborate preparations for the first test at Alamogordo (with additions like the immense – and eventually unused – steel containment vessel known as 'Jumbo' for example) could have been used for preparations for an atomic attack on Berlin instead. Last, but not least, if intelligence did confirm that the Germans were indeed moving ahead in 1942 in the effort to build an atomic bomb, the Manhattan Project would have started earlier and moved more surely to get there as quickly as humanly possible.

An interesting thought: If Hitler had not been a rabid anti-Semite and he had not murdered or driven out all of the Jews within his reach, he could have had the services of many more of the finest physicists in the world – the same ones who made the Manhattan Project successful.

Bibliography

Bernstein, Jeremy, *Hitler's Uranium Club*, (American Institute of Physics Press, Woodbury, New York, 1996).

Dornberger, Walther, *V-2* (Viking Press, New York, 1954).

Eisenhower, Dwight David, *Eisenhower's Own Story* (Arco Publishing, New York, 1946).

Gunston, Bill, *Bombers* (Grosset & Dunlap, New York, 1978).

Irving, David, *The German Atomic Bomb, The History of Nuclear Research in Nazi Germany* (Simon and Schuster, New York, 1967).

Jackson, Robert, *Unexplained Mysteries of World War II* (Smithmark, New York, 1991).

Moore, Mike, The Incident at Stagg Field, *The Bulletin of Atomic Scientists*, www.bullatomsci.org/issues/1992/d92.moore.html

Mosely, Leonard, *The Battle of Britain* (Time-Life Books, Alexandria VA, 1977).

Powers, Thomas, *Heisenberg's War* (Alfred A. Knopf, New York, 1993).

Rhodes, Richard, *The Making of the Atomic Bomb*, (Simon and Schuster, New York, 1986).

Weather Factors in Combat Bombardment Operations in the European Theater (US Strategic Bombing Survey (Restricted), US Department of Defense Military Analysis Division, 1945).

Notes

1. Heisenberg met with Niels Bohr in Copenhagen in 1941, ostensibly to assure the senior physicist that Heisenberg would not pursue bomb development. Bohr was not convinced.
2. In actuality, the Allies went even further: General Leslie Groves, the head of the Manhattan Project, even went so far as to forward suspected atomic research targets to Washington to try to kill Heisenberg and all those around him. A remarkable man, that Gen. Groves!
3. As spoken to MajGen Dornberger, Commander of the A-4 (V-2) project, 1942.
*4. Herr Figge, Reich Director of the Supply Committee for Special Projects stated that sufficient material for the third and fourth weapons was scheduled to be available by October 1944 but, 'This was not achieved, due, chiefly to the interruption of processes and the destruction of transportation as a result of air raids.'
5. See Dornberger, *V-2*, for details of that takeover.

10
ROMMEL VERSUS ZHUKOV
Decision in the East, 1944–45

Peter G. Tsouras

Dachau, 2 July 1944

Rommel vomited. He leaned against the barracks wall emptying his stomach until only the green bile was left. The staff officers around him were deathly silent, ashen faced, save for those who were similarly sick.

The field marshal straightened himself, wiped the filth from his lips, and swung his gaze to the SS commandant standing behind him, white as a ghost. Rommel's eyes were two red coals, his body trembling with rage. He drew his pistol and shot the man dead on the spot.

'I did not believe you, Stauffenberg. God forgive me. God forgive us all.'

The one-eyed, one-armed colonel was a repeated hero, as attested by the maiming he had received on the Eastern Front. He was also a patriot and a devout Christian, two qualities which had led him to risk everything in the successful plot to kill Hitler, the anti-Christ. Though he had not the central almost suicidal role in the assassination originally planned, he had been a vital link between Rommel's chief of staff, Major General Hans Speidel, and the Berlin plotters. He had insisted that Rommel stop here on his flight to Berlin after his victory in Normandy. Now a thousand things needed to be done to save Germany from the Red wave advancing from the East. Yet the most important was confronting them with a vile immediacy. Stauffenberg said, 'We must care for the survivors, Herr Feldmarschall.'

The piles of emaciated bodies, the stench coming from the barracks, and worst of all, the nightmare olfactory assault from the huge ovens as they spewed out black, oily clouds of smoke screamed that it was all beyond help, was beyond atonement. Yet Stauffenberg's simple statement gave Rommel something practical and direct to grasp. 'Yes.' He turned to the commander of a nearby training unit that Stauffenberg had arranged to be present. 'Colonel, arrest every SS swine in the camp. Put them in some of these barracks and put them on the same rations these people have had. Get your men in here immediately and disarm these creatures. Strip them of German uniforms. I charge you with saving as many lives as you can here.' Then he ordered the immediate transfer of the nearest army medical units to the camp. The colonel was as overwhelmed as everyone. He mumbled about not being able to feed or care for so many quickly. In a rage, Rommel turned on him, raising his baton in the air. 'Then let the good people of Dachau help! By God, order the whole damn town up here to help!'[1]

The drive back to Munich was not pretty. Rommel's anger was still white hot at what he had seen. That anger was not enough though to override his sense of the importance of immediate action. That day and the next, every Nazi death factory came to a halt as the army moved in. Courts-martial followed immediately for the senior officers and the more sadistic of the guards. Another fate was in store for the rank and file of the guard force, that collection of brutes from prisons and asylums, in whom humanity was so absent as to arouse not one spark of empathy or pity for all those they had tormented.[2]

Suddenly it's a new game

The more thoughtful and intellectual type of officer would have been overwhelmed by this experience and the new burden of national leadership. Luckily Erwin Rommel was not that sort. It is the intelligent man of action who sees things through, and this was Rommel. He had been on top of the world after defeating the *Amis* (Anglo-American Allies) in Normandy. Hitler had brought his entourage to gloat at the overthrow of Perfidious Albion and view the masses of wreckage and the endless columns of prisoners. For Rommel, this was a heaven-sent opportunity to arrest Hitler and stop the war. After all, the Allies, particularly the British, had suffered a defeat beyond measure in the Norman countryside. An offer of an armistice in the West was vital if Germany was to hold off the Bolshevik hordes grinding their way towards the Reich. For a straightforward man of honour, this seemed like the only correct solution, and Hitler's trial before the nation would seal it properly.

Fortunately, Speidel was far more worldly and took matters into his own hands. While Rommel was treating with Eisenhower for an armistice, Speidel arranged for the demolition of the wing of the Château La Roche Guyon, Rommel's army group headquarters, where Hitler and his cronies were feasting in its great hall. At one stroke, Speidel eliminated any prospect of recalcitrant Nazis rallying round or attempting to rescue an imprisoned Hitler. The explosion that killed the Führer also killed almost all the important National Socialist leaders, including Himmler, Göring, Goebbels, and the particularly dangerous Martin Bormann. The rest were rounded up in Berlin and elsewhere by the anti-Hitler plotters. After that, the Nazi Party simply collapsed. The German people were simply too orderly-minded for civil war. It was obvious to everyone, as well, that one war at a time was more than enough.[3]

The terms of the armistice of the First of July were also enough in and of themselves to dispel any lingering affection for National Socialism. At first glance it seemed the Allies had won. Rommel pledged to evacuate all the occupied territories in western and southern Europe and to cease the U-boat campaign against Allied shipping in the Atlantic and Mediterranean. He also pledged to suppress the Nazis. The Allies pledged not to resume the bomber offensive against Germany, which had been suspended in any case to support the battle in Normandy. The Allies would be allowed to deploy troops in the evacuated countries, but without heavy equipment and only enough to keep order if so requested by the returning governments. In any case, no Allied troops would be allowed nearer than 50 miles of the German border. Most importantly, for the German people, all military prisoners on both sides would be immediately returned. That meant almost 300,000 German fighting men would be coming home.[4]

Montgomery's defeat had taken the wind out of the British. They had been strained to the utmost by the war, and the British Army had scraped the bottom of the manpower barrel by the time Overlord had begun. At that time there were fewer than 4,000 infantry replacements in the United Kingdom. Montgomery was conscious that he had Britain's last army, but he had lost it in the catastrophe of Rommel's great counter-attack. Without that army, Britain simply could not wage war on land in Northern Europe. With the disaster had come a massive letdown at home. Exhausted by the war and seduced by the prospect of retrieving their army as well as achieving the liberation of Western Europe, the British public rationalised an acceptance of the armistice. Churchill was a broken man, and his office soon slipped from his fingers into the eager grasp of Lord Halifax who was all too eager to end the war on such terms. The shockwaves of the disaster triggered a vote of no-confidence in the Government almost immediately, bringing Labour to power with Clement Attlee as Prime Minister.

The Americans wanted to keep fighting; their lodgment built around their Utah Beach landings had been rapidly expanding while Rommel and Montgomery fought it out around the British and Canadian beachheads but their combativeness was useless without the partnership of Britain. It was with an unsubdued rage that they obeyed the orders of President Roosevelt. Roosevelt's death from a stroke three days later on 4 July further unsettled their national councils. The swearing in of Vice President Henry Wallace created chaos in Washington. The new president was so left-wing that even most Democrats thought he was dangerous. The ensuing constitutional crisis paralysed American leadership until the election of Republican moderate Tom Dewey in November. The Germans also played their hand well by immediately releasing all British prisoners captured in Normandy. To say that the Anglo-American Alliance had soured would have been a major understatement.

The most delicate issue for the Allies was their now awkward alliance with the Soviet Union. The Germans had insisted that they would withdraw their U-boat fleet from the seas only if aid to the Soviets was stopped. Admittedly, by July 1944, the submarine arm was no longer the collection of ravening wolf packs of 1941–42. The Allies had in turn insisted on maintaining Lend-Lease and its British counterpart; their only concession was to stop shipments via Murmansk, but by then most aid was funnelling through Iran and Vladivostok. Attlee tried to salvage something to save the Labour Party's darling cause of aid to the Soviet Union. The issue convulsed the more radical and outright Communist elements of the party. Trying to ride this tiger made this timid man downright unbending. In the end, the Germans gave way. The Allies had already conceded the one gift beyond price – the strategic freedom to concentrate on only one front.

The Kremlin, 4 July

Stalin remained a centre of icy calm in the blast wave of anger and betrayal that surged through Moscow. He was always at his calmest when he plotted revenge. Hatred seethed behind the stolid, grim faces of the members of the Stavka (Soviet military high command) arrayed around him in the Kremlin conference room. He just quietly puffed on his pipe as the briefings rolled on. The NKVD boss, Lavrenti Beria, his pince-nez glasses so ludicrous an affectation for a paedophile and mass-murderer, was coldly excited at the prospect of 'liberating' more Western POWs of the Germans the further west the Red Army drove. The *Gulag* could expect new ethnic spices for its stew of misery. The briefings from the Red Army's general staff were more matter of fact assessments of how the armistice would strengthen the German forces they faced. Marshal of the Soviet Union, and the most brilliant and brutal of Stalin's fighting generals, Georgi Zhukov, took the floor to summarise the estimates.

> 'We have dealt the Germans a crippling blow in Operation Bagration, far beyond what we expected to be able to do. As of now, we have destroyed at least 20 of the 38 divisions in Army Group Centre, effectively wrecking four Fascist armies, and pushed them west of Minsk. The continuation of the offensive operation should inflict irretrievable damage on this army group. Subsequent offensive operations against Army Groups North and South should add further strain to the Fascist position. Army Group North is especially vulnerable to being cut off now that its hinge with Army Group Centre has been thinned and pushed back almost to the Baltic.
>
> We can expect the Fascists to reinforce their forces by as much as 40 per cent now that the so-called Second Front has failed. Given the suspension of the Anglo-American bombing campaign, the enemy should be able to repair their transportation system quickly and transfer those forces to the east in two months. Unfortunately, this reinforcement will begin just as our offensive operations are exhausting themselves. By the time we resupply and are ready to resume the offensive in the autumn, the Fascists will also have been strongly reinforced. At that time, the effort required of the Red Army will be much greater and success less assured.'[5]

Stalin and Beria were the only two at the meeting who knew exactly how much more difficult it would be. The Soviet intelligence source within Hitler's entourage had ceased communications. Beria had privately briefed Stalin that the same explosion had probably killed the source as well as Hitler. The source's information had been invaluable, even decisive on many occasions. Had he known about Ultra, he would have called the source his one-man Ultra, able to relay Hitler's orders to Moscow even before they reached his own commanders. And now the dependable duo was gone — Hitler with his foolishness and the source with the ever timely news of it.

Stalin was now concerned with tallying up the pieces on the board. The Soviet Union must not lose any more pieces after the Anglo-American perfidy had removed the Second Front. The biggest piece was Lend-Lease. He had to restrain Beria from killing any more British and American aid officers, at least until victory was assured. He had come a long way as a military strategist and leader since 22 June 1941, the day of the German invasion when he had had a nervous breakdown. The Soviet peoples had unfortunately paid a horrific price for his instruction. He knew that the Soviet Union by the middle of 1944 had little need of combat equipment and ammunition from the West. Soviet factories had been rebuilt in areas safe from the Germans and now were in full war production, an achievement of quality and volume that was historic by any standards. But every last Soviet resource was funnelled into producing the sharp end of the Red Army's needs. The soft but vital sustaining logistics of war were beyond Soviet resources. Already much of the population outside the armed forces and vital industries was seriously malnourished. That part of the war effort poured across the seas from the United States and Britain.

When it became clear in 1942 that the Red Army needed desperately to restore the authority of rank to its officer corps and downplay the corrosive power of the commissars, old tsarist shoulder boards of rank had been reintroduced. It was then that the Soviets had surprised the British by requesting a million metres of gold braid for the new rank insignia. Now, it was common for the canned food the Red Army soldier opened to contain beef that had grazed in Texas or pork raised in Iowa. The Americans dedicated the complete production run of the Studebaker Corporation to supply the Red Army with the mobility to carry on high speed armoured warfare across vast fronts and at great depths. Monthly truck deliveries were averaging 11,500 vehicles, enough to equip nine infantry or two tank armies. Twelve thousand trucks had been required for the immediate needs of the armies taking part in Bagration. Now Soviet formations were being equipped on a scale undreamed of before the war. Fronts possessed truck brigades of 1,275 vehicles; armies had 1,200 in all including a 348-truck transport regiment. The new mighty tank armies were even more lavishly provided with 5,340 vehicles.[6]

These fleets of remarkable and reliable vehicles ran often on British oil pumped up through the great Middle Eastern oil fields. American radios and signals equipment linked the fronts and tank armies with a speed and efficiency that the prewar Red Army had thought was only a theoretical possibility. Often as not, the Soviet infantry trudged forward on American and British leather boots and were clothed in American and British cloth. That the useful idiots in the British and American governments had bargained to continue Lend-Lease had been the fruition of a long-term investment Stalin had made in subverting left-leaning elites in both countries. He must play that hand carefully – there were even more dividends to be reaped here.

He puffed on his pipe again and let the silence penetrate the moment.

> 'I shall remind you of what I said to you all in December 1941 when the Fascists were at the gates of Moscow. The Germans are only a temporary enemy. The main enemy, the *glavnyy vrag*, is the United States. When Lenin declared war on the Capitalist world before he died, he clearly recognised the centrality of the imperialist circles of the United States as the great bastion of the enemies of Socialism. That is even more true today.'

He knew he had their attention. But then, he always had their attention. The inattentive ones did not last long. But he had also confused them. Good. It would prepare them for the political-strategic lesson he was about to deliver.

> 'The cowardly armistice that the West has made will, indeed, make the immediate victory of the Red Army more difficult, much more difficult to attain. But, comrades, once achieved the victory will be all the greater – the victory of which Lenin dreamed – the final victory of socialism over capitalism will come with surprising speed.'

He was on his feet now, slamming his fist on the great wooden table.

> 'It will be the Soviet Union alone, ALONE which will conquer Germany, all of Germany, and make it a faithful subordinate of the Socialist camp. The rest of Europe will fall to us like rotten fruit. When the war ends, Soviet Power will be planted from Norway to Gibraltar to Crete!'[7]

Rommel at the front

Rommel's Junkers transport was more of a sieve than an aircraft when it belly-landed on the muddy field. His *Luftwaffe* escort had been jumped by a flock of Stalin's Red Falcons as they approached the front. The Yak-3s were aggressive and outnumbered the Focke-Wulfs three to one. One after another had sought out the Ju-52, clawing past the Focke-Wulfs, and sending streams of shells into the transport, burning out one motor, killing the pilot and wounding his co-pilot who barely got it on the ground without crashing.[8]

Rommel stumbled out followed by Gehlen, his intelligence chief, and the other survivors. They had landed near a Panzer company retreating west. A Kubelwagen sped over to the plane. A rumpled captain, Knight's Cross at his throat, jumped out of the car as it stopped by the survivors. A hard veteran at 25, the captain thought he had seen everything in three years on the Eastern Front. But he had to admit he had never seen the leader of the Third Reich, or whatever they were calling Germany in the last week, fall out a shot-up aircraft. He barely had time to salute before Rommel jumped into his jeep, ordered Gehlen to follow, and said. 'Hauptmann, where are the closest Russians?'

The story would shoot across the fluid front in hours. Rommel had escaped death by an eyelash, and his only thought was to find some Russians to thrash. The fact that he arrived at 20th Panzer Division and led its pitiful remnant into a counter-attack that savaged the Russian tank corps spearheading the pursuit grew quickly into a legend that grew and grew with the retelling. The truth was a bit more modest. Both the Panzer division and the tank corps were shells of themselves and exhausted. But the magic of Rommel's name had worked wonders with the German troops. He seemed to be everywhere among the retreating columns, showing himself, and turning them east. Goebbels may have been dead, but his propaganda machine was still working and picked up the story of the victory at Baronovichi. In these hands it became another miracle. The Desert Fox had brought his magic with him to the Eastern Front.

If Field Marshal Walther Model, commander of the remnants of Army Group Centre, had any complaint with the head of state interfering with his conduct of the retreat, he kept it to himself. After all, he had worked with Hitler who only caused him trouble. If Rommel wanted to play division commander, he would not object, especially when it helped. Their meeting had gone surprisingly well. Rommel showed a good grasp of the situation and concurred with Model's overall handling of the retreat and then outlined his plans for the immediate future. Within those plans, Model had a free hand. 'Trade space for time. Save as many men and as much equipment as you can. The decisive battle will be fought on the Vistula–Narew line. But you must buy me the time to prepare for it and mass a Panzer reserve.' Then he was gone.

Zhukov at the front

Zhukov did not allow himself to become elated when signal intercepts reported that Rommel had been shot down approaching the front. First reports were usually wrong, and he had more important things at hand, such as bullying his flagging armoured forces forward. He was a much-feared man and with good reason. He was completely ruthless. Rumours had it that he had personally shot more than one general who failed. Only recently, disgusted with the failure of an attempted river crossing, he had ordered the corps and division commanders involved sent to penal battalions. His staff had intervened to save the corps commander. The former division commander was allowed to redeem himself by leading a suicide attack. Generals physically feared him, but the troops seemed to have a great confidence and affection for him. Though he spent their lives like a spendthrift, he had a reputation for fair treatment of the lower ranks. Anyone who shoots generals usually looks good to privates.

He did allow himself some guarded optimism, though. Operation Bagration had destroyed or wrecked four German armies. Stalin would be pleased with the 50,000 POWs who were destined to be marched through Red Square. His job now was to guarantee the destruction of the remnants. With luck the Red Army would crush them and throw itself over the Vistula and Narew Rivers before his forces completely outran their logistics. Then a few months' rest, and the offensive would resume, now across the flat tilled Polish plain as its right brushed the Baltic through East Prussia and its left the Carpathian Mountains. The blow would fall upon broken German forces and sweep them aside as the Red Army made its lunge across the Oder to Berlin itself. And after Berlin there was the Rhine, and beyond the Rhine...

Remagen Bridge, 15 July

The railroad control officer was a retread from the 1914–18 War. Strangely enough, he had been working the same Rhine River railroad bridge control point in late November and December 1918. The troop trains then had been full of German troops returning to the fatherland. This time there was a difference. This time they were the victors, not the defeated.

The officer, like millions of other Germans, had been euphoric over the victory in the West. The news of Hitler's death had followed and stunned the nation. But the Armistice in the West had followed so quickly as to submerge Hitler's sudden disappearance from the stage in a wave of euphoria. Since Stalingrad and the disaster in Tunisia, the news had been getting worse and worse. A sense of doom had formed in the minds of the German people, growing daily as the propaganda could no longer explain away the constant retreats and as the rain of death from the sky had increased. The destruction of Hamburg in its firestorm from hell had stunned the elites, although everything possible had been done to hide the extent of the disaster from the public. Now the skies were clear again, and he, as a railroad control officer, found his job infinitely easier. No more constant interruptions of the schedule by damaged and destroyed track and rolling stock. It was almost like peacetime.

The Army had moved quickly and almost instinctively to shed the obnoxious attributes of National Socialism. The up and coming 'National Socialist' politicals quickly found themselves transferred to the more dangerous assignments where their previous and enthusiastic support of Hitler's 'hold or die' orders took on new meaning. Himmler's death left the SS without a head. One of Rommel's first acts was to abolish its national establishment and subordinate its fighting arm directly into the Army. *SS* General Sepp Dietrich's quiet support in the days before and after Hitler's assassination had proved vital in getting the *SS* under control. Most Germans were too concentrated on the implacable Bolshevik enemy to have any taste for civil war. As the fantastic days of early July sped by, the German people clung to obedience and duty.

The railroad officer also had to admit that the sudden disappearance of all those swastikas and the return of the old Imperial colours had been a welcome change. He also gathered from the movement orders that his little operation was only part of an incredible shift of forces across Europe, dwarfing the transfer of over a million German troops from the Eastern Front in 1917 after the defeat of Tsarist Russia. He was right. The movements truly dwarfed 1917 in scope and speed. At the beginning of June, the German ground forces were stretched far too thin along a great circle. Hitler's conquests in every direction had left him with an immense area to garrison, as shown by table below. Everything was important to Hitler who thereby dissipated the fighting strength of Germany in every direction. The consequences of a two-front war were devouring the substance of Germany's ability to continue fighting at an alarming rate.

German Ground Forces, 1 June 1944[9]

	Eastern Front	Finland	Norway/ Denmark	West	Italy	Balkans
Army	149	6	15	47	23	18
Luftwaffe	–	–	–	3	3	–
SS	8	1	–	4	1	7
Totals	154	7	15	54	27	25

The commitment to build up the West to counter the Allied invasion had sucked fighting forces from the Eastern Front which by June stood at only 2,160,000 men, barely two-thirds of the force with which Hitler had launched Operation Barbarossa in 1941. The total *Wehrmacht* forces in France at the same time were almost 1,400,000 of which 900,000 were in the field formations of the Army and *SS*. Another 340,000 were in the *Luftwaffe* of which over 30,000 were in its field divisions and paratrooper units and 100,000 were flak troops. The remainder were naval personnel.[10]

Theoretically, the Germans now had an additional 121 divisions available for commitment to the Eastern Front, almost doubling their order of battle. That included 1,030,000 men from France and the Low Countries, 500,000 from Italy, 300,000 from Scandinavia, and 500,000 from the Balkans,[11] altogether 2.33 million. Practically, it would not be quite as impressive. At least half of these divisions were not first-class units, nor were they fully equipped or trained.

Zhukov's appraisal of the German strength that would flow to the Eastern Front was exaggerated, but it was still massive enough to give

Germany a fighting chance. For any Germans and Russians, though, the parallels to 1917–18 were unsettling. The Germans had freed themselves of a two-front war in 1917 when the new Bolshevik government in Russia had made a craven peace. The massive transfer of German forces to the Western Front had still not been enough to win the war, even in the last desperate gamble of the Ludendorff Offensives of 1918. Would history repeat itself in 1944–45? A few of the more perceptive would argue that the last war's analogy had broken down. In 1918 the flow of American reinforcements to the Western Allies had negated the new German strength transferred from the Eastern Front. In this war, the Soviets would have no reinforcement beyond what they already had – and the ongoing flood of Lend-Lease equipment and supplies. Still, it would be a race. If the Germans were to receive a vital reinforcement, it would be in a context, not of a stalemated front in 1917–18, but of a crumbling front already reeling back from crushing Soviet blows. Hitler's 'hold or die' orders had already sacrificed huge numbers of German troops and infected the rest with an encirclement syndrome that corroded them with fear and panic. Even where troops had escaped, the retreat orders had often come too late. Vast amounts of supplies and irreplaceable heavy equipment in the Army's tail had been abandoned.

Sorting it out

Rommel faced twin problems of incredible magnitude at the same time. He had to allocate and manage the flow of men and equipment east while at the same time staving off collapse of the Eastern Front. His first conclusion was that he could not do it all himself. He bypassed the senior officers of the Army and appointed Speidel as chief of a combined staff of *OKW* (*Oberkommando der Wehrmacht*) and *OKH* (*Oberkommando des Heeres*). By doing so he put an end to the absurd division of power by which *OKH* ran the Eastern Front and *OKW* ran everything else. Speidel and he had worked hand in glove together in Normandy, and Rommel felt he needed someone he could trust and someone with deep experience of operations. Speidel was that man. If Rommel was the intelligent man of action, Speidel was the military intellectual of great operational and administrative ability. As Chief of Staff of *Eighteenth Army* in 1940, Lieutenant Colonel Speidel had received the surrender of Paris. He served two years on the Eastern Front as an army chief of staff in von Manstein's *Army Group South*. When Rommel had assumed command of *Army Group B* in France in early 1944, he asked for Speidel, even though they had never met, because the Army grapevine had carried only good things about his fellow Württemberger. More than a few observers commented that their relationship was similar to the 'happy marriage' between Hindenburg and Ludendorff in the 1914–18 War.

If Rommel stopped to think about it, the situation facing him would break down any man. Even his enormous self-confidence and energy were having to come to grips with his equally powerful realism. For the first time, Erwin Rommel was having to take account of his own limitations. To this point in his life his talents and experiences had served him well at every level of command. But each step had been a military one and a largely operational one. The realms of politics, diplomacy, and national strategy had never been his concern or of much interest. Nor did he have General Staff training or higher education to fall back on. What he did have was good judgment and a talent for picking good subordinates and trusting them. Speidel was one. And now there would be many others.

A flurry of orders recalled to active duty a number of the brilliant Army officers forcibly retired by Hitler – Field Marshals Erich von Manstein and Wilhelm von List, and General Hermann Hoth and many others. A similar flurry went out relieving the officers whose primary qualification had been loyalty to Hitler. Adolf Galland was jumped up from General of the Fighters to command of the *Luftwaffe*,[12] but the *Kriegsmarine* was left in the capable hands of Grossadmiral Karl Dönitz. The competent fence-sitters and trimmers were retained. Generaloberst Heinz Guderian kept his position of Inspector General of Armoured Forces. No one could reorganise and train the depleted Panzer arm better than he – especially now that he had something to work with. Albert Speer was also confirmed in office and given even more authority over Germany's war production as the last of the Party and service satrapies were abolished.

Rommel quickly realised that as a grand strategist, he was clearly outclassed by Stalin. An instinctive tactician and leader at heart, he now found himself thrust into the role of Hindenburg as supreme leader of the nation in war. And Hindenburg had failed. Also unlike Stalin whose command and staff team had stabilised at a high level of efficiency, the German counterpart was in shambles. Hitler had purged it of men of character and filled it with sycophants and party loyalists. The anti-Hitler plotters had begun to squabble among themselves. Not only did he need to get a grip on a war effort in free fall, but he had to suppress the Nazis and form a government as well. Then there had been Dachau and the horrific briefings on how deep the cancer ran. That filthy mess would have to be concealed while the fighting was still going on.[13] The courts-martial would continue, but the German people would hear nothing. All in all, he would rather be back in the Western Desert, crawling up to an outpost line under fire to get a feel for the battle against his old, chivalrous British adversary.

Digging in

Stalin was a realist. Soviet logistics played out sooner than expected by the middle of July, and even the mass of American trucks could not be everywhere at once. And the Germans had not cooperated. Since Stalingrad he had become used to Hitler's assistance to the Red Army. It had been all too easy to demolish German units which had been nailed to the ground by a Führer order. Now the rules seemed to have changed. The Germans eluded the grasp of his marshals everywhere, striking where they could and moving ever west, holding ground only to allow others to escape. Soviet military intelligence, the GRU, informed him that captures had fallen off dramatically since the initial encirclement of *Army Group Centre*. But now the Germans had finally come to a halt and turned about on a front on the line Kaunas–Grodno–Brest–Lvov.

Army Group North had begun an immediate evacuation of the Baltics. German troops and hordes of refugees were flooding through into East Prussia and western Lithuania and being evacuated by sea from Courland. The sudden appearance of the *Kriegsmarine* in strength in the Baltic had beaten the Soviet Baltic Fleet back into its bolthole in Leningrad and protected what the Germans had the black humour to call *unsere kleine Dunkirk* ('our little Dunkirk'). Although Soviet armies had fallen upon the retreating Germans, they had not been able to halt the evacuation and had in turn been stung by German counter-attacks. In a surprise move, the Germans had informed the Finns of their intention to evacuate the *Twentieth Mountain Army* from northern Finland. The Finns immediately began negotiations with the Soviets. Stalin would drive a hard bargain and transfer his forces where they would be more useful as well.[14]

Stalin had hoped the Germans would make the mistake of abandoning the Romanians as they had the Finns, but they had not. There was a different logic at work. In the north, *Army Group North* and *Twentieth Mountain Army* had extended the front enormously with no strategic gain. *Army Group South* (formerly *Army Group South Ukraine*), however, served very useful purposes. To have withdrawn from Romania would have opened the door for Soviet armies to flood through the Balkans and threaten the Germans on an enormous and porous front. By holding the line along the Dniester River, the Germans could anchor one flank on the Black Sea and the other on the Carpathian mountains. Already strong forces evacuated from Italy and the Balkans were heavily reinforcing *Army Group South*.

Intelligence reports were also painting a picture of massive German reinforcement and reorganisation deep behind the front in Poland. Air reconnaissance was becoming especially difficult as *Luftwaffe* strength ballooned. Red Air Force bombing missions had suddenly become very expensive and had to be curtailed.

Along the entire front, German strength swelled. And the Germans dug. Belt after belt of anti-tank defences echeloned in successive lines from in front of and behind the Vistula–Narew River line to the west halfway across Poland. In front of *Army Group Centre* the front ran on a line Bialystok–Brest–Lvov. Von Manstein personally chose its name, the Loki Line.[15] Another, stronger line, the Scharnhorst Line, was begun 30–40 miles east of the Vistula and Narew Rivers. A third belt, the Gneisenau Line, ran along the western banks of the those rivers. Amazing results were achieved in two short months as every available German and most of the adult Polish population were put to work with spade, shovel, and bucket. Anti-tank weapons, still caked with French mud or Norwegian bracken, were sewn thickly to great depth while all Panzer divisions disappeared from the front.

New production flowed into the gashes of fresh earth. The growing defences presented a deadly thicket of anti-tank weapons, machine guns, anti-tank ditches and obstacles, and mines − interlocking defences in depth. Large armour concentrations were also growing in East Prussia, to the west of Warsaw, and elsewhere.

The GRU also reported a fundamental change in German organisation. Many of the surviving German divisions in the East had become mere shells, having been kept in the order-of-battle simply because Hitler liked to see large numbers of divisions on his battle maps. The best of these units, especially the infantry divisions, were brought up to strength by breaking up garrison divisions from Scandinavia, France, and the Balkans and feeding their personnel into the experienced front-line formations. Göring's pet *Luftwaffe* field divisions were also broken up, and their personnel reassigned to Galland's reorganising efforts or to Army units. The creation of new units was halted immediately and personnel in these forming units were also sent to reinforce existing divisions. Panzer and Panzergrenadier divisions were withdrawn from the front and grouped into strong reserve formations where they were joined by formations arriving from other theatres. Everywhere, anti-tank defence in depth was stressed, with mobile formations held in reserve for counter-attack.

The Western Allies continued to feed Stalin intelligence which filled in many of the blanks left by his own intelligence services. None of the information was encouraging. German reserves of fuel were at their greatest since 1940. German synthetic fuel production was steadily increasing and could expect greater increases now that the bombing campaign had ended. Rommel's victory in Normandy had forestalled the post-invasion 'Oil Campaign' planned by the Allies to smash fuel production.[16] In fact, the air campaign had ended just as it had begun to inflict serious damage on German war production and on the Reich air defenders. Now aircraft production could continue accelerating, quickly reaching 4,000 fighters (mostly Bf 109Gs and Fw 190s) in August, at the same time as the *Luftwaffe* speeded up its training to produce more fighter pilots. An added bonus of the Armistice was the return of thousands of aircrew captured in the Battle of Britain and North Africa. There was also a wholesale conversion of the remaining bomber units to fighter commands as the aircraft became available. In fact, almost all of the resource-wasteful super-weapon projects favoured by Hitler were cancelled, expect for the Messerschmitt 262 jet fighter. Galland would get the best out of the *Luftwaffe*'s new lease on life.

The Armistice in the West kept on giving. The end of the bombing campaign also freed the *Luftwaffe*'s massive flak resources that had been vainly attempting to fend off the rain of Allied bombs. The 100,000 flak troops from France joined the endless troop trains heading east picking up hundreds of thousands more in Germany itself, swelling the flood of 88mm anti-aircraft guns that quickly began to thicken the front. Literally thousands of these superb guns were being sent east. Their dual-purpose capability as the ultimate anti-tank gun of the war further strengthened the German ground forces.

The warlords return

Another disquieting discovery for the Soviets was the reappearance of some of the best of the German commanders. Model had retained command of *Army Group Centre*. List assumed command of *Army Group North* to shepherd it to safety in East Prussia, and Kleist took over *Army Group North Ukraine*. Unknown to Stalin, though, Rommel had invited von Manstein to assume operational command of all three army groups. It was obvious that these three army groups would constitute the main theatre of the war; it was absurd to control each from the newly reorganised *OKW*. Manstein's advocacy of this very solution to Hitler had done much to ensure his relief. He flew to Warsaw immediately to begin putting his new headquarters together – *Oberkommando Ost*. Rommel had promised him his pick of staff officers. There was much to do.

Rommel had another meeting. Field Marshal 'Smiling Albert' Kesselring was not smiling when he heard what Rommel offered – command of *Army Group South*. The two had had a stormy relationship during the African and Italian campaigns but had remained grudgingly respectful. 'And what have I done that I deserve to be saddled with more Latin allies?' Kesselring asked. Rommel broke out laughing, 'Well, you know how to get the best out of them, and if that fails, you have had practice in disarming them.' Then seriously, he said, 'The main battle will be fought in Poland, Herr Feldmarschall, but the south must be held on its short Romanian front. If it fails, the entire Balkans will collapse, and we cannot cope with such an extension of our front. Nor can we afford to lose the Romanian oil fields. Trade space for time and bleed them, but do not abandon Ploesti.' When he, left Kesselring really was smiling. A natural optimist, he was already exploring the possibilities.

A remembered conversation

Generalleutnant Fritz Bayerlein, commanding *Panzer 'Lehr' Division*, was surely the first Panzer commander in the east to understand the massive reorganisation. He had been Rommel's chief of staff in Africa. They had met again at Hitler's headquarters in East Prussia as the Kursk fiasco was unfolding. Rommel had immediately grasped the lessons of that *Totenritt* ('death ride') of the German Panzer divisions into the depths of the Soviet defences. Bayerlein remembered clearly what Rommel's opinion of what to do had been then.

> 'You know, Bayerlein, we have lost the initiative, of that there is no doubt. We have just learnt in Russia for the first time that dash and over-optimism are not enough. We must have a completely new approach. There is no question of taking the offensive for the next few

years... and so we must try to make the most of the advantages that normally accrue to the defence. The main defence against the tank is the anti-tank gun; in the air we must build fighters and still more fighters and give up all idea for the present of doing any bombing ourselves...

We must fight on interior lines... In the east we must withdraw as soon as possible to a suitable, prepared line... You remember, Bayerlein, how difficult we found it to attack the British anti-tank screens in Africa. It needed first-class, highly-trained troops to achieve anything at all against them. Now I've made a careful study of our experiences in Russia. The Russian is stubborn and inflexible. He will never be able to develop the well-thought-out, guileful method with which the Englishman fights his battles. The Russian attacks head on, with enormous expenditures of material, and tries to smash his way through by sheer weight of numbers.

If we can give the German infantry divisions first fifty, then a hundred, then two hundred 75mm anti-tank guns each and install them in carefully-prepared positions, covered by large minefields, we shall be able to halt the Russians... There is not the slightest hope of our keeping pace with the enemy in the production of tanks, but we certainly can in anti-tank guns, if the enemy is having to produce tanks for his attack... Now let us suppose that the Russians attack in a heavily-mined sector where our anti-tank guns are forming a screen, say six miles deep, then – for all their mass of material – they are bound to bog down in the first few days, and from then on, they'll have to gnaw their way through slowly. Meanwhile we shall be installing more anti-tank guns behind our screen. If the enemy makes three miles' progress in a day, we'll build six miles' depth of anti-tank screen, and let him run himself to a standstill. We'll be fighting under the cover of our positions, he'll be attacking in the open... Once it becomes clear to the troops that they can hold their ground, morale will go up again... Our last chance in the East lies in equipping the army thoroughly for an unyielding defence.'[17]

Reappraisal, the Kremlin, 2 August

By the beginning of August, the situation had changed so dramatically that Stalin ordered a fundamental reappraisal of planning assumptions. Again, Zhukov took the lead in the briefings. For the past three weeks the Germans had dodged the pursuing Soviets, turned to strike, and then retreated again. But that had stopped as new divisions from other theatres had begun strengthening their front. They had clearly been trading space for time until now. And that change was worrying for Stalin and Zhukov. Despite the loss of their prized spy in Hitler's headquarters, there was enough low level intelligence coming in to paint a vivid picture of German intentions. *Army Group North* was reassembling in East Prussia with its *Sixteenth* and

Eighteenth Armies. A reconstituted *Army Group Centre* ran from the East Prussian border to the confluence of the Vistula and San Rivers in southern Poland and now consisted of *Second Army* plus *Seventh*, and *Fifteenth Armies* from France. *Army Group A* (former *AG North Ukraine*) consisted of the German *Fourteenth* (from Italy), *Seventeenth*, *Twentieth Mountain*, and *First Hungarian Armies* and was the link between *Army Groups Centre* and *South*. Randulic's *Twentieth Mountain Army* was slowly moving into the Carpathian Mountains after its long trek from the shores of the Arctic. *Army Group South*'s line ran *Eighth*, *Tenth* (from Italy), *Fourth Romanian*, *Sixth*, and *Third Romanian Armies* Nowhere was there evidence of any of the Panzer armies along the front.

Zhukov explained the situation to the gathered Soviet leaders:

'They are planning a Kursk in reverse but a Kursk on a theatre-scale. The only difference is that they cannot be as strong everywhere as we were at Kursk.'

Stalin pointed to the south.

'There in Romania is where they are most vulnerable. We should let Timoshenko proceed with his attack. The Romanians are sick of the war and will fall apart. Once the Germans are unhinged there, they can never hope to fight over such a huge front. It will serve to suck resources away from their concentrations in Poland. Then we will strike.'

He took grim satisfaction that the full fury of the Soviet peoples was at white heat to begin this final push. In the back of his mind, though, was a worry. The power equation in the war had shifted since this Rommel had come to power. He missed Hitler. He understood Hitler. Already the first hints from the 'former' allies had come suggesting he make peace. How long would it be before those hints became hands squeezing off Lend-Lease? If something went wrong?

He turned back to Zhukov,

'You, Comrade Marshal, you will have overall command of the offensive operation in Poland.'[18]

Blood and oil

Timoshenko's offensive roared into life on 20 August. As Stalin predicted, the Romanians flew apart, but this time Kesselring kicked them back into line, and the line held. It buckled, bent, and drifted back, but it held. And every once in a while, it snapped forward in a deadly sting of a counter-attack. Timoshenko's two fronts with 929,000 men were a powerful force, but the reinforced *Army Group South* was no longer the beaten command it had been in June. The reinforcement was by no means complete, but the recuperative powers of the German Army had made the most of what had arrived, and the reinforcements continued to arrive as the battle ground on. Fighting a dogged but nimble defence, the Germans extracted an enormous price from the Soviets. The active presence of the *Luftwaffe* was considered to be a miracle by the German troops and did much to keep morale up. That and the strongly increased flak did much to lessen the ground support provided by the Red Air Force to Timoshenko's armies. Still, the Romanians bled away quickly because the Soviets especially targeted their divisions. Timoshenko could report that Bessarabia had been cleared of the Fascists, and Stalin could order another massive fireworks display in Moscow to celebrate the liberation of one of the last pieces of Soviet territory in enemy hands. But by the beginning of September, going had been so slow and costly for Timoshenko that another front from Stavka Reserve had been allocated to continue the operation. Losses in tanks had been particularly severe, and the German front did not seem to have suffered fundamental damage in its bloody fighting retreat. Soviet bomber attacks against the Ploesti oil fields were deadly failures. And the oil kept pumping.

Kesselring's 'Latin' experience was finally called on again. His success in holding the Soviets to a slow advance had done much to strengthen the hand of the Romanian dictator Marshal Antonescu. However, appalling Romanian losses triggered attempts by King Michael to unseat Antonescu and declare Romania out of the war. Kesselring politely but firmly took the king into custody by providing him a German 'Guard of Honour'.

Army Group South's success had contributed to a remarkable strengthening of Germany's positions in the Balkans. Bulgaria edged back closer to the Germans after nearly ordering the German mission out when the German position in the east had been on the point of snapping. Turkey which had also been on the point of breaking relations quietly shelved those plans and continued exports, particularly of chrome. In fact, as the months dragged on, the position of the Rommel government slowly but steadily increased among the neutrals. German propaganda went to great lengths to demonstrate the new government's desire for peace. This uncharacteristically Teutonic subtle approach had a positive effect, decisively enhanced by Rommel's de-Nazification programme. It was so easy to blame it all on Hitler and this message sold. Latin American countries quickly re-established relations and resumed trade, though it remained a cold armistice with the British and Americans. Sweden and Switzerland doubled their deliveries of war materials. Imports began easing critical shortages in Germany, though the volume of trade was not great. In September Sweden and Uruguay offered themselves as joint mediators between Germany and the Soviet Union, only to be turned down brusquely, but the door was left open.[19]

Final preparations

At the beginning of January 1945 a tense quiet hung over the front from the Baltic Sea to the Carpathian Mountains. Gehlen's *Foreign Armies East* had reported that the Soviets had massed along the entire Eastern Front '414 formations of division or brigade size in the fronts, 216 in front reserves, and 219 in reserves in depth.' Most of these were opposite von Manstein's three army groups in Poland. Against *Army Group North*, Second and Third Byelorussian Fronts massed in the north against East Prussia and northern Poland 1,670,000 men with over 28,000 guns and 3,300 tanks and assault guns. Against the remaining two army groups, the First Byelorussian Front, commanded by Marshal Koniev, and First Ukrainian Front, commanded by Marshal Vasilievskiy, counted 2,200,000 men, 6,400 tanks and assault guns, and 46,000 guns, including heavy mortars and rocket launchers. They were supported by over 10,000 combat aircraft.[20] Soviet propaganda fed the desire for revenge among the troops until it glowed a dull hot ember red. The months since the end of Bagration had been used well to amass huge stocks of supplies and train to a razor's edge for the final, brutal campaign. Stalin had released the huge stockpiles of supplies and equipment he had stored in the Far East for the war with Japan and drawn even more of the divisions from there to deepen his reserves. Nothing would be withheld from the Red storm, codenamed Operation Suvorov after the most brilliant general in all Russian history.

Kesselring now commanded 40 battle-tried divisions; Manstein's super-command controlled another 150, with the remainder in *OKW* reserve. *Luftwaffe* strength in the East had increased to 5,000 aircraft, supplemented by thousands of flak guns. Tank strength now exceeded 4,000 machines. The reinforcements sent to the east had swelled the German army groups to strengths they had not seen since the beginning of the war. *Army Group Centre* was now over a million strong. An immense confidence also grew from the *Luftwaffe*'s increasing ability to protect the German troops on the ground from incessant attacks. Training had also been constant and hard, reminding retreads from the last war of the defensive preparations on the Western Front. Central Poland seemed to be one vast trench system. Some of the infantry had not seen a tank in months.

The Panzer armies were key to von Manstein's thinking. He had fully agreed with Rommel's concept of creating a defensive morass to soak up the offensive power of the Soviet armies. He took it one step further. The rebuilding of the German Army in the east was finally creating a powerful Panzer reserve which had been grouped carefully behind the first deep defensive system. He had available four Panzer armies, all of which reported directly to him at *Oberkommando Ost*: *First Panzer Army* (Generaloberst Erhard Raus), *Third Panzer Army* (Generaloberst Georg Reinhardt), *Fourth Panzer Army* (Generaloberst Hermann Hoth), and *Fifth Panzer Army* (General der Panzertruppen Hasso von Manteuffel).[21]

Third Panzer Army was positioned to support *Army Group North*. The remaining armies he grouped from Warsaw to Krakow, the area of the front against which the Soviet buildup seemed to be directed. *First* and *Fifth Panzer* (newly created) *Armies* were massed behind Warsaw and *Fourth Panzer*

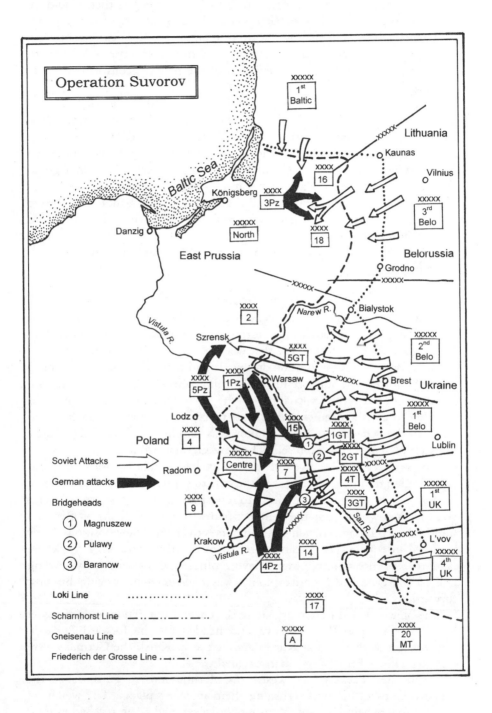

Operation Suvorov

Army was in the vicinity of Krakow. Substantial strength then would be available to counter a deep penetration anywhere along the front. Further to the west, the Polish earth was scarred in another vast defensive network, the Friedrich der Grosse Line, in a great bow from just south of Warsaw to Krakow. This was manned by divisions of the newly reconstituted *Fourth* and *Ninth Armies*.

It was the hardest thing Rommel had ever had to do – just sit there and listen as von Manstein delivered the final briefings at the front commanders' conference in Poland. For the man who always been on the speartip in battle, this had been his most difficult conquest. Then again, von Manstein and his subordinate commanders had left him little to do.[22] They were good, and he gave them all the slack they wanted – really not much different than letting a good lieutenant take on all the work he could handle. They were the final briefings. Gehlen had predicted that the Soviet offensive would begin within days.

Von Manstein had wanted it more precisely than that. And Gehlen delivered.

Furor Sovieticus

Gehlen had pieced together an accurate idea of the time of the Soviet attack by analysing the vast build-up of forces and supplies. Tens of thousands of Soviet guns were in place in the first week of January 1945, ready to be fed by carefully massed ammunition dumps. It had taken the Soviets months to mass the forces and support for the coming offensive. On 7 January von Manstein ordered the evacuation of the Loki Line. The relatively light German forces there quickly displaced rearward anything from 20 to 60 miles to the Scharnhorst Line. Zhukov was caught unprepared. His entire logistics plan was compromised. The new German front line was now far out of artillery range. Even if the guns had displaced forward, their ammunition dumps were too far to the rear to support them. Zhukov drove his logisticians to Herculean efforts to reposition their stocks forward as his commanders worked out the complex plans to move millions of men and hundreds of thousands of vehicles and horses to entirely new positions. They engaged in equally Herculean efforts to replan their attacks. Everywhere Zhukov was threatening, often relieving officers, and occasionally sending one to the camps. An entire month was consumed in moving his host forward.

The blow fell on 14 February along the entire front. Thousands of Soviet aircraft took off in the pre-dawn and headed for the forward *Luftwaffe* airfields just as they had at Kursk, and just as at Kursk the Germans were one step ahead. Ferocious air battles filled the skies.

As the Red Falcons flew west, tens of thousands of guns lashed the forward German defences, crushing them in many places. The weight of iron was overwhelming. Von Manstein, however, had again reached into his bag of tricks and made sure most of the Soviet metal was wasted. Good intelligence had alerted the Germans, in many areas giving 24 hours' notice of the artillery preparation. As planned the Germans again abandoned their forward positions and occupied secondary and even more powerful positions in the depths of the Scharnhorst Line. The attacking Soviet armies fought their way through the light screening forces for miles before encountering the main line of resistance. By then they had exhausted their impetus and did not have the crushing weight of massive preplanned fires to prepare the way. It was then the turn of the German artillery and close air support to take their toll. Nowhere did the Soviets penetrate more than a few miles on the first day.

The weeks burned through February as the Soviets ground forward leaving the blood trail of a nation behind them in the frozen Polish earth. By the end of the month they had barely reached the Vistula and Narew Rivers in a few places, and losses had been enormous. Thousands of burned-out tanks and assault guns littered their path westward through the Scharnhorst Line. The front line infantry divisions had been in many cases reduced to regiments. Everywhere the Germans had fought on until the point of destruction then withdrawn deeper into their endless defensive system. Tanks became as useless as cavalry in the trench system of the First War. Every time it seemed a penetration had been made in the system, the tank corps that rushed through the gaps found themselves in enormous anti-tank ambushes with Panzers in force waiting for the counter-stroke. The brunt of the battle fell to the infantry again, and Stalin was profligate but, as the month wore on, even he began to draw back and consider his dwindling human bank account. The British and Americans were also telling him that they could no longer justify continued assistance under domestic political pressure. 'Make peace,' they told him. 'You have already restored your borders. Expect nothing more after the end of this month.'

March began with more blood as the fighting slowly burned west, but by the second week the First Ukrainian Front made better progress as it fought its way first across the San then the Vistula at Baranow. First Byelorussian Front reached the Vistula south of Warsaw about the same time on 5–6 March. In one of the most costly and heroic actions of the war, the Red Army threw itself across the river at Magnuszew and Pulawy three days later to carve out a substantial bridgehead. By the third week, the good news was that the final belt of defensive systems of the Gneisenau Line had been breached by both fronts. The Soviets, however, had the utmost difficulty in widening the breaches against the Germans' determination to hold the shoulders in strength. Nevertheless, Zhukov ordered his tank armies forward, demanding a deep exploitation. Through the narrow breaches in the front on 17 March, Marshal Koniev released his 3rd Guards Tank and 4th Tank Armies and Vasilievskiy his 1st Guards and 2nd Guards Tank Armies. North of Warsaw, 2nd Byelorussian Front had gained a strong bridgehead over the Narew as well and was sending its 5th Guards Tank Army across.

Thousands of Soviet tanks drove west and north for the great encirclement of Warsaw, which at one stroke would take a 200-mile bite out of the front. Zhukov was determined finally to drive a stake through the heart of *Army Group Centre*. The deeper the Soviet tanks drove, though, the more dangerous became the rejuvenated *Luftwaffe*'s ground attacks and the less effective their own air support as the German fighters took a higher and higher toll. Deep behind the German front, the open ground suddenly ended as the tank armies came up against the deep defences of the Friedrich der Grosse Line on 23 March. Rage as they might, the Soviet tank masses were useless in this new maze of anti-tank weapons and obstacles. They were desperately short of the necessary infantry and heavy artillery. Neither Vasilievskiy nor Koniev had been able to widen the breaches in the main German line which still held and bent back strong shoulders.

Then von Manstein struck. The carefully husbanded Panzer armies appeared and hit the Soviets on 25 March at the base of their penetrations north and south of Warsaw, severed them, and then turned west to take the Soviet tanks in the rear and press them up against the German anti-tank defences. Hoth's *Fourth Panzer Army* closed in on Koniev's tanks in the south outside of Krakow, slicing across their rear. Raus' *First Panzer Army* cut down across the rear of Vasilievskiy's two tank armies. Both Panzer armies smashed into the Soviet bridgeheads. Those at Baranow and Magnuszew were broken, yielding thousands of prisoners. It was Fritz Bayerlein's *Panzer 'Lehr' Division* (*XLVII Panzer Corps*) that threw the last of the Russians into the Vistula at Magnuszew. Bayerlein had little time to contemplate the carnage, but it was obvious that the Russians had paid an appalling price getting across the river and then grinding their way through the German defences.

> 'I was struck by the endless number of destroyed enemy armoured vehicles caught up in the anti-tank defences and by the numbers of dead infantry they had not bothered to bury. I could only think how prescient Rommel had been.'[23]

Hoth and Raus immediately turned their forces west in the rear of the tank armies still only vaguely aware of the threat to their rear. They soon found out. The battles raged across south-central Poland as the Soviets were struck in the rear and turned to fight, caught between the Friedrich der Grosse Line defences and the Panzers. Then von Manstein committed *Fifth Panzer Army* (less one corps) on 27 March. Vasilievskiy's tanks were now fighting front and rear. Day after day hundreds of vehicles gushed smoke and flame up into the sky. Zhukov ordered an all-out attack by the Red Air Force to support his embattled tank armies and instructed his other front commanders to reestablish the bridgeheads. In the sky the greatest air battle in history raged over the greatest tank battle as planes in their hundreds and thousands fell to the earth. It was at this critical moment that Galland unleashed his carefully-husbanded Me 262 jet fighters. The Red

Falcons were jumped even before they reached the Vistula, their squadrons savaged and disrupted.

The only bright spot for Zhukov was the successful breakout of 5th Guards Tank Army north of Warsaw. He ordered it to swing south behind Warsaw and into the German rear. Manstein then released his final Panzer reserve – *Fifth Panzer Army*'s remaining corps – the *II SS Panzer Corps*.[24] They had fought these Russians before – at the great tank engagement at Prokorovka at Kursk in 1943 and been stopped. There were a few men left from both sides who had been there, but it would not be a happy reunion. The two tank masses met at Szrensk northwest of Warsaw on 28 March in a titanic meeting engagement.[25]

Moscow, 12 April

Foreign Minister Vyacheslav Molotov cordially met the ambassadors at the door and ushered them into his offices. He was a master diplomat and could put on any face required. This time it would be that of a genial and cooperative host. It ate at his gut like a bellyful of glass. He remembered the morning almost four years ago on 22 June 1941 when the German ambassador had delivered the German declaration of war to this very same room – after the invasion was well underway. Then Molotov had spat upon the German paper and ordered the Germans shown out the back entrance.

Now he had to hint that the Soviet Government, in the interest of the international working class, would be pleased to employ the good offices of the Swedish and Uruguayan governments. The debacle on the plains of Poland, had made all this necessary.[26] It was 1914 all over again – the two Russian armies destroyed at Tannenberg now writ much larger. And the Germans had been quick to make the analogy. The church bells had rung all over that cursed country. Central Poland had been the graveyard of Russian revenge – more than 4,000 tanks lost and the cream of the tank force destroyed. The offensive arm of the Red Army had been broken. The spring thaw had come early, encasing both armies in a sea of mud. At least Zhukov had been sent to chop wood in Siberia.[27] Now Molotov must smile and beg help from these fools to end this war. Of course, Stalin would portray it as a victorious war – after all the Fascists had been driven completely out of the Soviet Union and had suffered great losses. The border, he suspected, would essentially be the one drawn over the body of murdered Poland, the one he had helped draw, in 1939 – an ocean of blood spilled to come back to the same spot. He smiled again.

The reality

Of course, the pivot point of this alternate history is the defeat of the Western Allies in Normandy. It was the only plausible scenario, however remote, in which Germany could have survived World War II, and it was one which Rommel identified in his papers. The extensive comments by Rommel to Fritz Bayerlein about how to deal with the Soviets were the most common-sense approach, given the circumstances. Common sense, however, was the one critical resource disallowed the Germans while Hitler remained in power.

This alternate history has attempted to explore the optimum scenario in which Germany could have escaped destruction that late in the war. Irreplaceable elements in this scenario were the removal of Hitler, the cessation of the Allied bombing campaign, and a one-front war. The industrial resources and the military manpower remaining to Germany, even after the disaster of the destruction of *Army Group Centre*, if intelligently used under these circumstances (admittedly a big 'if'), could well have stalemated the Soviets in the east. The Soviets were approaching the bottom of even their vast manpower barrel, despite being flush with Lend-Lease equipment and their own war production. In the final assault on Berlin in 1945, Stalin cautioned both Zhukov and Koniev that there were no replacements.

This alternate history also clarifies the mutually supportive roles of the Soviets and the Western Allies. The Soviets rightly claimed to have fought the overwhelming part of the German ground forces, but they went on to assert that they essentially won the war. The truth is that they were successful because the bombing campaign, the Allied campaigns in the Mediterranean, and ultimately the Second Front so dissipated German resources that they could only fail everywhere.

Bibliography

Chant, Christopher, ed., *Warfare and the Third Reich: The Rise and Fall of Hitler's Armed Forces* (Salamander, London, 1998).

Lewis, George G., and Mewha, John, *History of the Prisoner of War Utilization by the United States Army, 1776–1945*, Department of the Army Pamphlet 20-213 (Department of the Army, Washington, DC, 1953).

Rommel, Erwin, *The Rommel Papers*, Liddell Hart, B.H., ed., (Collins, London, 1953).

Mueller-Hillebrand, B., *Das Heer 1939–1945*, vol. 3 (Mittler, Frankfurt-am-Main, n.d.)

Seaton, Albert, *The Russo-German War 1941–1945* (Presidio, Novato, CA, 1993).

Seaton, Albert, *The German Army 1933–1945* (New American Library, New York, 1985).

Tsouras, Peter G., *Disaster at D-Day: The Germans Defeat the Allies, June 1944* (Greenhill, London, 1994).

Tuyll, Hubert P. van, *Feeding the Bear* (Greenwood Press, New York, 1989).

Ziemke, Earl F., *Stalingrad to Berlin: The German Defeat in the East* (Office of the Chief of Military History, Washington, DC, 1968).

Notes

* 1. Stauffenberg, Claus von, *Saving Germany* (Verlagshaus Hindrichs, Potsdam and Leipzig, 1949), pp. 49–53. Von Stauffenberg's account of Rommel at Dachau owes nothing to the postwar Rommel myth. If anything, other eyewitnesses state that von Stauffenberg understated Rommel's rage.

* 2. The fate of the death camp staffs is treated well in Eva von Bartelsmann, *A Reckoning With Shame: Germany's Hideous Secret* (Collins, London, 1963), pp. 132–50.

 * 3. Peter G. Tsouras, *Disaster at D-Day: The Germans Defeat the Allies, June 1944* – the definitive work on the Allied defeat in Normandy and the roles of Rommel and Speidel in Hitler's assassination.

 * 4. By July 1944 there were 173,980 German prisoners interned in the continental United States. Most of these were men captured in North Africa. See Lewis and Mewha, *History of the Prisoner of War Utilization by the United States Army 1776–1945*, pp. 90–1. Large numbers of prisoners were also kept in the United Kingdom who were quickly returned in response to the immediate release of British prisoners by the Germans. The most useful of these were the several thousand aircrew captured mostly in the Battle of Britain.

 * 5. Quoted in Zhukov, Georgi, *The Great Patriotic War* (Progress, Moscow, 1958) p. 477.

 6. Hubert P. van Tuyll, *Feeding the Bear*, pp. 63, 69.

 * 7. Quoted in Zhukov, *op. cit.,* p. 491.

 8. There had been barely 40 operational Luftwaffe fighters supporting *Army Group Centre* when Operation Bagration had begun. In his flight to the front, Rommel's escort comprised a high proportion of surviving operational aircraft.

 9. Mueller-Hillebrand, *Das Heer 1939–1945*, vol. 3, Table 62.

 10. Seaton, *The Russo-German War 1941–1945*, p. 547. See also Seaton, *The German Army 1933–1945*, p. 223.

 11. Ziemke, *Stalingrad to Berlin: The German Defeat in the East*, pp. 369–70. The Southeastern Theatre forces in the Balkans 'had a ration strength of 900,000, including naval and air contingents and what the Germans called "*Wehrmachtsgefolge*", the technicians, bureaucrats, police, and mere hangers-on who followed the armed forces into occupied countries. The ground combat strength was, roughly, 600,000... ' There were 300,000 men, mostly German, in *Army Group E* in Greece. Subtracting Bulgarian troops leaves a figure of approximately 500,000 German troops for the entire theatre.

 *12. Jon F. Collins, *General of the Fighters: The Rise of Adolf Galland* (Military Publishing Co., Richmond, VA, 1963), p. 236. The meteoric rise of Adolf Galland who began World War II as a captain and ended it as field marshal commanding the *Luftwaffe* is well-documented in this book. As the brilliant innovator of fighter operations, he was just the man Rommel needed to lead the *Luftwaffe* in the final battle in the east against the overwhelming numbers of the Red Air Force.

 *13. It was only after the war that Reich Chancellor Rommel officially informed the German people and the world of the Final Solution. A full accounting was made of the four million put to death in the camps up to their closure in July 1944. Unfortunately, as critics charged, the Rommel government was all too quick to emphasise the restoration of German honour in this matter rather than the original loss of it. Nevertheless, it was the Rommel government that sponsored the creation of the State of Israel in 1952 and provided the military support that was critical in defeating the initial Arab attempts to destroy the Jewish state. 'I can never forget what I saw,' Rommel was reported to have said on a number of occasions.

 *14. Dr General Lothar Rendulic, *The German-Finnish Cobelligerency, 1941–44* (Amesbury House, London, 1956), p. 322.

 15. Loki was the Germanic-Norse trickster god.

 16. Chant, *Warfare and the Third Reich*, pp. 413–14.

 17. Rommel, *The Rommel Papers*, pp. 451–3.

 *18. Quoted in Zhukov, *op. cit.,* p. 509.

 *19. Dean Acheson, *German Diplomacy under the Rommel Government* (Courtland Press, New York, 1956), pp. 63–6. Alger Hiss, *Soviet Foreign Policy in World War II* (Bellmont Books, New York, 1953), pp. 334–9.

 20. Ziemke, *ibid.*, pp. 416–18.

*21. Von Manteuffel's rise to Panzer army commander had been meteoric. An early protégé of Guderian, he was a brilliant and aggressive tactician and leader, known as the 'Lion of Zhitomir,' for his destruction of the Soviet 16th Army in 1943. It was at the urging of Guderian and Hoth under whom he served in the *XLVIII Panzer Corps* that he was jumped to command the newly formed *Fifth Panzer Army* made up largely of divisions which had served in the Normandy Campaign. He served after the war in his mentor's wartime position of Inspector of Panzer Forces 1949–52.

*22. Rommel, *Decision in the East* (Greenhill Books, London, 1960), p. 364. Rommel's self-control did have its limits, however. In this first English translation of his best-selling memoir written after his retirement as Chancellor, he relates with obvious glee of his visits among the troops from Romania to East Prussia in these hectic months of desperate preparation. The image of Rommel among the troops before and during the great battles of 1944–5 became the leitmotif of the final campaign. Privately, von Manstein was chagrined to have Rommel steal the limelight, but he did admit that if he had to choose between the limelight and the substance, he would still choose the latter.

*23. Fritz Bayerlein, *Panzer Sieg* (Allstein Verlag, Frankfurt-am-Main, 1954), p. 244. A brilliant Bavarian, Bayerlein, served as Chief of the German Army General Staff 1950–56, personally selected by Rommel.

*24. *II SS Panzer Corps'* two divisions had been the *1st SS Panzer Division 'Leibstandarte Adolf Hitler'* and *2nd SS Panzer Division 'Das Reich'*. The former had originated, as its name indicated, as Hitler's bodyguard detail. Hitler's assassination made the honorific somewhat indelicate. It was renamed *1st SS Panzer Division 'Deutschland'* and as such accompanied *2nd SS Panzer Division 'Das Reich'* into the meeting engagement at Szrensk. However, its men still wore their old AH armbands into battle. After the war, Rommel demobilised the *SS* fighting arm and incorporated its most distinguished units into the army in 1947. With that act the last element of the *SS* and its infamous twin runes passed into history. Nigel Bromfield, *History of the Waffen SS* (Caulfield and Michaels Ltd, London, 1969), pp. 290–5.

*25. Hasso von Manteuffel, 'Meeting Engagement at Szrensk', *Armor*, March 1963, p. 34. Although von Manteuffel characterised the engagement as a tactical victory, Soviet accounts were more correct in depicting it as a drawn fight. It was an operational and strategic victory of the first order, however, in that it stopped Zhukov's last chance to rescue his tank armies in what history has called the great 'Rommel Pocket', to the intense annoyance of von Manstein whose brainchild it was. Rommel could not help dominating the public's impression of the war in the East as he had in North Africa and France and the name 'Rommel Pocket,' coined by a soldier at the front, stuck. Although heaped with honours by Rommel after the war, von Manstein retired immediately.

*26. Oskar von Blutfeld, *Casualties of the Second World War* (Greenhill Books, London, 1989), p. 737. Citing German and Soviet sources, this German military historian asserts that the Soviets lost over 4,000 tanks, 3,000 aircraft, and 536,000 men in the fighting west of the Vistula alone, including 253,000 prisoners. German losses amounted to 102,000. For all of Operation Suvorov, Soviet losses exceeded 1.4 million, and German losses were 339,000 including 47,000 prisoners.

*27. Zhukov was Stalin's scapegoat for the disaster of Operation Suvorov. He spent the next eight years in a concentration camp near Magadan until Stalin's death. He was rehabilitated in 1956 under the destalinisation campaign and has taken his proper place in Soviet military history, his defeat in Poland balanced against his numerous earlier victories which drove the Germans out of the Soviet Union. He died quietly in retirement in 1960, his health broken by his treatment in the camps.